UNDERSTANDING AQUACULTURE

UNDERSTANDING AQUACULTURE

By

Dr. Amita Sarkar

Dept. of Zoology

Agra College

Agra (U.P.)

(India)

DISCOVERY PUBLISHING HOUSE PVT. LTD.

NEW DELHI-110 002

Published by:
Namit Wasan
DISCOVERY PUBLISHING HOUSE PVT. LTD.
4383/4B, Ansari Road, Darya Ganj
New Delhi-110 002 (India)
Phone : +91-11-23279245; 23253475; 43596065
E-mail : discoverybooksindia@gmail.com
discoverypublishinghouse@gmail.com
namitwasan9@gmail.com
web : www.discoverypublishinggroup.com

Edition: **2020**

ISBN: 978-81-8356-548-6

Understanding Aquaculture

Printed at:
Infinity Imaging Systems
Delhi

Preface

The present title "Understanding Aquaculture" has been written for those students interested in careers in diverse fields of biological sciences. It provides a structured approach to learning by covering all the important topics in a uniform, systematic format. The book has been comprehensively designed incorporating recent advances in this fast moving field. It also provides accessible information on molecular biology in compact form for undergraduate students in biology and related life sciences. It is intelligible to the educated layman, though it deals with some complex ideas. It is an adequate text for all the requirements of students in this area. In addition, busy lecturers who require a quick reference compendium will find it useful, particularly for tutional planning. Simple, yet hopefully clear figures and tables are provided throughout the book.

The over-riding goal of this book, and indeed of the whole *Understanding series,* is to present the essential information concering molecular biology in a compact, readily accessible form which leads itself to student learning and revision. The convergence of various approaches has generated a rich panorama of detail, the significance of which we are still attempting to unraval. The present text has been written as an introduction to this rapidly growing field.

To make the work more comprehensive and informative, the author has consulted many authoritative books, research journals, abstracts, monographs etc., so there can be no claim to originality except in the manner of treatment.

The author expresses his thanks to his friends and colleagues whose continue inspirations have initiated him to bring out this book.

The author expresses his gratitude to Mr. Wasan and staff of M/s Discovery Publishing House Pvt. Ltd. for their whole hearted cooperation in the publication of this book.

In the mean time, the author will remain sincerely responsible for any shortcomings of the book and be grateful to the readers for their suggestions and constructive criticism for the continuous betterment of the book. He takes this opportunity to appeal to the readers to send their suggestions straightaway to his Publisher.

Author

Contents

1

INTRODUCTION

The environment in which fish live in captivity is made up of a complicated mixture of various factors—*physical*, *chemical* and biological—*covering* many areas of knowledge. Of these factors usually only the less complex ones are under the direct control of the aquarist, and judicious manipulation of these can often *compensate* for any *inability* to adjust in other *directions*.

An unsuitable environment quickly emphasises the difficulties which are inherent in the basic situation of containing a fish in a relatively small volume of water, whereas correct and *knowledgeable* treatment will *assist* the fish in adapting to the rather *unnatural* conditions in which it *finds* itself.

The fish in the usual *aquarium* community are many and varied and may come from quite different parts of the world and yet they are expected to live together *peacefully* and *happily*. Their *individual requirements* may vary in the extreme but there are fortunately many basic factors which are common to almost all species.

Fish can be divided into categories and classified in terms of the *environmental* factors which form the most noticeable differences in their ways of life. For example, a particular species may be described as being *freshwater* rather than *marine*, *tropical* rather than *coldwater* (ie *temperate*),

livebearing rather than egglaying, and so on. By *signposting* its environmental and biological characteristics in this way we immediately know roughly what sort of fish it is and broadly what its requirements will be when kept in *captivity*. The important point to *emphasise* is that it is essential to *establish* an *environment* which is tailored to a

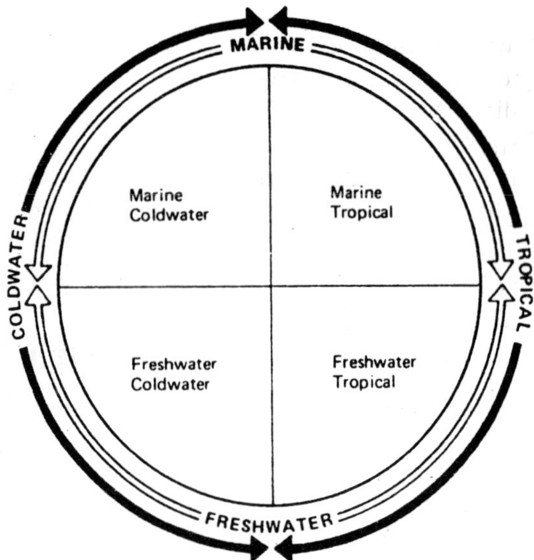

Figure 1.1: The major types of aquatic environment.

particular type of fish or collection of organisms if they are to be *encouraged* to display or carry out that part of their lives which the aquarist most *wishes* to *study*.

Figure elsewhere in this chapter illustrates *diagrammatically* the major types of aquatic *environment*. The principal factors in each of the four sectors are absolutely *fundamental*, because almost any fish which is kept under *inappropriate* conditions will almost *invariably* die *sooner* or *later*.

In other words, the correct *choice* of *salinity* and *temperature* is so basic to the fish's well-being that it is vital for its survival. Other environmental factors are not always quite as demanding as this, and in this respect it is often quite possible to keep a particular type of fish for its normal *lifespan* in conditions which do not suit it at all. For instance, it is well known that fish grow to their full adult size only if enough space is made available to them.

There is no reason at all to suppose that a stunted fish is any 'unhappier' or suffers in any way in comparison with its fully-grown counterpart, but it is surely bad *fishkeeping* to provide *insufficient* space for a fish to achieve its-full *expectations*.

The usual test for the suitability of an environment is the readiness with which a particular species will reproduce itself in a given set of conditions. As a general rule this would seem to be a fair test, as long as the characteristics of that fish throughout its whole life are taken into account and not merely those which *predominate* at its normal breeding time.

All waters in nature change their *characteristics* in *cycles*, usually annually, and the fish's ways change with them. Thus their breeding period is usually influenced by the *conditions* which *successfully* promote the growth of their young and not necessarily those which are to their own *advantage* over a long period of time.

SPACE

The adult body size of a fish, within the limits of its natural maximum, is largely determined by the space available to it. If this space is *restricted* by the use of a small container or by overcrowding, then the fish will be *stunted*.

It is not easy to give *minimum* volumes of water required per fish-inch or similar *criteria* since the other factors, eg the condition of the available water, affect the result, but if the problem is acknowledged it will be seen that due *allowance* must be made. An important starting point is to allow as much space as possible by providing an *aquarium* of adequate size.

Aquaria are hardly ever big enough to house anything but small fish, and not even large quantities of those. Of course, if an aquarist only has, say, a 20gallon (90-litre) *aquarium* and wishes to keep, for example, Tinfoil Barbs, he will usually do so and *eventually* come to realise that there is no chance of seeing the fish grow to their full *potential*.

It is difficult for many aquarists to keep in their homes a *container* with a capacity much larger than 20 gallons (90 litres), and there is no real reason why they should not keep Tinfoil Barbs in an aquarium of this size, but the same *argument* does not really *excuse* those who keep *goldfish* in *goldfish* bowls.

Space is also important in the relationship between fish or groups of fish whose interests conflict. Territorial fish are good examples. The area of a species' *territory* depends upon the environmental *requirements* of that fish and is *instinctive*.

Hence, if two fish of this type are put together in a container with adequate space for only one of them, either continual fighting will result or the weaker fish will be killed or spend its whole life being harassed. *Equally*, fish which school up will be seen to do this only if the swimming space available is larger than that usually taken up by the school when *swimming normally*.

If the container is of the ame size or smaller, then the fish, from their own viewpoint, will be in a school already, but this may not be apparent to the *aquarist*.

The volume of an *aquarium* is also an important factor in the stability of any *biological* balances which may be set up, such as those between fish and *aquatic* plants.

If a container of large volume has good biological conditions and is not *overcrowded* then changes in balance have a minimal effect and the *environment* may recover without too much trouble, but in small containers or in overcrowded conditions troubles multiply *alarmingly* and in bad cases almost any minor difficulty can be enough to ruin the whole *aquarium*.

Water surface area, which is well known to be an important factor in fish growth and biological balances, will be discussed fully later but here it is necessary to question the *commonly* held view that a large surface area can entirely *compensate* for lack of space or volume.

Water surface area can always be increased effectively by a reasonable amount of surface *turbulence* caused by an ascending air-stream, but lack of space is not so *easily rectified*.

The only situations in which small *containers* are useful are those *requiring sterile conditions*, eg for spawning egglaying fish, or for isolating single fish or small groups for various *reasons*, and these arrangements are usually only *temporary*.

There are no real *biological* disadvantages in using a large container, but there may well be *practical* reasons such as weight, available space or cost which make it *undesirable*. However, if aquarists are to progress in this hobby in a satisfactory manner then their *permanent aquaria* should be as large as possible.

WATER

The water in any aquarium is obviously fundamental to the whole exercise of fishkeeping and while it is possible to create almost any kind of environment from whatever water is at hand, it is far better to use water which in its original *characteristics* is as close as possible to the ideal.

Preliminary thought at this stage will save much time later and will minimise the need for *complicated* methods of *maintaining* the water in its proper condition. There are various kinds of easily available water, including *tap-waters* (these being the most commonly used), natural waters from *rain*, *ponds*, *streams* or the *sea*, and *distilled* water

Table 1.1: Commonly available waters and their characteristics.

Type	*Characteristics*	*Disadvantages*	*Method of Use*
Mains Tap-water	Hardness and acidity vary with geographical area. Clean,well oxygenated	Contains dissolved chlorine. May carry copper from pipework	Dilute with mature waterorallow maturing period
Rain-water	Softand neutral. Basically clean and well-oxygenated	May be polluted by chemicals from atmosphere or collecting surfaces	Filter if dirty. No maturation needed
Natural Fresh Water	Hardnessand acidity vary with geographical area. May contain life	Maybe polluted by chemicals or organics. May contain diseases or parasites	Examine thoroughly. Stand in darkness 14 days before use
Natural Sea-water	Stable with little geographical variations. Contains life. Usuallywell-oxygenated	Polluted around coastline. Microscopic life dies quicklytofoul water. May contain marine diseases	Collect offshore. Stand in darkness 14 days before use. Aerate thoroughly
Artificial Salt Water	Stable characteristics and proportions when properly made up. Clean and pure immediately	Expensive in quantity. Some trace elements may be missing	Must be thoroughly mixed in correct proportions with good tap-water
Distilled Water	Soft and neutral. Clean and pure	Too pure for biological life when new	Usedtomixwith otherwatersas neutraliser

from commercial sources. The major characteristics which determine the nature of any water are: *salinity*, *hardness*, *acidity*, *cleanliness*, unwanted *inclusions* and desired *omissions*.

Sea-water is an obvious example of a water of high salinity. Hard waters are characteristic of chalk and limestone areas, while soft waters occur in regions where rocks such as granite are found.

Hard waters contain dissolved minerals and are generally *alkaline* while soft waters do not and are generally acid. Tap-water drawn from the mains supply requires a period of time to '*mature*' before it can be used in a *completely* new *environment*.

Not only is it too pure for biological purposes, but it also contains dissolved chlorine which will harm the fish. Water from recently installed supply systems may also contain copper, and this must be avoided at all costs, since even very small *concentrations* of copper can be lethal to fish and other *creatures*.

Salt is, of course, absent from tap-water and must be added to achieve the required degree of salinity, while *hardness* and acidity are fixed characteristics of any given water supply area. *Information* on this last point is generally freely available from the relevant area water authority and should be sought even if the *aquarist* never intends to modify the water.

If fishkeeping activities can be confined to environments which suit the local water a great deal of trouble will be saved. This is not as limiting as it sounds, as almost all common freshwater aquarium fish live happily in *mature tap-water* of most kinds, providing that other *environmental* conditions are correct.

Less common fish will, however, often require water of a particular type. Tap-water used in a marine evironment is so altered by the inclusion of the necessary salts that its initial *characteristics* are of little *importance*.

In all waters hardness and acidity values usually run together, ie a water will be hard and alkaline or soft and acid. This is desirable as it represents the states which occur in nature. Both *hardness* and acidity can be adjusted by the aquarist by means of chemical additions, and rough measuring methods are readily available.

As mentioned above, tap-water should be matured before use in a new environment. When an existing *environment* similar to the available tap-water requires the immediate addition of water, usually in an emergency, up to a 50 per cent change by volume is often permissible, *providing* the temperature of the added water is equalised.

The *minimum* maturing period recommended for a completely new environment is one week. During this time the dissolved chlorine will pass into the atmosphere and the water will age to a *biological condition* which is *acceptable* to animal and plant life.

Stirring by aeration and standing for a further period will improve the water even more, but most of us do not always have much patience and, except in special cases, for instance where a sensitive fish is to be moved from a long established environment into the new one, a week is usually sufficient providing a *container* with a *reasonably* large surface area is used.

During this period of maturation the water must, of course, be protected from external *fouling* and other sources of pollution. Rain-water is probably the purest form of natural water when it starts its journey *downwards*, but on the way it may pick up all sorts of constituents from the *atmosphere* and from any surfaces on which it may fall before being *collected*.

In industrial atmospheres all manner of toxic and undesirable products may be collected, and treatment of the water is not always *possible* by *ordinary* means. To be safe, this kind of *rain-water* should not be used.

Collecting surfaces for rain-water should be free from *pollutants*, particularly metallic compounds. Rain-water which is clean and *properly* collected from a clean, inert surface, will be soft and *neutral* and ideally suited to many *freshwater* environments. It will not need a *maturing* period, and in any event will usually have had one in the collecting container.

If it is accessible to birds it should be inspected for fish *parasites* before use. *Planted* aquaria and such fish as the popular barbs and tetras usually benefit from the use of good rain-water where the local tap-water is hard and *alkaline*. However, its use in spawning tanks is not to be *recommended* as *bacteria* which attack eggs may be present.

Other natural waters from inland areas or from the sea must be treated with extreme caution as they may contain pollutants in far greater concentration than *rain-water*, and even if *chemically* clean may abound in fish *parasites* and disease *spores*.

There are also many small creatures in natural waters which, while they do no harm at all in an aquarium, are of no *benefit* either and may develop in sufficient numbers to spoil the character and appearance of the *environment*.

Natural waters are most useful when they normally contain the fish and other organisms with which the aquarist is *concerned*. However, even in this *instance*, a natural water should not *automatically* be considered as the very best for a particular creature.

It may well be that in its natural state a creature is able to cope with pollutants which, due to the sheer volume and the movement of the water, are *massively diluted*. In the much smaller volume of an *aquarium* container use of such water may build up dangerous concentrations of such *pollutants*.

Even with regard to this argument, however, when *aquatic specimens* are collected from the wild and their habits and *requirements* are not known, as much as possible of their natural water should be collected with them and, at least *initially*, used while accustoming them to life in the artificial environment.

Also, if possible, the temperature at the depth at which the *specimens* normally live should be measured and any other relevant environmental factors should be noted. In this way the aquarist will be able to *reproduce* the natural *situations* as closely as possible.

It must be pointed out that if natural waters of any kind are used to set up an aquarium, the continued addition of the same water may or may not be necessary to maintain that *environment*, depending on the *circumstances*.

In a marine situation, for instance, the continual addition of sea-water to replace evaporation losses would obviously result in an undesirable build-up of salts, as these are not lost to the *atmosphere* with the water. On the other hand, if hard, alkaline tap-water is added to a soft, acid *freshwater environment*, the water will tend to become neutral and the benefits of the soft water will be reduced.

In soft-water environments any gravel or rockwork present will in any case gradually tend to *neutralise* the water, or even change it completely over a long period of time, so that '*topping up*' with the original soft water is *desirable*.

If, however, the aquarist is specifically setting out to change the character of the water by artificial chemical additions any good available water can be used provided there is an attempt to compensate for its deficiencies and regular tests are run. These *procedures*, however, can be *time-consuming*, require experienced operation and are only *recommended* to *confirmed dabblers* or those with special situations to cater for.

One last point on the use of natural waters concerns *biological* filtration, which is fully described later. *Suffice* it to say here that mature natural water in good condition is useful in initially setting up a *biological* filter as it will help to seed the bed with the *required* bacteria.

Also where an old bed is being washed before being used again, *mature* water will scour away far less of the desired bacteriological *population* than would fresh tap-water, particularly if the natural water is of the same type as that to which the bed is *accustomed*.

Distilled water is usually only used to alter conditions in existing environments or to modify unsuitable waters when setting up a new environment. As produced *commercially* it is of no use to *aquatic life* as it is chemically and biologically pure. Its addition to any environment tends to neutralise the water by dilution and it is thus useful in arresting extreme degrees of *hardness* or acidity.

In some cases it is used as the basis of artificially *constructed* waters for specialised purposes, such as *spawning* environments for difficult fish, but generally it should be *considered* as a *neutraliser* and nothing more.

AIR

Two air-water interfaces exist in most aquatic environments, namely, that between the water surface and the atmosphere above the aquarium, and that between the water and any air *artificially injected* into it. All air which comes into contact with the water must be clean and free from *pollutants* which might either become dissolved in the water or cover the surface and thus prevent the normal *interchange processes* from taking place.

In domestic surroundings, paint fumes, insect sprays, hair lacquers and other household *sprays* frequently cause trouble simply because they are used in the same room as the aquarium. *Pumped* air can easily become poisoned if the situation of the pump is such that it draws in pollutants or if it is *oil-lubricated.*

Precautions against these troubles are simple but mandatory; the ability of the water to dissolve substances is so great as to make this a matter of *supreme* importance. *Domestic garden* or *industrial sprays* must not be used where they may be carried into the air and thus into the aquarium.

Dust can be kept out effectively by a cover glass, but chemicals must not be allowed into the air of the room where the aquarium is

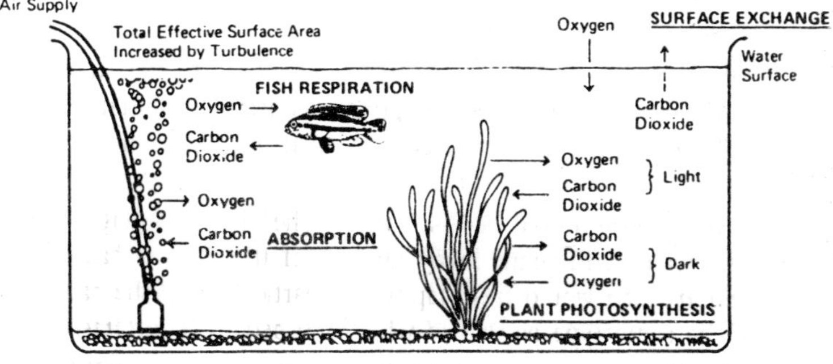

Figure 1.2: The oxygen-carbon dioxide exchange processes in the aquarium.

situated. One of the most important processes which must be controlled in any aquarium is the exchange of carbon dioxide (CO_2) and oxygen (O_2) with the atmosphere.

In brief, sufficient levels of oxygen must be maintained to support the fish, while the concentration of CO_2 must be kept low. Figure elsewhere in this chapter summarises the major exchange processes which take place.

Although aquatic plants produce oxygen by photosynthesis in bright light during daylight hours, it is only in extreme situations, in what could more properly be called plant aquaria, that this *phenomenon* is of any significance.

The aquatic *environment* therefore usually relies on its air-water interfaces for the *replenishment* of oxygen and the expulsion of carbon dioxide by the exchange of these *gases* between the water and the air.

The efficiency of the interface for this purpose will depend on its size, its state of cleanliness, any movement of air across it and the temperatures of the air and the water.

It is often suggested that so many square inches of water surface will support so many inches of fish life in an aquarium. Any recommendations of this kind are presumably arrived at by considering 'average' situations in mixed tanks and contain large safety factors.

The aquarist who blindly follows these figures will never realise the full potential of the available water surface. The surface area of the water is *automatically* increased by *turbulence* such as that caused by a stream of air bubbles or a filter return system; but, of course, this *situation* exists only while the pumping equipment is switched on and working properly.

For this reason it is unwise to crowd an aquarium to the point where such equipment is essential to keep the fish alive, as emergencies occur in even the most reliable *systems*, and most aquarists' set-ups fall rather short of this.

An environment should therefore be planned, whenever possible, to provide an excess of water surface area *sufficient* to cater for the needs of the *inhabitants* without artificial assistance. Also, if the inhabitants are not fully mature when *installed*, allowance should be made to cope adequately with them when they have grown to full size.

If this requirement cannot be met or if the likely final population is unknown (eg when fish are collected gradually in a community aquarium), careful observation coupled with *experience* will be necessary in order to enable full use to be made of the environment, especially if the fish are still growing.

Fish kept in an environment which suffers from oxygen deficiency will lie at the water surface with fins *folded*, *gasping* and *sucking* in *atmospheric* oxygen. They will not feed or remain active and if this state persists for any appreciable time, they will invariably die.

The *absorption* of oxygen from air by water is a continuous process which takes place in the surface layer until the water is *saturated*, ie full of all the oxygen that it can hold in a dissolved state. In a static situation, that *oxygen* slowly *diffuses* into the lower levels of the water and is replaced from the surface.

It can thus be understood that if the surface layer is *continuously* changed by circulation the process of oxygen acquisition will be *speeded* up. Also, the associated stirring action spreads oxygen more easily to all levels in the *container*. By this means, an otherwise barren volume of water can be completely *saturated* with oxygen.

In populated aquaria it is essential to ensure that the oxygen is replenished more quickly than the *inhabitants* use it up, preferably in such a way that even if the *circulating* equipment is not working the water surface area alone can cope, at least for a *reasonable* time.

Despite this advice many aquarists will, of course, continue to rely heavily on pumping equipment, but they should at least realise the risks they run and should have *suitable* back-up *equipment* available for *emergencies*.

Water does not dissolve a large amount of oxygen by comparison with its volume and this amount decreases with increasing water temperature. Hence, *tropical* environments are more critical than coldwater ones and, as fish activity generally increases with water temperature, a 'full' tropical *environment* may require more artificial assistance than an *equivalent coldwater habitat*.

There is one condition, however, which is to be carefully avoided, and this is the supersaturation of the water with oxygen. In this predicament more *oxygen* is present than the water can dissolve and the excess takes the form of small *bubbles suspended* in the water.

In a static situation these bubbles would rise and break at the surface and the excess would eventually pass to the atmosphere. However, if this state is induced continuously by the injection of *pumped* air in overlarge quantities, the wader surface may not be able to release the bubbles *quickly* enough.

Furthermore, the associated high *turbulence* may encompass the whole water volume and, by a *swirling* action, keep much of the excess oxygen away from the surface.

Fish which take in excess *oxygen* are subjected to the same effects as if they were forced to obtain oxygen directly from the air, and suffer accordingly. This *situation frequently* occurs when aquarists set up their first marine *environment* and, due to the relative expense of the inhabitants, decide to play safe by *providing* more air than would ever be needed.

There are also sound *recommendations* from various authorities that marine aquaria need more air than others. The result in some cases is that much damage is caused through this effect. The detection of excess oxygen due to supersaturation is very simple.

Small bubbles readily show up against a dark background in the aquarium. Any piece of black non-toxic material can be used and the air supply should be *reduced* until the small bubbles *disappear*, although this may take a little time.

Environments with small populations are, in theory, more easily supersaturated than those in which oxygen consumption is high, although this effect is rarely noticeable.

The air-water interface is vitally important for the removal of carbon dioxide given off by fish and other animals in their respiratory processes, and by plants in the dark hours. The passage of carbon dioxide from the water to the air can be artificially *influenced* in the same way as is oxygen *acquisition* and it is similarly *dependent* on the interface area.

Since carbon dioxide is more soluble in water than oxygen, it is not so easily removed, a biological excess occuring long before its supersaturation point is reached. Also, a static body of air above the surface does not remove carbon dioxide as quickly as a moving one and this effect is *exaggerated* by the very low levels of carbon dioxide which are *normally* found in air.

Unfortunately, in a tropical aquarium with artificial heating any continuous air currents would cause appreciable heat losses, but in a coldwater environment a steady flow of air above the *aquarium* can be used to *advantage*.

The exchanges of carbon dioxide and oxygen are so similar, although in opposite *directions*, that they are usually treated as one *problem*, and it is often not apparent which is responsible for any particular difficulty. However, high levels of carbon dioxide in the water produce the *characteristic* result of high acidity.

As more and more carbon dioxide is dissolved, the acidity of the water increases and may become so high as to be *dangerous*. This behaviour explains the experience of aquarists whose planted *environments* apparently alter their acidity values with light intensity, because when the light is strong the photosynthetic action of the plants temporarily reduces the acidity by *large-scale absorption* of *carbon dioxide* from the water.

LIGHT

All life on earth exists on food which is directly or indirectly formed from the light energy emitted from the sun. Light is at the bottom of all food chains and is of *paramount importance* in all natural *environments*.

In artificial *aquatic* environments, light is usually provided to promote plant growth and to allow the aquarist to see the inhabitants, but the relationship between the applied light and the requirements of the inhabitants is rarely *considered*, *although* some interest is being shown now that more people are able to keep *anemones* and living corals, whose well-being depends on the correct *application* of *light*.

Of all the factors involved in the successful *maintenance* of planted aquaria probably no other single *subject* has created as much controversy amongst *experienced* aquarists, or *despondency* amongst beginners, as the matter of how much and what kind of light should be provided.

Lighting *arrangements* are often blamed for entirely unconnected plant failures (eg the *clogging* of plant pores by dirty water) and everyone's opinion on the subject seems to vary. *Individuals* whose planted *environments* are successful often cannot give any real reason why this is so.

If a small *planted aquatic* environment, such as a garden fishpond, is studied, it will be seen that there is a critical biological *situation* at the time in its cycle of existence when plant *growth* is *strongest*.

At this point the major plant growth will have expanded to fill all of the available light-catching areas and secondary plant species, such as algae and weaker plants, being deprived of the light by the stronger plants, cannot thrive, although they may continue to *survive* until another part of the *natural cycle*, when conditions may be more *favourable* to them.

In an artificially *illuminated* environment it is not *ordinarily* possible to reproduce annual or seasonal cycles of light intensity and character, for reasons of *equipment complexity*. It is therefore usual to try to reproduce only that part of the cycle which best *conforms* to the aquarist's requirements. Wherever light falls something living will usually develop. In aquatic environments, algae of various types will appear, either on fixed surfaces or floating free in the water, and, unless some *regulating* factor is at work, in all illuminated environments all the available light tends to be used up by the algae.

In an aquarium this produces the 'pea-soup effect', which is obviously undesirable. Algal growth is generally regulated by plants of a higher order which can *absorb* or shield out much of the light; by various *aquatic* animals such as snails and certain fish which eat certain types of *algae*; and by artificial methods such as filtration which *physically* remove some types, especially the *free-floating* kinds.

Thus, in a planted *aquarium*, it should be ensured that the plants selected dominate the algae present and *discourage* too much new algal growth. Algae should not be eliminated altogether, even if this were possible; they are a very necessary feature of all *artificial environments* which are meant to be natural rather than *sterile*.

Furthermore, algae are the only readily available plant growth for marine environments. Where algae live in *association* with more *desirable* plants they must be kept in a secondary position. To achieve full growth of the *major* plants, the light available to them and their *population* in the *environment* must be such as to represent that time in the cycle of the wild environment when the plants are at their best.

Figure elsewhere in this chapter illustrates the seasonal changes in a *natural*, planted pond. In winter the pond is in a *static* condition in which plant growth is either *stationary* or reduced to dormant root-stocks in the base *medium*.

Temperatures are at their lowest, daylight is dim and does not last long, and any animals present are inactive and do not feed enough to provide any *appreciable* wastes. When spring comes, daylight and temperature increase, the animals '*wake up*' and feed and produce wastes, and a *plantoriented* condition develops.

Those plants which may have retained their last year's growth will now carry on, but the other plants whose old growth is non-existent or useless remain only as *root-stock*. These plants need to grow all the way from the bottom to the surface or near it to make the most *efficient* use of light and this takes some time, especially if the plant food around the *root-stock* is poor.

In the meantime, in the absence of any regulating influences, algal growth is promoted by the bright spring *sunshine* and develops *quickly*, covering all available surfaces and *eventually appearing* as free-floating

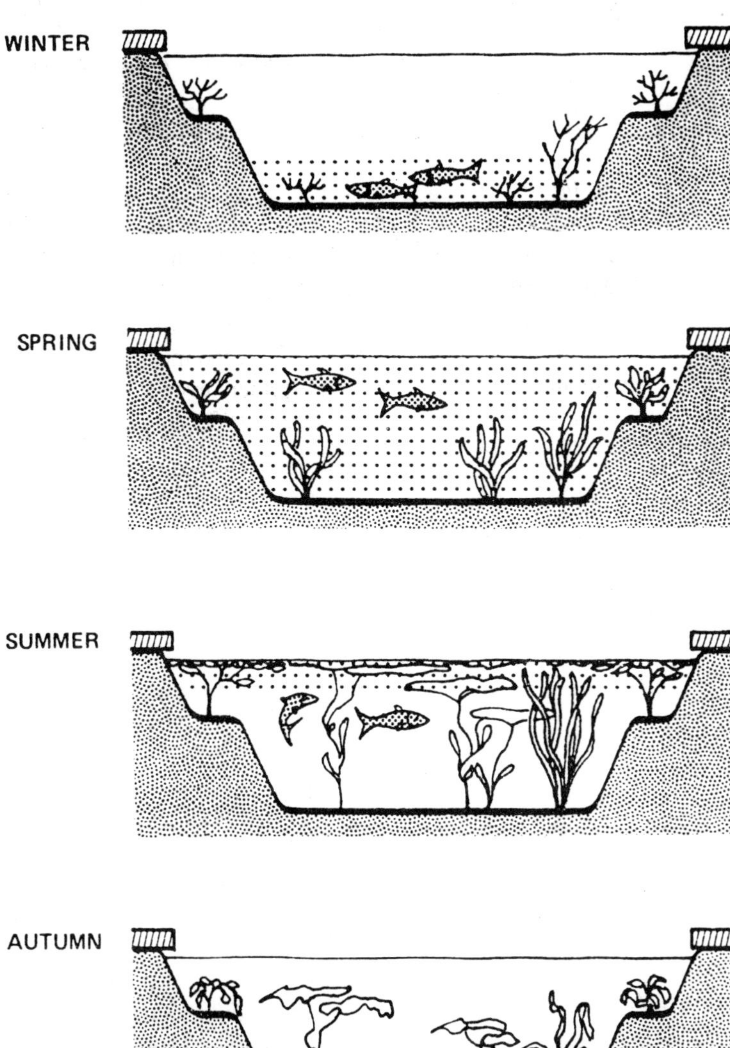

*Figure 1.3: The seasonal changes in a planted pond.
The dots represent green algae.*

forms. The pond then has that familiar 'pea-soup' consistency and appearance.

With the coming of late *spring* and *early* summer the fish have their breeding period and are very active, producing much waste, while daylight and *temperature* increase further and finally the rooted plants appear from the deeps in search of light.

The algae now go into a decline and a balance is created whereby the major plants fill all the space they can reach and the *algae* grow strongly only in the remaining spaces. This situation continues through the summer with a decrease in algal growth as the major plants develop further.

Throughout this period the water is clear and only surface-fixed algae are noticeable. In the autumn everything starts to rot down or just stops growing, ready for the next year. The whole of this *amazing* cycle is controlled by seasonal changes in daylight and *temperature* with only minor *variations* due to other *environmental* factors.

It is clear from the example of the fish-pond that we should seek to reproduce and stabilise in freshwater planted environments that summer period of *luxurious* plant growth *coupled* with clear water and *minimal* algal population.

The main requirements are plenty of light, both in terms of intensity and duration, high temperatures and sufficient well-fed plant growth initially to ensure domination over the algae. This last point is usually the one which most *aquarists* neglect.

Instead, the tendency is to start with a virtually sterile, gravel base medium, often with *plant-disturbing* influences such as a subgravel filter, and to install only a bare minimum of plants on the *assumption* that they will grow to fill the container in no time at all.

This is a great mistake, because if the environment does not initially have sufficient plant life installed in a suitable feeding base medium, strong algal growth will *flourish* and *dominate* the higher plants. The environment will then be a *simulation* of the spring condition rather than the *summer* period and may not *progress* as it does in nature.

Fish do not require absolutely fixed intensities or durations of light, but they do have preferences which presumably reflect the fact that they come from various natural *environments* and have many *characteristics* which are strongly *influenced* by light.

The popular range of aquarium freshwater fish can be divided roughly into those which delight in intense light and swim and feed just below the surface and in the *middle waters*, those which inhabit the bottom and dark corners and are suited to dim lighting, and those which are usually *nocturnal*. The intensity of light definitely seems to have an effect on the '*happiness*' of some of the more sensitive fish.

Some cichlids, for instance, will not do at all well unless they can hide in caves or under plant growth away from strong light. If these *facilities* are not provided the fish may become '*neurotic*' and illness or death may follow because they do not feed properly.

Generally the tetras, danios and many barbs and similar fish, particularly those which *shoal*, like or tolerate strong lighting, while cichlids, catfish and the more individual species prefer *shady* hiding places in *bright environments* or *dim lighting* in more open environments.

It is surprising how a change of lighting will alter the balance between fish in a community *aquarium*. For instance, a previously meek, nervous specimen may bully the whole population if the *lighting* is altered, while a bully used to dim lighting may be *virtually* driven 'underground' by an increase in *intensity*.

Also, the colour of a fish alters with the strength and type of light falling upon it, so that a particular fish will look at its best only in the right light. Many fish completely change their colours and *camouflage patterns* with changes of light.

The duration of illumination in artificial situations determines either partially or wholly the length of the fish's day. Within reason this can influence their feeding habits and hence their rate of *growth*.

Certainly the application of regular amounts of light coupled with the usual constant high temperatures tends to keep fish in a *perpetual summertime* condition, so that they should grow faster and *stronger* than in nature.

This is not necessarily desirable but it is virtually inevitable where all the available light is artificial. Also, fish do not receive the annual *cyclic rest periods* to which their bodies are adjusted and it could be argued that this may *shorten* their life-span.

One feature of *domestic life* which always affects fish which have previously lived in natural surroundings is the sudden switching on and off of *artificial lamps* in the room in which the aquarium is kept. Nervous fish such as large angels have been known to dive straight into the gravel base or crash against the sides of the tank and suffer severe *injuries*, if not *death*, when this *happens*.

Lighting should always be changed gradually or in steps, for instance by switching off the aquarium light, say, fifteen minutes before the room light, and vice versa when switching on. *Domestic* lamp dimmers are now readily available and are ideal for aquarium use.

FOOD

Any *artificial* environment requires the inclusion of food in one form or another and in such a manner as not to spoil its longterm stability. It should be such that it can be absorbed easily and *quickly* by the *inhabitants* without any serious effects such as fouling, and of course it must be *nutritious* and efficient in *promoting* growth and good health.

Ideally, food should be given as often as the animals will take it. Many creatures, including various fish, are adapted to *continuous* feeding while others, particularly the *predators*, feed less often but in larger quantities at one time.

Some effort should be made to cater for these requirements, especially in young, growing fish which need to feed *continuously*, otherwise the loadings on their digestive systems will be *excessive*. The correct quantity and quality of the food given can be learned only by experience and *demands* a regular involvement on the part of the aquarist.

One of the *pitfalls* of keeping any kind of livestock is the need to attend to feeding requirements with often *inconvenient* frequency and regularity. Most of the troubles encountered in artificial *environments* can be traced back to excessive or incorrect feeding, *especially* where small *containers* are used.

There are fundamental differences between the feeding habits of aquatic and terrestrial life-forms. *Terrestrial* animals expend large *amounts* of energy in searching for and obtaining water which fish obviously do not have to do.

The water in which they live is a rich fluid of many dissolved salts and gases fairly evenly distributed throughout, so that many valuable *chemical* substances can be *absorbed* directly, for example through the fish's gills, without any direct *feeding* action at all.

This is partly the reason why fish can go for long periods without actually ingesting food and not suffer severe damage, although their growth rate may be slowed or *stopped* and their *overall condition* may slowly *deteriorate*.

Whether they can do this in an artificial environment will depend on the prevailing conditions. Fish may be *herbivorous* (*vegetarian*) or *carnivorous* (meat eating), or more likely both, and most species will take a wide variety of foods of both kinds when hungry, but it is *surprising* how they show preferences for *certain* items when they are well fed.

In natural surroundings each species has its own way of acquiring the food which suits it best but in captivity it is dependent on the offerings of the aquarist. In an enclosed *artificial environment* the fish *theoretically* has far better feeding *conditions* than it ever does in the wild because it does not have to go foraging for its food, or compete seriously for it with other fish, or keep a constant watch for enemies whilst feeding.

If its dietary requirements are understood and it is offered the right type and size of food it should come to a better condition than in the wild, *assuming* that all other *environmental* conditions are satisfactory. Good feeding helps wild *imported* fish to settle *quickly*, especially if they can be given something with which they are already familiar.

Young fish are particularly sensitive to feeding *arrangements*; as an example, *aquarists* who raise fish in quantity for sale or for the selection of breeding *specimens* can usually rear them to the size at which they are sold by most *aquatic* shops within ten to *twelve* weeks, depending on the species.

Details of particular foods, feeding and preparation techniques are dealt with in other chapter of this book. It only needs to be noted here that although a great deal of time is wasted by *aquarists* through inefficient and *unnecessary maintenance* methods, this is rarely the case with *feeding practices*.

Once a certain feeding technique has been proven, nothing should be too much *trouble* in putting it into operation, and the regular involvement necessary for the right attitude to feeding cannot be overstressed.

TEMPERATURE

Fish are *cold-blooded* animals and as such have only a limited control over their body temperatures, which vary with the temperatures of the surrounding water. They employ the same processes for the conversion of food into energy and heat as other animals, but any excess heat is quickly dissipated into their *surroundings* with the result that, for *practical purposes*, their body temperatures can be said to be equal to that of the water.

A fish's functions such as its feeding *activity*, *health and growth*, its activity level and the *workings* of its *internal processes*, are all affected directly by the temperature of its *immediate* environment.

Each species tolerates only a relatively narrow temperature range which reflects the prevailing *climatic* conditions in its natural *habitat*.

Outside this range a further band exists in which the fish can live, but not very well—it easily becomes sick, does not grow *properly*, and may not reproduce. Beyond these outer limits the fish dies, through the *slowing* down at low temperatures of its *metabolism*, or its *inability* at high *temperatures* to cope with the additional load on its *system* coupled with *problems* caused by the lack of oxygen in the water.

Table 1.2: Preferred and tolerated temperature ranges of some common species.

Species	Preferred	Tolerated
Goldfish (coldwater)	55°F-65°F	35°F-95°F
Guppy	65°F-75°F	40°F-95°F
Angelfish (tropical)	72°F-82°F	60°F-90°F

Table elsewhere in this chapter shows the preferred and tolerated temperature ranges of three common species. It should be noticed that this table demonstrates the two major divisions of aquarium fish, namely, tropical and coldwater, reflecting the *overwhelming importance* of environmental temperature in their lives, but also shows the *guppy* as an *interesting exception* which can live in both temperature ranges.

Because of the limitations of available equipment, artificial environments which require heat are usually maintained at some more or less constant value, rather than being allowed to wander over a limited range in *daily* and *seasonal cycles*, as in *nature*.

This is *particularly* true today due to the use of electrical heating methods. In former days, when gas and solid fuel boilers were used to heat fish houses for instance, cycles could be *arranged fairly* easily and in fact often could not be *avoided* due to the *greater* influence of ambient temperature on these systems.

This, however, was probably the only advantage of the old methods and it is doubtful whether it was often exploited *intentionally*. The temperature of the environments in which tropical fish are kept is usually *maintained* within about 4°F (2°C) of the chosen point.

It is possible to obtain thermostats which produce a differential of only 1°F (0.5°C) but this is unnecessary and is certainly of no benefit to the fish.

The selected temperature should be representative of the fish's daytime surroundings in its natural environment during the summer period of its *annual cycle*. A middle temperature of 76°F (24.5°C) with a *differential* range from 74°-78°F (23.5°25.5°C) is the basic *temperature* band generally used in *tropical fishkeeping*.

This is based on the long experience of many aquarists as being that best suited to the common *community type* environment and a good starting point for *tropical fish* whose temperature *characteristics* are unknown.

Obviously a few degrees either side of this range will not harm healthy fish as long as there are no rapid changes, but a sudden drop of only 5°F (3°C) can be fatal as a result of shock or the development of disease.

The so-called coldwater group of fish shows several interesting aspects of temperature tolerance. The *common goldfish* and most of its varieties are unusually adaptable to *gradual* temperature changes. They are frequently kept in tropical *conditions* yet also survive winters in *iced-over ponds*.

Some of the fancier varieties tend to favour the warmer ranges but generally the goldfish seems able to succeed in all *situations*. On the other hand, various wild *coldwater* fish do not survive in aquaria or shallow ponds because they require colder *temperatures* than can be provided with normal *equipment*.

The perch is a good example of this and many native marine fish suffer from the same disadvantage. As no suitable refrigerating equipment for aquaria is readily available, these fish cannot be kept very *successfully*, which is a great pity because, for instance, a perch in good condition in a truly *representative environment* is probably as attractive as any other *freshwater fish*.

Once a satisfactory temperature has been arrived at for a certain species this will normally be altered only to induce reproduction or to combat disease. Otherwise temperatures are usually *maintained* automatically around this *fixed value* and the *fish grow* accustomed to a virtually constant temperature.

Whether this is bad for them is difficult to say. It would seem that as long as the value is within the normal range of their natural adaptation they should cope, but it is questionable whether an old fish having spent all its life at one temperature could survive a permanent change of say 5°F (3°C) and also whether *aquarium-bred fish* could cope with the *fluctuations* encountered in nature.

Once fish have become accustomed to life at constant temperatures then it is wise to take every precaution against *sudden* or *permanent* changes. In mixed environments of fish, plants and other aquatic animals the situation may become more difficult unless the inhabitants all live naturally within the same *temperature* range.

Plants do not seem to adapt well to unnatural temperatures and the requirements of many of the more exotic animals are not well known at the moment.

THE NITROGEN CYCLE

In any enclosed container of mature water, organic material such as fish excreta, uneaten food or dead bodies is automatically converted into mineral form by *heterotrophic bacteria*. These *organisms* feed only on organic substances and develop quite easily and naturally wherever *sufficient* food of this kind is *available*.

For *practical* purposes the result of their activity is the production from waste material of substances such as *ammonia*, which in sufficient quantities are toxic to fish and other *animals*.

This process of breaking organic matter into simple chemicals is a fundamental part of what is known as the nitrogen cycle and when the cycle is completed the wastes are eventually *converted* into *nitrogen* and nitrous oxide, both of which are *harmless* to the *inhabitants* of the environment.

Alternatively, the *nitrogenous minerals* (*nitrites* and *nitrates*) are absorbed by plants, and then by some animals, thereby completing the cycle.

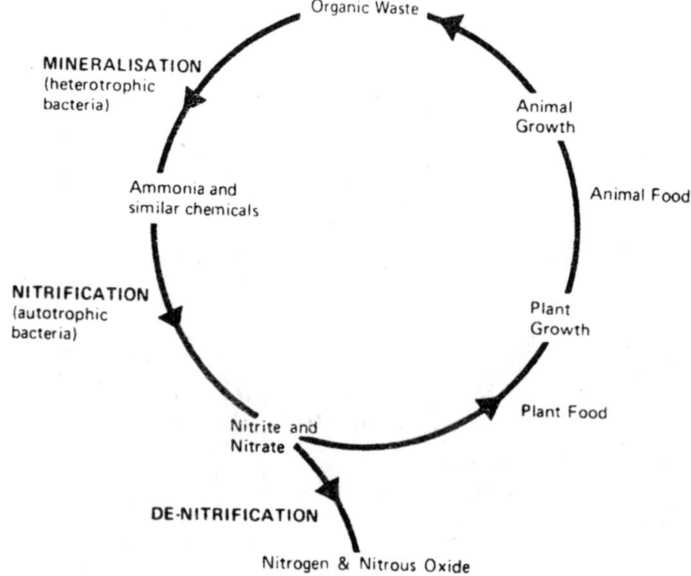

Figure 1.4: The nitrogen cycle.

Table 1.3: Progress of the nitrogen cycle, the relationship of various cleaning methods and their application.

Process	*Resulting Products*	*Relevant Methods*	*Mode of Operation*
Accumulation of dead animal and plant remains, excreta and urine, uneaten food	Organic waste as visible detritus and dissolved organic chemicals	a) siphoning and manual removal	Removes large accessible pieces.
		b) mechanical filtering with straining materials	Removes small pieces to reduce turbidity.
		c) adsorption by activated carbon	Removes dissolved organics
Mineralisation of organic waste by heterotrophic bacteria	Ammonia compounds typical toxic level 0.5mg/litre	a) water changing, completely, or partially	Dilutestoxic concentrations.
		b) de-ionising resins water.	Absorbsammonia unsuitable for salt
		c) air-stripping with bubble columnsand protein skimmers	Oxidises ammonia by air contact. Skimmercollects scum residue.
		d) ozonisation by Ozone contact air containing triatomic oxygen organisms	oxides ammonia killsmicro

(Table 1.3 Contd.)

(Table 1.3 Contd.)

Process	*Resulting Products*	*Relevant Methods*	*Mode of Operation*
Nitrification of ammonia by autotrophic bacteria	Nitrite: typical toxic level 15mg/litre. Nitrate: typical toxic level 150mg/litre	a) biological filtration by sub-gravel filters or external beds	Sufficientinorganic material in aerobic conditions promotes large nitrifying bacteria colony.
		b) plant and algal growth	Absorbs nitrates as food
Nitrification of nitrite and nitrate by both heterotrophic and autotrophic bacteria	Nitrous oxide and nitrogen. Both harmless	Nitrogen cycle completed	

The problem in completing the nitrogen cycle comes at the second stage where by various means the highly toxic ammonia is converted to the less *harmful nitrates* and nitrites by *autotrophic bacteria*, which feed on inorganic substances and use carbon dioxide in the conversion process.

Whereas the development of' heterotrophic mineralising bacteria depends on the quantity of waste available, nitrifying bacteria cannot develop in large quantities unless *sufficient inorganic material* of a suitable type (eg *rocks*, *glass*, *gravel*) is present.

If the aquarist does not include enough of this material, or some substitute for it, the nitrogen cycle will only be partially completed and the only protection against increasing *toxicity* in the aquarium will be scrupulous cleanliness and the *exclusion* of all wastes. This is a lengthy and tedious process which can usually be *avoided* by *careful management*.

The third stage of the process, in which *nitrates* and *nitrites* are converted to free nitrogen and nitrous oxide, is carried out by both *heterotrophic* and *autotrophic bacteria* and is *automatic*, providing the second stage has been *satisfactorily* completed.

A further requirement for the completion of the cycle is that aerobic (oxygen-rich) conditions should occur wherever the autotrophic bacteria are situated. *Anaerobic conditions*, familiar to aquarists as black smelly gravel in over-fed, *neglected environments*, must always be avoided.

There are various methods of completing or substituting for the difficult second stage of the cycle, thereby ensuring *continuous purity* of the water. Table elsewhere in this chapter *summarises* the methods. The *measures* adopted depend on the severity of any likely pollution and how much time and effort the aquarist is *prepared* to spend.

The obvious straightforward method is to change a proportion of the water periodically, thus regularly reducing the concentration of toxic ammonia to acceptable levels. This procedure has the *disadvantage* that otherwise useful mature water is thrown away, chlorine is introduced with new tap-water, and that water changing is hard work.

The second remedy, where the environment is suitable, is to grow submerged aquatic plants and/or algae in such quantities that the plants use up mineral salts as food at the same rate as they are produced from organic wastes, thus *maintaining* the *purity* of the water. Generally, this system is practical only in *habitats* in which the fish do not eat the plants.

Table 1.4: Methods for the completion of the second stage of the nitrogen cycle.

Method	*Disadvantages*	*Comments*
Siphoning and manual removal	Removes only that visible	Useful for removal of large pieces or accumulations
Mechanical filtration (straining)	Removes only materials which water circulation system brings into the filter body. Must be frequently cleaned. Dissolved organics remain	Reduces turbiditywhere inhabitants dig or are messy. Strong and continuous action possible
Activated carbon	Holds dissolved organics for disposal. When' full' can suddenly release load back into water. In use must be pre-washed to remove dust and changed often. Adsorbs medicines and other additives	Extremely efficient when properly operated. Can be re-used following steam pressure cleaning. Removes urine
Water changing	Hard work. Partial changes only give proportionate dilution. Continuous or frequent newwater inputs not always beneficial due to chlorine content and temperature matching, and salt depletion in marine environments	The only reliable method for fast action in emergency situations or where a pollutant is synthetic
De-ionising	Removes too many valuable elements from salt water. Subject to fouling by unabsorbed organic substances. Some resins toxic themselves	Expensive. Study of available types essential. Not generally recommended
Air-stripping	May increase pH value by removing weak acids normally present. Foam must be regularly removed from skimmers. Effective only against substances sensitive to surface reaction	Oxygenates water. Bubble columns are decorative. Skimmers are quite bulky, so are best fitted externally

(Table 1.4 Contd.)

Method	***Disadvantages***	***Comments***
Ozonisation	Ozonised airshould not be directly injected as it is harmful to the inhabitants in close contact. Removes trace elementsfrom salt water. Difficultto estimate injection Excess ozone harmful	Best used in conjunction with a protein skimmerfor high efficiency. Useful in sterile systems, correct regulation must be achieved rate.
Biological filtration	Requires maturation period to achieve full efficiency. Medicines and additives may kill filter bacteria. Clogs up eventually if too much mechanical place	Sudden loss of bacteria brings about toxic con ditions. The most efficient system except where inhabitants dig or disturb bed. Should be primary method
Plant growth	Requires deep growing bed with plant nutrients	Very decorative. Additional urine removal needed in freshwater
Algal filtration	Uses large trays and intense lighting with complex water circulation system	Impractical in domestic situations

Further methods of dealing with ammonia utilise various items of specialised equipment, either to complete the nitrogen cycle or to make its completion unnecessary by *directly* removing ammonia from the environment. All types of *filters* and *skimmers* fall into this category and are fully discussed in other chapter of this book.

Their use and *reliability* depend on available power supplies and the degree of *maintenance* they require to keep them operating. Many of the gadgets available are little more than *complicated substitutes* for simpler methods which have been available for a long time but were never fully understood.

By intelligent application of simple equipment, some attention to the total population of an environment and proper feeding, it should be possible for the average aquarist to keep a *container* of water in good biological condition for at least one year *without* any complex *routine procedures*.

It should be remembered that the simplest *method consistent* with success will be the most reliable and *rewarding*. The best and most convenient method for general use in most types of *environment* is probably a biological method involving a sub-gravel filter. The filter itself and its action are described later but its advantages are considered here.

It requires a minimum of external equipment, no routine maintenance, is inconspicuous and will function *satisfactorily* for years. The only restrictions on its use are in planted environments, where plant growth is important to the aquarist, and in aquaria *containing* fish which dig into the gravel.

The alternative *methods* all have advantages in specific situations. Natural methods are a far truer representation of the normal environment because of the inclusion of animals and *organisms* with which the fish *normally* associate.

In other systems the food which these creatures need might not be readily available. Sterile methods are the best means of *ensuring* protection against disease or pollution and may be considered useful where a *large specimen* or a *small group* of a single species (such as discus) might in any event live in total isolation from other fish.

2

Aquarium Systems

If the *environmental* factors detailed in the previous chapter are carefully considered it can be seen that all of them are common, in varying degrees, to all aquatic *environments*, *depending* on the required *conditions* and the nature of the *inhabitants*.

The aquarist's objective is to select and manipulate these factors in order to arrive at a near-perfect solution to a particular problem. It is important to realise that, in the long run, the critical factor which *determines* the success or failure of any *aquarium project* is the degree to which the nitrogen cycle is *satisfactorily completed*.

Other factors, such as temperature and illumination, are readily adjustable but the method used to complete the *nitrogen cycle* is best thought out beforehand to suit the type of environment planned, since once a *particular method* is adopted it is often difficult to change to another without *considerable trouble*.

As already outlined, there are three basic types of nitrogen cycle systems which can be used—*natural*, *biological* and *sterile*, to use current popular *terminology*. Each system is described below in some detail, with an account of the various *advantages* and *disadvantages*, the purpose of any specialised techniques *concerned* and the *equipment* used in each case.

There are many instances in which equipment and methods peculiar to one system are used in another, sometimes *beneficially* and sometimes not, and a thorough *understanding* of the *basic systems* should help to avoid incorrect selection and unnecessary *duplication*. It is perhaps worth mentioning that the present-day emphasis on new environmental methods and the use of various technological innovations has been *accelerated* by the growth of interest in marine aquatics and the resulting need for a more careful study of these fish's *requirements* than was previously undertaken for *freshwater* fish.

The knowledge and *understanding* acquired, however, provides a useful background for all kinds of *fishkeeping* and with proper application can benefit everyone.

THE NATURAL SYSTEM

Environmental systems are said to be natural when they reproduce the wild aquatic environment as closely as possible and use nature's own methods to ensure stability and completion of the nitrogen cycle, without the use of artificial methods and external equipment.

The natural system is the successor of the *old fashioned* concept of the 'balanced aquarium' and at its best it can approach in many respects this *theoretical ideal*.

A large container, equipment to provide the required amounts of heat, light and air, and enough water of the correct type in a matured state are necessary if the setting-up of a *natural* system environment is to be *considered*.

The main objective, coupled probably with the need to produce a decorative and pleasing aquarium, is to ensure that the gap in the nitrogen cycle between the automatic stages of mineralisation and *denitrification* is filled by a suitable *nitrifying process* so that wastes and other unwanted organic debris are *rendered harmless*.

For a successful natural system the inhabitants must be fed with extreme care and any dead bodies or large lumps of uneaten food removed as soon as possible so that the nitrogen cycle is run with a fairly *constant loading* and is not subject to excess mineralisation.

The reason for this is that even though every inorganic surface in the environment eventually acquires a population of *autotrophic nitrifying* bacteria the total area is simply not large enough to provide sufficient bacteria for *unusually large* rates of nitrification, and so the nitrifying potential of the environment as a whole is low; however, it is able to cope with a *reasonably* constant medium loading.

The acquisition of nitrifying bacteria takes some time and initially a new environment will have virtually no *nitrifying potential*. The basic objective is to avoid the introduction or build-up in the environment of

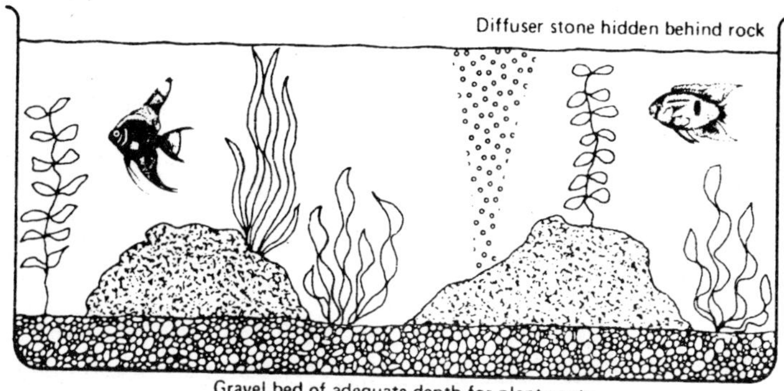

Figure 2.1: The freshwater natural system. The nitrogen cycle is completed by natural methods involving plant growth and the use of scavengers such as snails and other organisms which are found in the fish's natural habitat. A fertilising medium may be included in the gravel bed to encourage a lush growth of rooted plants. The air-bubble column ensures adequate gaseous exchange and provides natural turbulence.

quantities of organic waste and to install functional inhabitants, plant or animal, whose activities help in the control of this waste and so reduce the work-load on the *nitrifying bacteria*.

In freshwater aquaria, lush plant growth can be used to absorb mineral salts and should be set in a deepish gravel bed which contains enough plant food to establish the *plants initially*.

If the plant growth is good and aerobic conditions are present in the bed this will provide extra *inorganic* surfaces for population by autotrophic bacteria, with a consequent increase in the nitrifying potential. It is usually recommended that gravels should be washed, or even *boiled*, as a safety measure in case any chemical pollution is *present* but, ideally, when gravel is first used it should be *biologically* mature with at least a partial *population* of *bacteria*.

Mulm, debris and so on should also be present to provide immediate plant food. If absolutely clean gravel must be used, it should be 'dirtied' by rubbing with *good garden soil* (*insecticide free*) or by leaving it exposed to the *weather*.

If these precautions are taken, plants can root and grow quickly, and subsequently other animals, such as snails or insects, can be introduced. Snails help the process of mineralisation by eating large pieces of organic debris, some of which they *digest* and some of which they excrete in a more convenient form for bacteria to *absorb*. Other creatures may not be particularly *beneficial* to the system but if *harmless* can be included for *decoration* or *interest*.

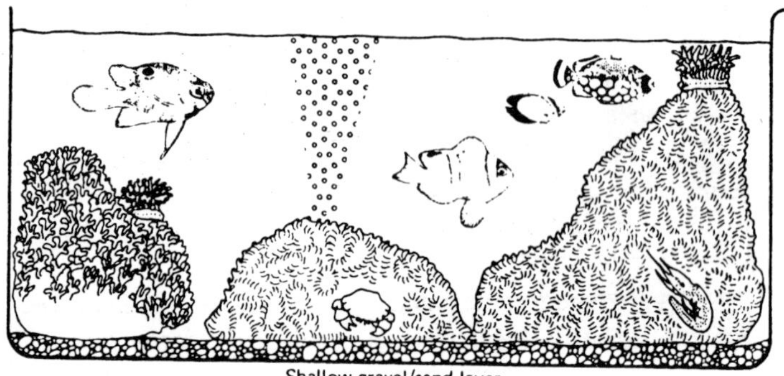

Figure 2.2: The marine natural system. Scavengers such as crabs and other crustaceans search out uneaten food, while filter-feeding invertebrates such as living corals remove organic material from the water. In this way the nitrogen cycle is completed, provided no heavy loadings occur. The air-bubble column provides natural exchange functions and turbulence.

In marine aquaria it is not usual to establish and propagate a heavy plant growth. It is interesting to note, however, that in the sea many *creatures* and organisms are found which effectively perform the same function as the plants in natural freshwater aquaria. Live *coral*, *tubeworms*, sponges and various other *creatures*, all known as *'filter feeders'*, continually *circulate* the water through their *bodies* and *remove* matter for their own use.

A large population of these organisms effectively *removes organic* substances from the water and reduces the rate of mineralisation. This is especially important in natural marine *environments* because the *nitrifying* potential is usually low compared with that *available* in freshwater gravel beds, due to the lack of any *appreciable inorganic* surface area.

Gravels in natural marine aquaria should be *shallow* (ideally one grain deep) since, without the presence of plants or other means of producing *oxygen*, *anaerobic* conditions can easily *develop* and *ruin* the whole environment.

Gravels are in fact only of limited use in natural marine systems since most filter feeding organisms prefer to be situated on rock rather than on loose gravel and some anemones, for example, will move on to the walls of the container if a suitable hard base is not provided.

Dead coral material or Westmorland stone (which is *geologically* similar) with *fairly smooth* surfaces are satisfactory and anemones will not change position if they are initially sited to their liking. Even with plenty of rock as a base for the filter feeders the *nitrifying* potential will still be low, so the environment must be kept clean. Fish and other organisms which die must be removed *quickly* and any *rotting organic* matter must be scoured from *rockwork*, *dead coral* and other material such as shells before *installation*.

Other marine creatures such as *crustaceans* and *starfish* are all useful to the nitrogen cycle and are suited to the *natural system*, provided of *course* that they are *compatible* with one another and with the other *inhabitants*.

It takes some time to build up a suitable population of *nitrifying bacteria* in both freshwater and *marine environments* since the autotrophic bacteria develop only after *sufficient mineralisation* has taken place to ensure enough food for them.

There are two basic methods of populating the available surface area: either a small animal population can be kept initially while the population of bacteria is allowed to build up slowly, or a single large animal or a large population of smaller animals which are tolerant of the *resulting* temporary build-up of *toxic materials* can be installed *immediately*, while the *nitrifying bacteria* develop.

This latter method encourages the speedy development of the bacteria due to the resulting high rate of mineralisation, but great care must be taken during the *intermediate toxic stage*. On balance, the first method, which is slower, is more suitable for use in a *natural system*, *especially* a marine one in which the filter feeders would have to be *installed* after the toxic stage in the second method.

Any large, hardy animal, for instance a turtle, can be used in this second method, and would normally be removed afterwards rather than becoming a *permanent part* of the *natural system* since its *copius wastes* would *probably overload* even the final *bacterial population*.

A good, easily understood example of a natural system is a successful goldfish pond, where all the points given above are satisfied and the only regular involvement on the part of the aquarist is to provide food. A thorough study of such a *situation* will be of benefit to aquarists involved in other types of *fishkeeping*.

It should be pointed out here that fish parasites and disease organisms can live as easily in a natural system as in their home waters, so care must be taken to exclude them *completely*. A diverse living *population* makes medication extremely difficult, since a cure for one *organism* often poisons another.

It is better to remove isolated cases of infection or *sickness* for treatment elsewhere, and all new additions must be *thoroughly* and effectively quarantined before *inclusion*. Where contagious epidemics are encountered, which *necessitate* treatment of the whole volume of water, plants or filter feeders are probably best *removed* before treatment as they are sensitive to many of the medicines used.

Often an *epidemic* will ruin a particular environment and the only cure will be to scrap everything and start again after the container has been purified. Algae in one form or another are inevitable inhabitants of all *natural systems*.

Brown algae, which grow in *poorly-lit situations*, are not *particularly* beneficial and usually not encouraged. *Green algae*, on the other hand, particularly the soft, brightly coloured types, grow in good light in *situations* devoid of plant life and give the same benefits as the higher plants, although on a *lesser scale*.

Algae are especially useful in marine environments because of the lack of higher plant life. They also form an *important* part of the diet of many fish. Algae must, however, be kept in check and limited to a useful *function* only. In freshwater environments, strong algal growth can smother plants, which die as a result of *blocked* leaf *pores* and *poor* light. Similarly, *gravels* are grown over and become *anaerobic* and *foul*.

Small *light-dependent* organisms called *Zooxanthellae* are present inside many marine filter feeders and their well-being, and thus that of their host, depends on their living in properly *illuminated* surroundings.

This fact is well illustrated by the observation that in dim lighting the host creatures lose their natural coloration and become pale, often acquiring algal growth, a condition which is a sure sign of ill-health. Light has an important *influence* in all natural systems because of the inclusion in these environments of light-dependent organisms. (The remarks made on this subject, and the methods of application recommended must be particularly noted.)

There are a few techniques commonly used by *aquarists* in natural systems which help to keep the level of *toxic materials* below that which the available nitrifying *bacteria* can deal with.

These methods might be considered '*cheating*' by some, but anything which improves the *inhabitants*' way of life is good and as long as the reason for their use is understood and they are not *detrimental* they must surely be used.

In many environments the aquarist *periodically* changes part of the water to reduce the *toxic* content. The water added should be mature and similar in character to that which is being replaced. *Mechanical* filters may also be used, either *temporarily* or *permanently*, to remove swirling debris which may never settle as a result of *turbulence*. *Periodic siphoning* to remove mulm and large pieces of *uneaten food*, and the cleaning of the front glass for good *visibility*, are both often *necessary*.

The use of a column of air bubbles to induce water movement and avoid the effects of thermal stratification also helps to *oxygenate* the water and in fact to some extent duplicates the action of a *protein skimmer* in *breaking* up *toxic wastes*.

The problem of uric acid is one instance in which the *marine* environment has an advantage over the freshwater one. *Freshwater fish* excrete *large quantities* of *urine* because their bodies have a greater salt content than the surrounding water and to maintain an *internal balance* they must frequently discharge *unwanted substances*.

With marine fish the flow is in the opposite *direction*. Although they '*drink*' and *purify* large quantities of sea-water to maintain the internal balance, and also *continuously* excrete large volumes of liquid, this does not contain much uric acid. For this *reason*, *uric acid* is not present in significant *concentrations* in marine environments and in fact for practical purposes can be considered absent.

Activated charcoal filters are often used in *freshwater* environments to absorb urine. Oxygenation in natural environments is assisted by *photosynthesis* in the higher *plants* and *algae* in strong light, and by the *Zooxanthellae* present in filter *feeders*.

Also, some form of air injection by pumping is usually necessary to provide water movement so *oxygenation* is not a problem unless the environment is *overstocked*. In nature, *marine habitats* are often very rich in oxygen because of the swirling currents found around *coral reefs* and the wave activity at the surface; thus some marine *creatures* may be more *sensitive* to *oxygen shortage* than might be *expected*.

On the other hand, many marine organisms are easily *damaged* by entrapped air caused by *supersaturated* conditions (or by *handling* out of water) so oxygenation must not be *overdone* and a fine *balance* must be *struck*.

THE BIOLOGICAL SYSTEM

In the biologically filtered environment, use is made of the fact that if aerobic conditions exist nitrifying bacteria populate all *inorganic* surfaces. Normally, as detailed earlier, the available inorganic surface area in any *aquarium* is insufficient to allow for the development of a really good *nitrifying* potential.

In the biological system this problem is overcome by using a deep gravel bed, with a large total grain surface area, through which the aquarium water is *continuously circulated* by a *sub-gravel* filter, thereby producing aerobic conditions and *exposing* as much of the water as possible to bacterial action.

The *efficiency* of any biological system depends on various criteria and these will now be considered in turn. The great majority of *autotrophic bacteria* occur in the top 3in (8mm) of the gravel bed and only a small increase in the *population* is gained by using a bed *deeper* than this.

It follows, therefore, that a bed of this depth which covers the whole area of the container base will give *satisfactory results*. The gravel particles used should be of irregular shape so that they have a large surface area, and they should be *fairly small*, but not so small that the water *circulation* is impeded.

A suitable size range is 0.1-0.4in (2-5mm). The depth of the gravel should be uniform over the whole area and the bed should be *horizontal* so that *water flows evenly through* it in all regions. Areas without good circulation may *develop anaerobic* conditions with consequent

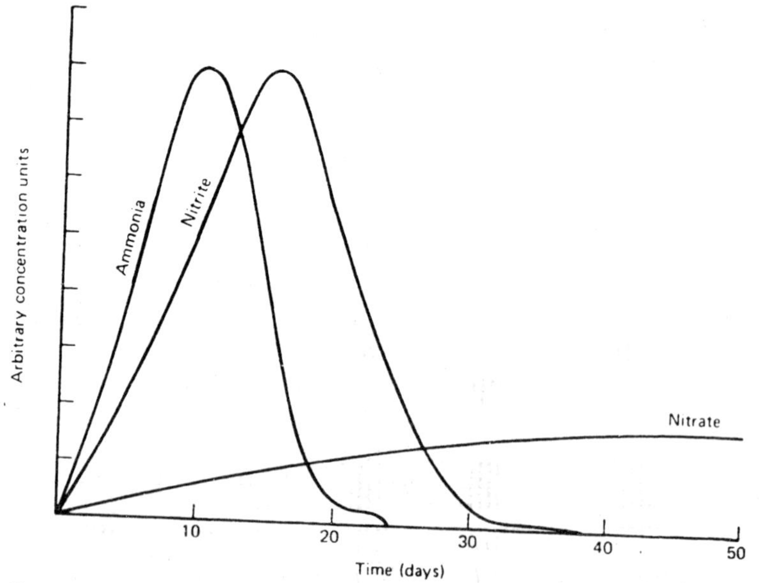

Figure 2.3: A diagrammatic illustration of the changes in concentration of the various components of the nitrogen cycle during the maturation period of a typical biological system.

problems. The circulation rate of the water through the bed should be such that the water is not so rich in oxygen as to be *supersaturated* but must be fast enough to *maintain aerobic conditions*.

A figure of half a gallon per square foot of bed per minute is usually a good starting point, measured most easily at the air-lift output tube. Care must be taken to ensure that there are no points at the edge of the bed against the *container* walls where *channels* of fast flow can develop, thereby *bypassing* the filter bed.

The usual cure for this is to bond the edges of the filter to the walls with an inert adhesive such as silicone rubber. In *setting* up a *biological system* the filter plate is installed on the base of the container and the gravel bed is laid on top. Either mature material or new *material* '*seeded*' with a portion of an old *successful* bed may be used.

If only new material is available the 'turtle' method described elsewhere in this chapter can be used to advantage, since the fantastic total surface area available makes the nitrifying potential extremely good and the *acquisition* of bacteria can be that much faster than in a natural system.

It is possible to populate a new bed simply by putting a piece of meat or fish into the aquarium and allowing it to rot, but this process would probably take longer than the *turtle* method as the meat would not be in such a convenient form for *bacterial assimilation* as would the *faeces* from a turtle or a larger fish. If *rotting* meat has to be used it should be ground up for best *results*.

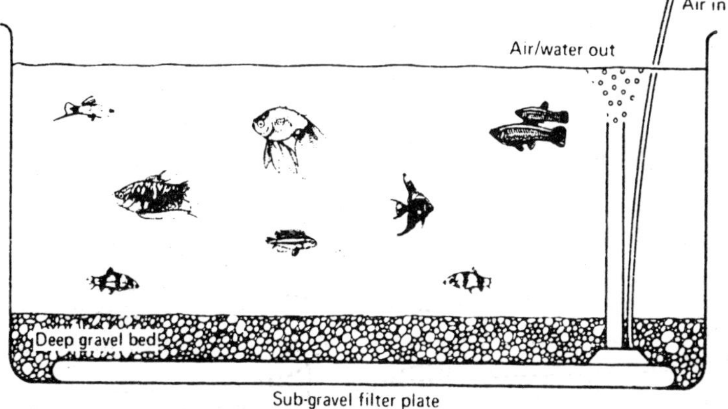

Figure 2.4: The freshwater biological system. This figure shows an aquarium in which a number of young fish are successfully being reared in a container which would be overpopulated if it were not for the biological system. No ornamental inclusions or plants are present in this specialised environment.

It must be stressed that while the population of *autotrophic bacteria* is growing, the environment may become temporarily toxic for creatures which are sensitive to high levels of *ammonia* and they should therefore not be *included* until the system is at, or near, its full nitrifying potential.

If for some reason such inhabitants are to be included shortly after installation of a biological system the *environment* must only be stocked lightly until the *temporary toxic* stage has passed. The level of concentration of *ammonia products* present can be *measured* by means of a *nitrite* test kit.

Finally, when the environment is at its full nitrifying potential it can be stocked quite heavily and any reasonable amounts of *uneaten* food and even the odd small dead fish need not be removed from the water.

Remember that the system is dependent on the circulation of the water through the bed to maintain aerobic conditions and continuity of the air supply to the *subgravel filter* is vital. The supply should not be switched off or lost through *breakdown* for any length of time and reliable equipment should be used with an emergency air *supply* always *available*.

In marine *environments* the *biological* system has the added advantage that natural coral sand can be used instead of stone gravel and this sand helps to maintain the chemical *stability* of the salt water. However, some coral sand on sale has a rather small grain size for efficient *circulation* and it is worth while taking the *trouble* to obtain a larger size if possible.

As well as acting as a biological filter the *gravel* bed is also an efficient mechanical filter. *Gradually* the *spaces* in the bed fill up with detritus from the water and this material is also *colonised* by bacteria, thereby adding to the *nitrifying potential*.

Clogging can occur where an excess of detritus is present but in this event the real problem is usually caused by using gravel with too small a grain size. The *design* of the filter plate itself and its associated air-lift system also affects *efficiency* and this is *discussed* further in other chapter of this book.

If a bed is washed for any reason after a period of use, this should be done with *mature* water of the same type as that normally used with the bed, since otherwise most of the *bacterial population* could be scoured off and lost. *Washing* removes a lot of the bacteria anyway but reasonable care will leave enough for a good start to be

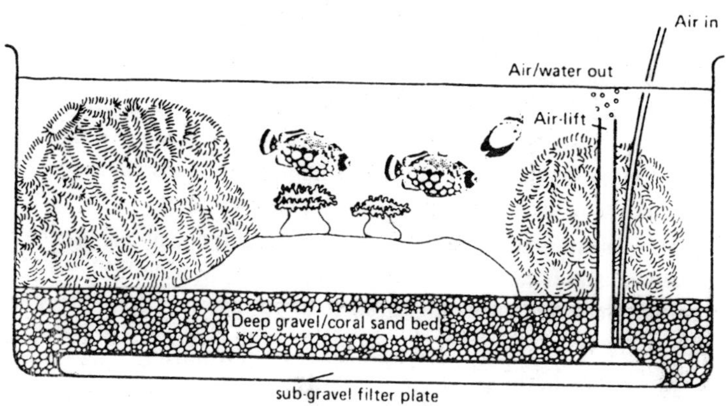

Figure 2.5: The marine biological system. The nitrifying potential of this environment is so high that some overfeeding, and even dead fish, can be tolerated. These happenings are not to be encouraged, but they do demonstrate the system's capacity to cope with common emergencies.

made on *reinstallation*. When emptying an *aquarium*, try to keep the water, if in good condition, and use it to wash the *gravel*. This procedure is particularly useful with marine gravels since these will be thoroughly scoured by fresh tap-water.

Changes in conditions in the environment *temporarily* affect the efficiency of a *biological* system but the system usually recovers and carries on as before. Acidity, temperature, fish population and so on all produce temporary changes.

Changes in the specific gravity of salt water due to *evaporation* losses should not be allowed to exceed 0.002 before adding fresh water, otherwise the bacteria will be affected.

The efficiency of this kind of system and its state at any *particular* time can be tested by measuring the *nitrite* content of the water with simple equipment. A reading which indicates a very low content or none at all means that the *environment* is '*clean*' and that the nitrogen cycle is being completed.

Other filters may be. used in *conjunction* with a *biological* system but their use is encouraged only when absolutely necessary. For example, in a very dirty *situation*, where the condition is likely to be permanent, a mechanical filter may alleviate clogging.

Also, if any activated charcoal filtration is required it can be carried out in the *mechanical filter*, thereby having no effect on the bacteria in the bed. *Neglected mechanical* and carbon filters take on a biological characteristic if left long enough without cleaning, as a result of the eventual population of their surfaces by *nitrifying bacteria*, but the available areas are not usually large enough to add significantly to the *nitrifying* potential of the environment.

The *biological system* is probably the best overall method for general use. Its large nitrifying potential allows the aquarist more time to concentrate on the fish and there is no need for *constant surveillance* and removal of waste, except in very extreme cases.

The system is adaptable to all kinds of environments, is particularly economical and is easy to understand and to use. Marine fishkeeping has *definitely benefited* from this system as its use has done away with much of the *mystique formerly* associated with this *branch* of *aquatics*.

Its serious development is in fact probably a result of the need to simplify the previously complicated methods used in marine fishkeeping. The *biological* system is, however, *unsatisfactory* in environments where a lush plant growth is *required*.

The plants do not seem to be able to tolerate the *circulation* of water around their roots and it is thought that such highly aerobic *conditions* may be too rich for them. It can also be argued that plants which feed heavily from their roots suffer from a *deficiency* of *essential* salts when the *nitrifying action* is good.

In those cases where *environments* with sub-gravel *filtration* and good plant growth have been established, the biological system is probably either inefficient or *non-existent* for some reason, possibly as a result of low air flow, and the *environment* is in fact almost functioning as a *natural system*.

In cases where the animal population burrows into or lives in the gravel bed the system may be unsuccessful because the continual disturbance opens up fast-flow channels which bypass the bed. *Eel*-like fish may become *trapped* and die *beneath* the *filter plate* if it is not sealed at the edges, or may find their way down the *air-lift* tubes if the ends do not have a *mesh cap* or *similar device*.

THE STERILE SYSTEM

In this system, developed mainly for the keeping of expensive and delicate marine specimens, the only creatures present in the environment are those for whom it is designed. There are no secondary animals or any other *biological lifeforms* and all *supporting* functions are carried out by *ancillary* equipment and the use of *stringent cleaning* methods.

Because urine presents less of a problem this method is more easily applicable to the marine *environment* but, even then, it is probably only the high cost of some marine specimens which justifies such an extreme approach to the problem of long-term *maintenance*. The methods are very technical and are totally dependent on the correct application of complex equipment.

The system is also artificial both aesthetically and biologically and by its very nature must be maintained in a spotlessly clean condition. *Aquarists* are advised to consider very carefully their own *requirements* and other available methods before becoming involved with a system of this kind.

It should be noted that the development of successful biological systems has made sterile methods somewhat redundant. As with the first two systems described, the basic *problem* is to achieve successful completion of the *nitrogen cycle*.

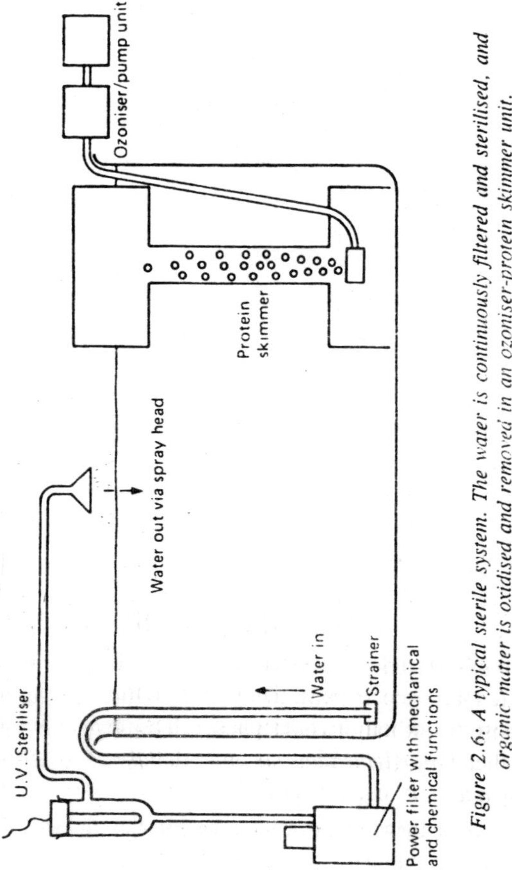

Figure 2.6: A typical sterile system. The water is continuously filtered and sterilised, and organic matter is oxidised and removed in an ozoniser-protein skimmer unit.

The equipment which performs this function in this system usually comprises a large *mechanical* filter, an *ozoniser* and a *protein skimmer*. In addition, an ultraviolet steriliser may be used to prevent disease. All of this equipment is expensive to *install* and *maintain* and the *aquarist* is totally dependent on it *functioning* correctly.

Feeding is carried out *sparingly* and carefully with artificial foods and nothing is put into the aquarium which has a remote chance of causing *pollution* or disease.

The main reasons for taking all this trouble are simply to minimise the risk of losing expensive specimens in imperfect natural *environments* and also to provide a method which, given the *availability* of specialised equipment, can be set up quickly for *commercial* purposes.

The container used should be as large as possible and should have smooth internal surfaces with any inside corners rounded to eliminate crevices which might hold dirt.

The only articles put into the environment, other than the inhabitants and the internal equipment, are either ornamental or perform a psychological function for the fish, such as providing hiding *places*.

These corals, rocks, or whatever, must first be cleaned thoroughly both chemically and biologically and this process should be *repeated* periodically throughout the life of the environment.

At such times a larger proportion of the water may also be changed to ensure dilution of any toxic compounds which may not have been removed by the *purifying* equipment.

No small objects or gravels should be included as these would hold dirt and make cleaning more difficult. One of the reasons for ageing water before installing the inhabitants in *natural* and *biological* systems is to ensure a population of bacteria and other organisms from the start.

In a sterile system any bacteria, *plankton* and so on, whether harmful or beneficial, are soon killed by the equipment and so there is no point in supplying mature water for this purpose. On the other hand, the ageing process may remove unwanted constituents such as *chlorine* and for this reason may be necessary.

When a solution of synthetic salt is being mixed for a sterile marine environment there would seem to be a case for using distilled water, since nothing else is required other than those ingredients supplied in the salt mix.

There would then be no organic substances or organisms present initially and this would get the system off to a good start. In a freshwater environment tap-water with the right qualities would be needed, since distilled water without additions would be unsuitable. Plants and filter feeding organisms cannot be kept in a sterile system since the strong cleaning action present destroys all suitable food and the system is therefore limited to those creatures which can be fed directly by the aquarist.

Uneaten food and dead bodies could theoretically be left in if the system were highly efficient but it is better that wastes are removed in case some breakdown of equipment occurs before the rotting substances can be made safe.

The specialised equipment used in this system—ozoniser, protein skimmer and ultraviolet steriliser—can only eliminate pollution of the water if the cleaning action is faster than the rate of regeneration of

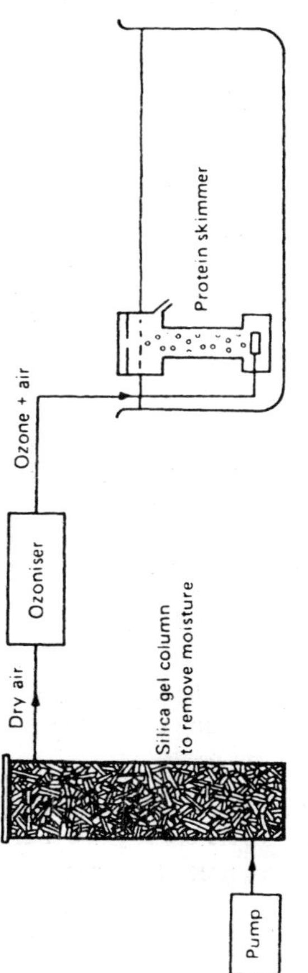

Figure 2.7: An ozoniser-protein skimmer system in detail.

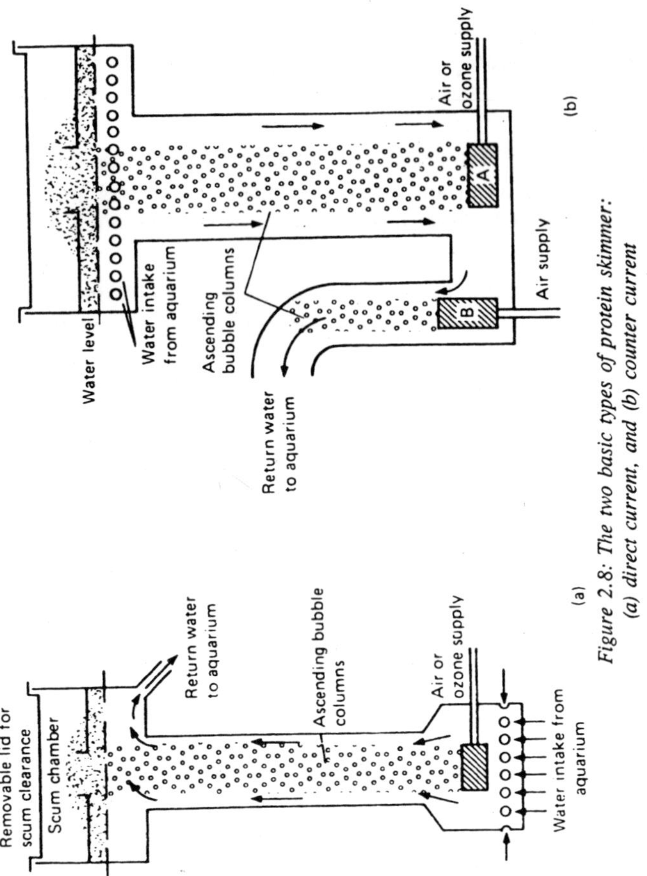

Figure 2.8: The two basic types of protein skimmer: (a) direct current, and (b) counter current

the pollutant; hence the need for large water throughputs, since a system which is slower will only dilute a problem and may never clear it.

This may be the reason why, even with all this complex equipment, periodic partial water changes are still advised and why some trial and error is required in adjusting a system to reach optimum efficiency.

The ozoniser converts oxygen in the air into ozone, an unstable poisonous gas which kills bacteria and also oxidises ammonia. The air supply for the protein skimmer is usually passed through the ozoniser, but the ozone may alternatively be injected via an airstone and thus into direct contact with the water.

In this case care should be taken that the fish do not come into direct contact with the ozonised bubbles. Assuming that the correct water turnover rates are achieved, all the water in the environment will frequently come into contact with ozone and will be cleansed of bacteria and some toxic compounds. Figure elsewhere in this chapter shows a typical layout of an ozoniser-protein skimmer system.

The silica gel column is used to ensure a dry air input to the ozonator to prevent damage to the internal components from any moisture present, with resulting inefficiencies. The silica gel crystals change colour when 'full' of moisture and can then be cleared by baking in a domestic oven.

The ozonator must not be contaminated by oil from piston airpumps, so if these are used preliminary oil filtering must be installed. The protein skimmer employs the same principal as an ascending column of bubbles from an airstone.

When such a column is passed through a solution of organic water, ie a dirty aquarium, the wastes are deposited as a foam or scum which in a protein skimmer is collected for removal. The skimmer is simply a method of passing the aquarium water continuously through an ascending air-stream and trapping the resulting residue at the top.

If supplied with ozonised air it will perform both functions and there will be less residue to dispose of as much will be broken down by the ozone. The two basic types of protein skimmer in use are shown in Figure elsewhere in this chapter.

In the directcurrent design the efficiency of the oxidation process is dependent on the available area of the air-water interface (determined by the size of bubbles and their quantity) and the longest possible contact time between the water and the air (maximum distance between diffuser stone and water surface).

In the counter-current design the water is made to flow in the opposite direction to the bubble columns from the diffuser. This results in increased contact time and thus more efficient oxidation. The process may tend to oxidise weak acids in fresh water and thus increase the pH value, and may remove trace elements from salt water.

Both the ozoniser and protein skimmer depend for their efficiency on a good supply of pumped air, which in a sterile environment should be filtered before use. On the other hand, with the ultraviolet steriliser it is necessary to pump the water through it and so it is usually used in conjunction with a water pump type of mechanical filter, often called a power filter.

The steriliser contains an ultraviolet lamp and the aquarium water is passed through in such a way that the water is irradiated by the lamp. The radiation kills all bacteria, good or bad, which pass through in the water and also various disease organisms.

Its efficiency depends on the rate of flow of water through it and on the intensity of the lamp. It has some advantage in that, unlike the ozoniser, it does not inject anything into the environment but only treats water which passes through it external to the aquarium.

It can also be used for medicinal reasons in systems other than the sterile type since it does not kill fixed nitrifying bacteria, which do not circulate through it. Lighting in sterile systems should not encourage the growth of algae (although the cleaning equipment should in any event minimise this), as by the very nature of the system even decorative algae are unwanted.

There is some speculation as to whether fish kept for long periods in sterile environments can return successfully to more natural conditions. It is likely that, having adapted to such clean surroundings, their immunities (some dependent upon internal bacterial colonies) may be degraded such that natural water is harmful to them.

On the other hand, certain fish, particularly those which inhabit coral reefs, may survive in captivity only in sterile systems. The reason for this is that the typical reef conditions—high turbulence and strong currents—probably maintain a very pure local environment which can be simulated only by the sterile systems.

For these fish all the time and trouble involved in setting up the system will be worth while. Finally, it is a good rule, when buying expensive specimens, to find out whether they have been kept in a sterile environment and, if so, to consider their chances of survival in a non-sterile system.

3

HEATING APPARATUS

Most *aquaria* depend almost totally on ancillary equipment in order to maintain a suitable environment for their inhabitants. The misuse of equipment or the use of unreliable devices can therefore have disastrous consequences and so it is essential to consider carefully the *quality* and ease of use of particular products before buying.

Price is not a dependable indicator of *reliability* and in fact similarly priced articles often show marked differences in quality. Most aquarium equipment is produced by specialist manufacturers and is generally of a high *standard*. There are, however, some products, particularly cheap imported ones, which are just not worth having.

It should be remembered that gaudy finishes and attractive packaging do not necessarily mean reliable performance or long life. Some items of equipment, for instance the aquarium *container* itself, can be constructed at home with the added advantage of being matched to the aquarist's requirements.

Equally, other items can be adjusted, modified or repaired by a handy aquarist who has a basic understanding of the principles and technical considerations involved. In this and the two following chapters the construction and working principles of examples of the basic types of *equipment* are discussed and recommendations for safe and simple installation, leading to reliable usage, are given.

It should be said here that all pieces of *equipment* used to maintain a given environment should be *complementary*. They should not normally

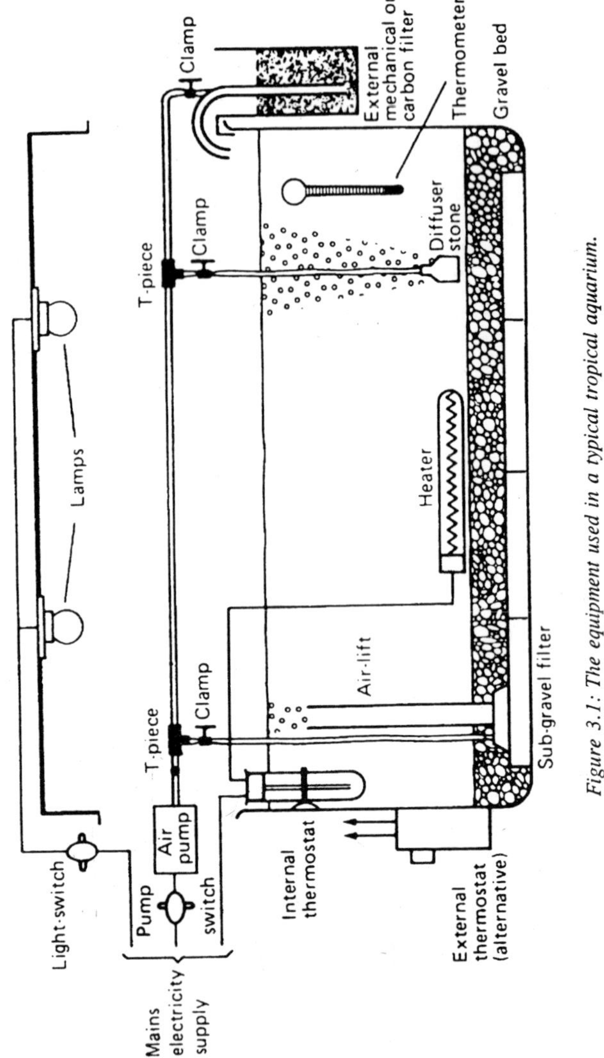

Figure 3.1: The equipment used in a typical tropical aquarium.

duplicate one another's functions and every care should be taken to make sure that the aquarium does not become loaded up with *redundant hardware*.

THE AQUARIUM CONTAINER

The aquarium container must be *watertight*, *strong* and *rigid* enough to take the *weight* of the water it will hold. It should provide a good view of its contents and should be made of *materials* which will not

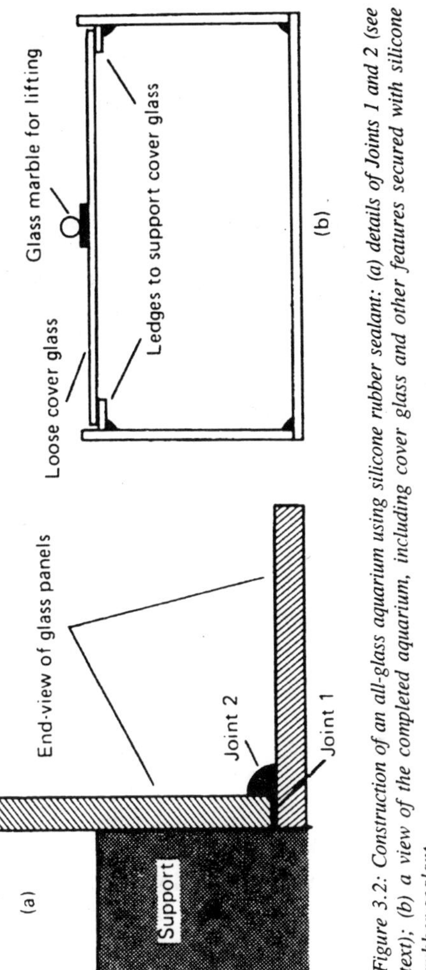

Figure 3.2: Construction of an all-glass aquarium using silicone rubber sealant: (a) details of Joints 1 and 2 (see text); (b) a view of the completed aquarium, including cover glass and other features secured with silicone rubber sealant.

deteriorate in use or prove *toxic* to the *inhabitants*. The best *commercially*—available aquarium container for general use is the all-glass aquarium made from sheets of *glass* butted together and jointed with silicone rubber *sealant*.

This method of construction invariably provokes scepticism in the uninitiated, but very large aquaria can be made successfully in this way. The glass must *necessarily* be thicker than that used in frame aquaria in order to give the same *rigidity* and to provide sufficient edge surface to bond to the *silicone rubber*.

Suitable *thicknesses* of glass for typical sizes of container are given below:

	Length	*Depth*	*Width*	*Glass thickness*
Up to	18in	12in	12in	4mm
	36in	151n	12in	6mm
	48in	18in	12in	6mm sides with 10mm base
	72in	24in	24in	10mm

NB Aquarium tanks in the United Kingdom are built in exact inches, whereas *glass thickness* is completely metricised.

The silicone rubber sealant must not contain fungicide additives and it should preferably be used in an open, *wellventilated* space as the fumes are unpleasant. After cleaning all edges of the glass with methylated spirits, joint 1 is made.

The silicone rubber is applied to the base plate and the side pieces are then placed upon it and *supported* in position for at least two hours. Joint 2 is then made *throughout* in order to seal all *inside* corners.

A neat finish can be achieved by running a finger along all joints to push the sealant into the corners and to remove any excess. The finished *container* should be left to air-cure for forty-eight hours. This type of *aquarium* can be easily made in almost any shape or size, is inert chemically, even with salt water, and does not conduct *electricity*.

Various other types of *aquaria* are available but none of them can be strongly *recommended*, and the only advantages they offer relate to price or decorative appearance. The *oldfashioned*, metal-framed painted aquarium has now been superseded, and with it the fears of leaks and rusting.

Polycoated aquarium frames are available, and are cheaper than nylon-coated frames, but there is some doubt as to their suitability for marine use. Certainly after a time some of them show a tendency for the coating to *split* and peel away from the metal *beneath*, possibly because of the presence of rust on the frames before the coating is applied.

Anodised *aluminium frames*, with either glass or plastic sides and base, are usually of flimsy construction and are comparatively expensive. Stainless steel frames are similar, and sometimes are not in fact rustproof, particularly with *salt water*.

For reasons of economy, both of these last two types seem to be made with as little metal as possible at the expense of rigidity and strength. All-*plastic aquaria* are widely available, either as a plastic frame with *transparent* sealed-in sides or as a one-piece *moulding*.

Plastic is not as transparent as glass, *particularly* in thick sections, and is easily scratched. *Algae* seem to get into rather than on to it, and it yellows easily with age.

A development for the future will probably be the glass-fibre tub with one side of *glass*, perhaps moulded in, and the whole *inner* surface made extremely *smooth* to *reduce algal growth*.

As already stressed, aquarium containers used for permanent environments should be as large as possible. In the larger sizes, strength and rigidity are critical *considerations*, especially as the depth of water increases.

The weight of water, rocks and gravel is an important factor, particularly if the aquarium is supported on a high stand and a '*sensitive*' floor. Domestic installations often suffer from the effects of slammed doors and children jumping on *wooden floors*.

A gallon of water weighs about 10lb and there are 6½ agal per cubic foot, so a container size 36 × 12 × 12in (90 × 30 × 30cm) holds approximately 185lb (85kg) of water, and to this must be added its own weight and the weight of *ancillary* equipment.

Aquarium stands must therefore be strong and rigid, and tall stands should be bolted to the wall to prevent them from tipping or rocking. The proportions of the container should suit the particular aquatic environment which is being created. For an ornamental aquarium, assuming it is big enough to provide the required volume and surface area, perspective and proportion can be important.

The standard shop size of 24in (length) × 12in (width) × 15in (depth) (60 × 30 × 38cm) illustrates the point. Although it is a small aquarium, its dimensions are such that it seems to give the impression of size and space, even when empty.

Long and narrow, thin and tall containers may not look so attractive and some effort to acquire a container of pleasing proportions is undoubtedly worth while. Triangular containers fill corners nicely and present a good frontal expanse to the *viewer*, but their surface area is limited, and so a properly populated *triangular aquarium* always seems to be short of fish in relation to the size of the front glass.

Round and spherical containers give a *distorted* view of their contents and the latter also have a poor surface-area: volume ratio. For this reason their use, especially as small *goldfish* bowls, is not recommended. Frequently attempts are made to make aquaria from acid carboys but these are rarely successful, *generally* due to maintenance problems associated with the *narrow neck*.

The depth of the *aquarium contributes* greatly to the total weight and also influences the growth of tall plants. These two points are fairly obvious but there are other more obscure considerations.

Where an environment is *inhabited* by fish which live near the bottom and compete with each other for territories it will be found that in deep water these *territories* do not extend to the surface but stop at some point in mid-water which corresponds to the *requirements* of the fish in possession of that *particular* volume.

If the number of fish present is greater than the number of available territories on the bottom, then in a deep aquarium the weaker fish can find some refuge by moving to the *upper waters* which are not claimed by the strong fish.

Thus, in a deep container, fish driven out of possessed *territories* always have somewhere else to go, whereas if the environment is only one territory deep an expelled fish must blunder into yet another possessed territory and suffer again. A fish which normally lives near the bottom, however, should only be made to live *permanently* in the upper waters when no other more suitable *accommodation* is available.

Deep water also gives *security* and a better appearance to *laterally compressed* fish such as *angels* and *discus*. Tall plants and vertical arrangements can be set up to give a background which suits the fish's *camouflage* patterns and their way of life.

Similarly, in community situations, populations of mixed fish share the environment better if the water is deep enough to enable individuals to inhabit the level at which they naturally live so that they are not *crowded* together within, say, a depth of 12in (30cm).

HEATING EQUIPMENT

In tropical *aquaria* in which the required temperature is above the prevailing ambient *temperature*, some form of artificial heating must be used together with a control system which maintains the temperature within certain limits.

Nowadays, artificial heating is carried out most cleanly and conveniently by electrical methods. In any *installation* which involves more than just a few aquaria, heating costs are an important item in the aquarist's budget, so attention to the *conservation* of heat and proper temperature control is amply repaid.

In the home, the aquarium is often situated in, say, a lounge, and in this situation heat losses are not *necessarily* so important, since they add to the warmth of the room. In fact, a large aquarium can usefully take the chill off an otherwise unheated room.

Heating systems can be classified into three basic types:

i. Those which heat the water directly from inside the *container* (*immersion heating*).

ii. Those which heat the base of the aquarium from *underneath* (*base heating*).

iii. Those which heat the air in the room containing the *aquarium* (*space heating*).

By far the most popular method makes use of a combination of immersion *heater*, *thermostat* and *thermometer*. This system is easily installed without technical knowledge, providing a few basic points are observed.

The Immersion Heating System

The combination of components used in this system comprises one or more immersion heaters, a simple thermostatic switch and a thermometer. Each item is simple and *reliable* and there has been little alteration in their basic design for many years as they are functionally ideal, although electrical regulations have *enforced* alterations to their containers. *Immersion* heaters consist *basically* of an *electrical heating* element contained in a *heat-resistant*, *protective tube*.

A *waterproof cable* carries current from the supply, a bung seals the cable into the tube and the air is sucked out of the whole device to create a vacuum by the manufacturers during assembly. These are efficient and difficult to fault.

For high wattages, say over 250W, the life of the element may be shortened because of the higher internal working temperature, and substitution by two units of lower power is better.

Heaters should not be moved about while hot and should not be installed in direct contact with the walls or the floor of the container, and are not designed to be buried in the gravel bed.

The power of the heater is measured in terms of its wattage and this should be *reasonably* matched to the volume of water which is to be heated.

If the wattage is low the heater may not be capable of the high emergency temperatures sometimes required for *disease* control or may not be able to cope with the extra demands if the *ambient* temperature should *suddenly* drop.

On the other hand, a *high-powered* heater in a small volume causes

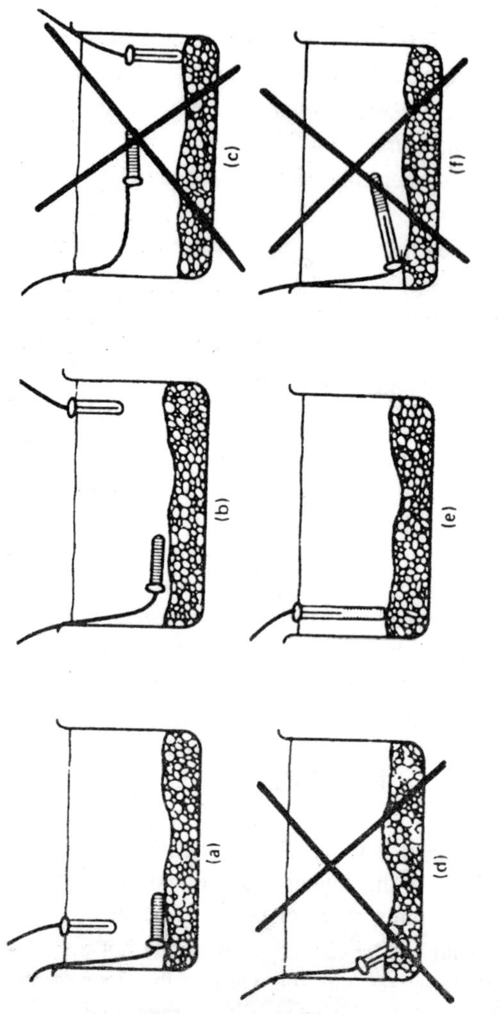

Figure 3.3: Correct positioning of heating equipment in the aquarium. Unsatisfactory arrangements are crossed through: (a) and (b) thermostat above heater. Two heaters should be used if the tank is very large; (c) thermostat below heater; (d) heater buried in sand; (e) and (f) a combined heater-thermostat with the thermostat section, respectively, above and below the heater.

the thermostat to work that much harder in order to control the *temperature* properly, and this reduces the life of the thermostat and causes excessive heat loss due to *cycling* temperatures. *Recommended* heater wattages are shown in Table elsewhere in this chapter.

These recommendations are for aquaria in warm locations and are only approximate, so that any slight variation from the sizes shown would be *adequately* catered for by the same value. In cold *locations* higher values should be used and generally, unless the *location* is *extremely* cold, that shown for the next size up is satisfactory.

Table 3.1: Recommended heater wattages.

Container Dimensions Length × depth × width	*Recommended Wattage*
18 × 12 × 12in	50W
24 × 12 × 12in	75W
30 × 12 × 12in	100W
36 × 12 × 12in	150W
48 × 12 × 12in	200W

The use of two small heaters instead of one large one has the advantage that there is still some heating capacity if one heater fails. To control the *temperature accurately* a *bi-metallic thermostat* is commonly used.

The bi-metallic switch consists of two long strips of different metals, for example steel and brass, *fastened* together face to face along their length. When a *temperature* change occurs both metals expand and the composite *strip bends* as a result of *differential expansion.*

An electrical contact is carried at the end of the bending strip and this meets another on the fixed part of the thermostat body to form a *sensitive switch.*

The bending strip is pre-tensioned by an adjusting screw so that when it is at or below the minimum *required* temperature the fixed and moving contacts *touch* and when it is at the maximum temperature required the contacts *move apart.*

The difference between these two temperatures is called the 'differential' of the thermostat and in high quality equipment is only a few degrees. *Adjustment* for the desired temperature is carried out by altering the tension on the *bi-metallic strip* by means of a *precision* screw *adjuster.*

A small magnet is fitted next to the contact points so that as the moving contact approaches the fixed one it is snatched quickly into contact and similarly, when trying to move away, it is released suddenly after acquiring a certain tension. This provision reduces arcing at the contact points and thus *maintains* them in good condition.

Aquarium thermostats are usually designed to fit either inside, immersed in the water, or outside, fitted flush against the glass side so as to sense the water temperature through the glass.

They are supplied supposedly set for an approximate temperature but this should not be *blindly* relied on, and the best results will be

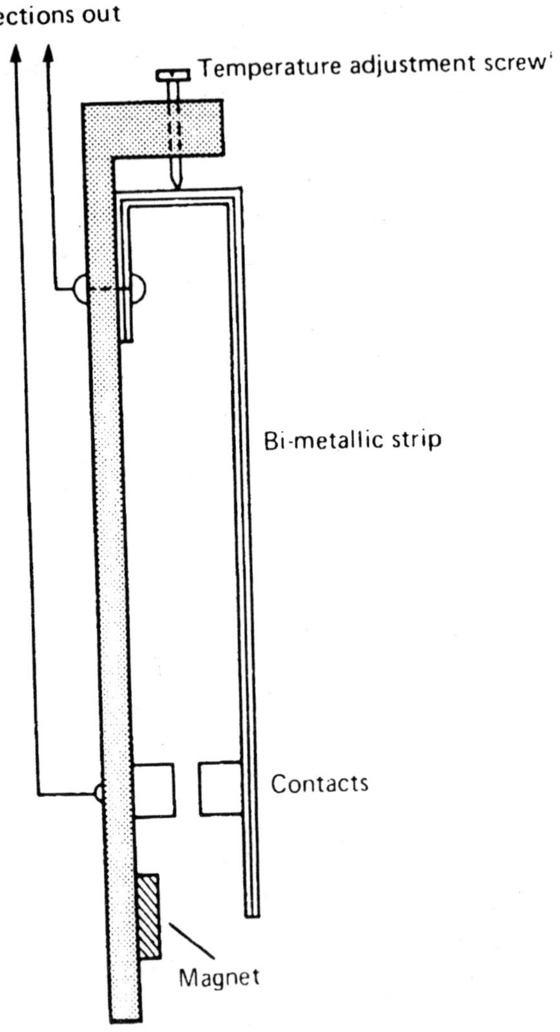

Figure 3.4: Internal construction of a simple thermostat.

achieved if the thermostat is adjusted to the particular requirements of the environment.

Most immersible thermostats are designed to be used in a vertical position and in any other position the action of gravity on the weight of the bi-metallic strip can upset control.

Externally-fitted thermostats are probably the best for small and medium-sized containers, where the glass sides are not so thick as to impair the thermostat's sensitivity. They are mounted flat and must be in contact with the surface of the glass over their whole face.

They are not reliable on patterned or frosted glass which is not flat all over. Any clip used to hold the thermostat on to the aquarium must be non-toxic if it fits over the top lip of the aquarium and this method is useful if the thermostat might need to be removed temporarily for some reason.

Clipped-on thermostats are, however, easily dislodged which then means that the heater will be permanently switched on. The use of an adhesive allows greater flexibility of positioning but makes the fixture permanent.

There is some advantage in mounting the thermostat near the bottom of the container (but not below the gravel surface) in case the aquarium is only partially filled at any time. External thermostats are safer electrically and can usually carry more current, but they must not be allowed to gather condensation or salt from marine environments and their performance can be affected by the ambient air temperature if this varies greatly.

As a result, they must not be fitted in very draughty locations. There are some important general considerations relating to all types of thermostat. The water level must always be at least three-quarters of the way up the tube of the immersible types and above the top of external types, otherwise they may tend to respond to the air temperature above the water surface rather than to the water temperature itself.

Where there is only one aquarium and no spare equipment the thermostat used must be thoroughly reliable. It cannot be repeated often enough that external thermostats must be kept dry and clean.

When a large aquarium or several aquaria using more than one heater are controlled by a single thermostat, the current rating of the thermostat contacts must be selected to avoid overloading and consequent damage.

This information is given by the manufacturers and is quoted in amperes. Small thermostats usually have IA contacts and these carry a maximum practical load of 200W at normal mains supply voltage. A simple calculation confirms this: watts = amps × volts. Thus, the maximum permissible load at 240V (mains voltage) and IA (thermostat rating) is 240W.

Some spare capacity is best allowed for and so a practical rating of 200W is obtained. Any loading above the maximum values induces severe arcing and produces heat inside the thermostat, which shortens its life and affects its reliability. Small neon indicator lamps are often fitted and require some understanding. Usually on separate immersible thermostats the neon is on when the heater is off and on external types it is on when the heater is on.

In combined heater-thermostats of the immersible type, the lamp is on when the heater is on. This situation is confusing and the aquarist should ascertain from the maunfacturer's specification which system applies. Neons in immersed thermostats can be frightening to nervous fish, especially in the dark.

With careful use a thermostat should last several years. Signs of deterioration are erratic temperature control, often coupled with varying differential. If arcing is taking place at the contacts they may require careful cleaning, although if they are badly pitted replacement is essential.

Neon indicators which flicker several times at each switch-over indicate that the contacts are not closing properly. When the temperature setting is being adjusted to a new value it is better to make several small steps rather than one big one, in order to allow the water enough time to respond and achieve the new temperature before further adjustments are made.

Large, sudden thermostat adjustments can cause untold trouble when fish are present in the water. External thermostats can be boxed in if they are likely to be affected by draughts or interfered with by children or knocked about during housekeeping. This provision also improves their temperature relationship with the water.

A thermometer is required to indicate the water temperature. Great accuracy and a fast response are not needed, so the immersible spirit-in-glass type is quite adequate, preferably with a paper scale inside the glass.

Immersible mercury-in-glass types are unnecessarily accurate and more difficult to read properly in a hurry. A new thermometer should be checked against one of known accuracy before use and rejected if the reading is more than one degree different.

Aquarium thermometers have always been calibrated in degrees Fahrenheit and most older aquarists will still use this scale in writing and conversation, but the change to centigrade is now accepted and the aquarist should know how to convert from one scale to the other. This is carried out using the following formula:

$$\frac{°C}{5} = \frac{°F - 32}{9}$$

For example, to convert 75°F to centigrade:

Thus °C = $\frac{43}{9} \times 5$ = 23.9, and 75°F = 24°C approximately.

Table 3.2: Temperature conversion chart.

°C	°F	°C	°F	°C	°F
0	32.0	13	55.4	26	78.8
1	33.8	14	57.2	27	80.6
2	35.6	15	59.0	28	82.4
3	37.4	16	60.8	29	84.2
4	39.2	17	62.6	30	86.0
5	41.0	18	64.4	31	87.8
6	42.8	19	66.2	32	89.6
7	44.6	20	68.0	33	91.4
8	46.4	21	69.8	34	93.2
9	48.2	22	71.6	35	95.0
10	50.0	23	73.4	36	96.8
11	51.8	24	75.2	37	98.6
12	53.6	25	77.0	38	100.4

Where several heaters in separate containers are controlled by one master thermostat the following points must be noted. If all the heater wattages are the same then all the volumes of water heated must be the same and must have similar heat losses, otherwise the temperatures maintained will vary from one container to another.

It is very difficult to balance up satisfactorily systems of varying volumes by providing heaters of various wattages and this kind of installation is not really worth while.

In any multiple system, should anything happen to the heater in the master tank, the thermostat will sense a drop in temperature and remain switched on. As a result the other tanks will become overheated. The thermostat must, of course, be reliable and have contacts capable of carrying the total load of all the heaters.

Many other variations of heater-thermostat systems are possible. Highly complex circuits can be evolved (see, for example, Figure 17) incorporating extra units to provide for all sorts of emergency situations, but this back-up idea usually fails because in properly installed systems emergencies are rare and the extra thermostats deteriorate from not being used.

As a result, they often become contaminated with damp and dirt

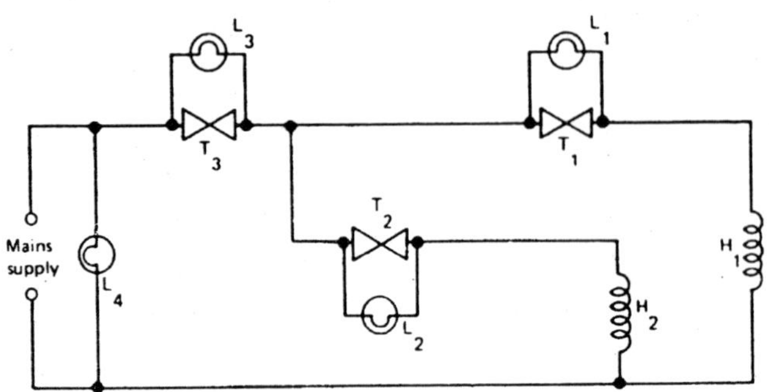

Figure 3.5: A typical circuit using three thermostats and two heaters to give protection against high and low temperatures.

L_1	L_2	L_3
Below 65°F	**Below 75°F**	**Below 85°F**
On-T_1 open-circuited	On-T_2 open-circuited	On-T_3 open-circuited
Off-T_1 switched on	Off-T_2 switched on	Off-T_3 switched on
Above 65°F	**Above 75°F**	**Above 85°F**
On-T_1 switched off	On-T_2 switched off	On-T_3 switched off
Off-T_1 short-circuited	Off-T_2 short-circuited	Off-T_3 short-circuited
or	*or*	
H_1 open-circuited	H_2 open-circuited	

so that when the emergency eventually arises they do not function properly.

Most temperature emergencies in anything other than very small volumes or very cold places develop slowly and should be spotted by a vigilant aquarist early enough to allow faulty equipment to be replaced.

Holidays and long weekends away are obvious danger periods, but the chance of trouble is still not enough to outweigh the inconvenience of complex multi-thermostat systems.

No circuit of this type can, of course, compensate for power failures, which cause most of the electrical emergencies that are encountered.

Heat losses from internally-heated aquaria are a function of the surface area available to radiate and conduct heat away, and not truly a function of the volume. As an example we can consider two containers of equal volume but with different dimensions.

Let the first container be a cube with 2-ft sides, that is a volume of 8cu ft, and the second container 16 × 1 × 0.5ft in size, also a volume of 8cu ft. It can be seen that the total surface areas are quite different being 24 and 49sq ft, respectively. Thus, the heat losses from the longer container will be far greater than those from the other.

Many aquarists insulate all the surface areas bar the viewing side but it must be remembered that many insulating materials are hygroscopic and so if used in a damp or wet situation will soak up water and lead to unpleasant conditions.

As heat rises, it is normally unnecessary to insulate underneath the base of an aquarium unless several are stacked one above the other, when it may be found that a lower aquarium overheats those above.

Base Heating Systems

Heating from below, through the base of the aquarium, was frequently practised in the past using various forms of power. Gas, electricity, steam pipes, paraffin—all have their uses and methods of application.

The main requirement is that the base of the aquarium container should be heat-resistant, yet obviously still waterproof and able to conduct the heat. Slate in quite thick sections was the most popular material while metals were less often used because of contamination problems.

Nowadays slate is expensive and hard to obtain, and commercially-built aquaria are certainly not fitted up this way. There are several inherent disadvantages in base heating. The transfer of heat is impeded by the base of the aquarium and any gravel layer above it.

Thermostatic control is easily applicable only to electrical methods, or to gas heating if a little trouble is taken. Insulation around the equipment is required to prevent loss of heat to the surrounding air and the transfer of heat to the container by the source must be slow and even.

Direct gas systems and steam piping methods require almost constant experienced hand 'trimming' to achieve steady temperatures and to minimise sudden changes caused by variations in the ambient conditions, and are only reliable if a responsible person is present most of the time, or at least is available quickly.

Paraffin, even the so-called 'clean' sort, produces fumes and odours and is only fit for emergency use. Gas fumes can also be troublesome and necessitate draughty conditions for their removal, which increases heat losses.

Base heating is usually used in situations in which an internal heating system might damage fry or creatures such as anemones, or where only minimal heat is required, such as when preventing coldwater

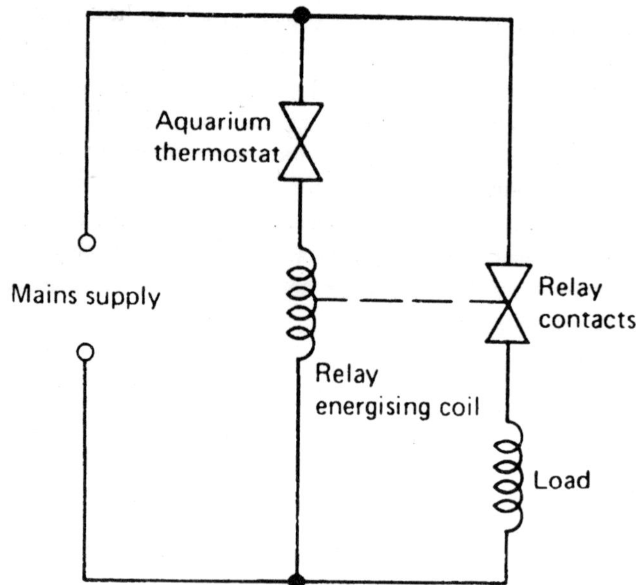

Figure 3.6: Circuit for using an auxiliary relay to allow the aquarium thermostat to control a heavy electrical load.

environments from freezing. It is not as wasteful as space heating and it can allow a more pleasant atmosphere for the aquarist to work in.

Electrical methods are the most suitable for a modern *baseheating* environment and some advantage can be gained over space *heating* if the aquarist is prepared to take a little trouble over the *installation*. The application of heat must be slow so that the base and gravel do not become a lot warmer than the water.

A normal thermostat *situated* in a master *aquarium*, which represents the temperature of all other aquaria, would be capable of adequate control if fitted with an *auxiliary* relay to carry the large currents expected.

When using an *auxiliary* relay the following should be noted:

i. The current drawn by the relay coil must be within the rating of the thermostat contacts.

ii. The relay contacts and their connecting wires must be capable of carrying the maximum current required by the load.

iii. The relay must be suitable for mains *voltage operation*.

Heat sources can be either low-power tubular *greenhouse* heaters or ducted fan heaters, both arranged to *efficiently* heat the tanks rather than the general *atmosphere*. If containers of different shapes and sizes are used, some adjustment will be necessary to account for differing heat losses so that a uniform temperature is obtained.

Even so, such a system would be worth while in a large fish house and would be a vast improvement on the hot, *humid conditions* associated with *space heating*.

It is clear from this brief *explanation*, however, that the subject deserves far more study and attention than it gets at present, because of its basic advantage of not excessively *overheating* the air in which the aquarist *spends* his time.

There are several types of commercial electric base heaters available with thermostatic control which are sold to gardeners for use in propagating plants. These take the form of an enclosed box or tray on which the plant *containers* sit, and they are quite suitable for use with small *individual aquaria*.

The handy aquarist could make this sort of device and produce something similar. The weight of the complete *aquarium* would, of course, have to be taken into consideration. In the past, aquaria were often *mounted* on an *insulated* box containing one or more light bulbs, which provide a lot of heat, but the bulbs have a short life because they are positioned *horizontally*.

They must also be far enough away from the bottom glass of the container to avoid cracking it through *overheating*. The method has the advantage that it is easy to construct and use, especially if an extra aquarium is required quickly and proper heating *apparatus* is not available.

Sterile environments would perhaps benefit from base heating as this would enable the heater to be placed outside the container, and the lack of any base *gravel* bed in this system would encourage good heat transfer.

Also, the very turbulent conditions which are present would counteract any tendency for the lower levels to be warmer than the top. *Stratification* generally, however, will tend to be reduced even in static water by the heat rising from the whole base area.

Space Heating Systems

With the advent of cheap and efficient electrical fan heaters for domestic and greenhouse applications there is a trend amongst aquarists to opt for space heating in even quite small fish houses. *Fan heaters* can provide a clean, *fast-acting supply* of heat and are readily suitable for thermostatic control.

The fan action allows heat to be directed horizontally and has a strong mixing function so that serious stratification does not occur. The heaters are simple to install and do not require complicated maintenance. They can, however, be very expensive to operate if used continuously, and this is their main disadvantage.

A basic principle which governs any comparison of internal and external methods of heating of aquaria is that it is far cheaper to heat the water directly and minimise the heat losses to the surrounding air than it is to heat the air in order to warm the water.

Water has a higher heat-holding capacity than air and it cannot therefore release heat as quickly or acquire it so readily. Also, glass is not a good conductor of heat and these two facts together make for inefficiency in space heating systems.

Obviously, to pass heat from one place to another the source must be hotter and so the air in a space-heated enclosure with thermostatic control might have to be at, say, 80°F (27°C) for much of the time in order to provide water at a constant temperature of 75°F (24°C). This temperature level is not pleasant for the aquarist and, in fact, cannot be tolerated for any length of time if it is coupled with high humidity.

Because of the rate at which such a high air temperature causes heat to be lost to the outside in temperate climates, the whole building needs to be insulated and ventilation is usually minimal. This results in the exclusion of natural air movement and light.

Also, aquaria must be covered to counter the high rate of evaporation and artificial lighting must be provided both for the environments and for the aquarist's workspace. All these requirements lead to a fairly complex installation which, even if it can be made reasonably economic, may be unpleasant and even unhealthy to be in, and will after a time inevitably become dank and humid.

Thus space heating systems are recommended only if the aquarist can afford the cost of the extra power required, if adequate ventilation is available and some natural light is let into the building. There are many methods other than the use of fan heaters but all have larger installation costs and require some sort of maintenance, and the general arguments made above apply to all systems.

Any domestic or greenhouse heating system is suitable as long as it is capable of maintaining the high air temperatures involved in heating fish houses. Extensions from existing domestic systems are often carried out with advantages of installation cost. Gas fires without proper flues, and paraffin heaters, must not be used, however, because of the dangers of toxic fumes. They also produce a scum or film on any water surface, which is difficult to remove. Boiler systems with steam pipes require experienced manual regulation for good control at all times.

CONCLUSIONS

Where individual aquaria are kept in domestic situations it is obvious that the only worthwhile heating system is that using electrical immersion heaters designed for aquarium use. The only exception is the possible use of base heating for sterile environments or fry-raising aquaria.

Recommendations are in order, however, for some optimum form of base heating system for use in fish houses and other collections of aquaria. The amateur aquarist, setting up a fish house for pleasure rather than profit, and requiring economy in running costs, will find the immersion system convenient as it will allow aquaria to be installed one by one, and each aquarium can be a complete individual environment with separate temperature adjustment, insulation and other features.

Heaters and thermostats can be bought as they are needed and, in fact, once the building and its electrical supply system are set up there need be no further large single expense. The advantages of flexibility and individuality in a multiple immersion heater system are gained at the cost of some unavoidable complexity in the electrical wiring system.

Each aquarium must have a power point and any other connections such as those between the heaters and any separate thermostats must be catered for. The total current involved in the event of all the heaters being on together, as well as the lights, pumps and other equipment may be considerable and must be properly allowed for.

Also, if the aquaria are well-insulated, some means of keeping the room temperature at a low but comfortable level for the aquarist in winter must be provided, either by insulation of the building or by some kind of background heating. In commercial establishments, where the aquarist is breeding fish in reasonable quantities in fairly crowded environments, many of which contain small fry, the immersion system can have disadvantages, as already mentioned.

There is also the problem that where frequent water changing and tank cleaning are carried out the numerous electrical cables involved may be a serious inconvenience, and if their condition is allowed to deteriorate they may become dangerous when water is spilled, as must inevitably happen sooner or later.

In this case, base or space heating should be considered, but it must be pointed out that, if profits are required, both of these systems must be fully loaded and used at maximum potential right from the start.

A space-heated building only half full will never pay unless the aquarist is producing some valuable rarity which renders all running costs negligible.

EMERGENCIES

It should be assumed that the responsible aquarist will always keep spare heaters and thermostats. If this is not done, and the thermostat has failed and cannot be replaced *immediately*, the heater can be wired directly into the mains supply and switched on and off manually, following reference to the *thermometer* reading.

This, of course, requires almost continuous close attention. During power failures only small aquaria or those in very cold surroundings lose heat quickly, and in fact loss of aeration is often more important than temporary loss of *heating*.

A large aquarium can usually withstand a power failure lasting for a few hours without serious results and, if needed, closed bottles of warm water can be put into the *aquarium*. This practice must not be overdone and, like all manual *methods*, it must be applied *gradually*.

Low voltage heaters and also small pumps which work from car batteries are available, while some pumps have their own internal batteries. In fish houses, *paraffin* heaters are probably the best emergency heat sources, *provided* every precaution is taken against fumes.

An insulated *building* does not lose heat too quickly if the doors and windows are kept shut, and old newspapers laid on the aquaria provide good temporary *insulation*, but if paraffin is used, *ventilation* must be provided and the expense of fuel should not be considered during an *emergency*.

If aquaria are *individually* insulated it is perhaps worth while to keep a stock of extra pieces of *insulation* so that the viewing sides can also be insulated if *necessary*.

4

AERATION

Air injected into aquatic environments has three basic functions: (a) to provide oxygen, remove carbon dioxide and break down toxic wastes by its contact with the water; (b) to provide motive power for the circulation of water by air-lift mechanisms; and (c) to induce water movement and general turbulence.

Ascending air-streams also provide an attractive feature. A typical installation is shown in Figure elsewhere in this chapter. It is well known that atmospheric pressure (average 14.71b per sq in) will support a water column 34ft high. From this fact it can be calculated that a column only lin high is supported by a pressure of only 0.0361b per sq in.

Therefore, to force air to a depth of even 24in, which is deeper than most ordinary aquaria. only a very small pressure is required. This conclusion is of great importance to aquarists for it allows the use of extremely simple air pumps.

The most popular type of small pump uses the vibrating diaphragm mechanism which pushes air through a simple automatic valve system and is operated by a magnetic coil fed directly from the mains supply.

These pumps are cheap, efficient, easy to repair and maintain, and the larger models supply considerable amounts of air and are quite adequate for multiple installations or for driving air-powered cleaning tools.

The most frequently encountered problem with this type is noise and vibration, generated by the diaphragm moving quite powerfully, usually at fifty impulses per second in sympathy with the frequency of the mains supply.

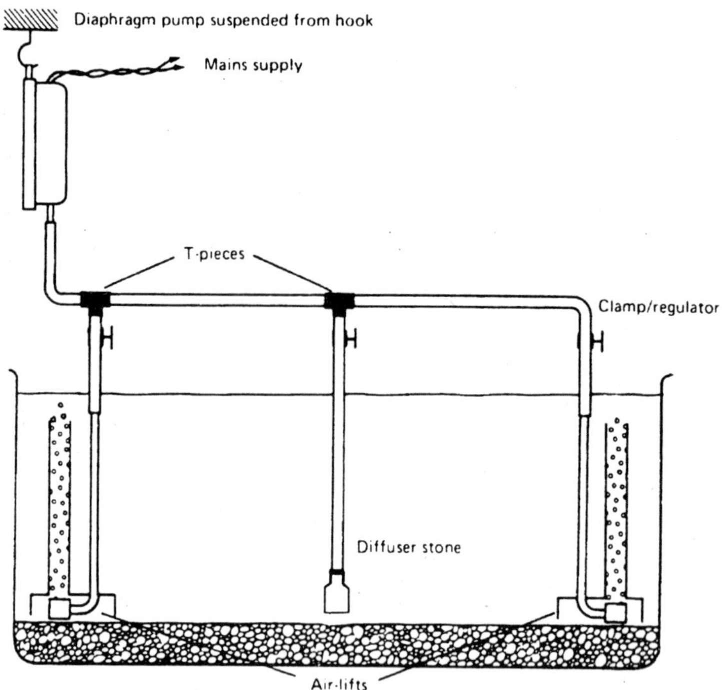

Figure 4.1: A typical air-supply system. The diaphragm pump should be positioned at least 6in above the water surface. All piping should be kept as short as possible to encourage the build up of a back pressure.

Recent models have been improved by positioning the diaphragm-actuating lever so that it is not in contact with the coil (in older models the coil was also the mounting for the lever) but though noise problems have thereby been minimised they have not always been eliminated.

Since, however, there is no comparable alternative to this type of pump, the aquarist is recommended to try to understand the problems and then to eliminate their effects, which in all but the worse cases can easily be achieved.

Vibrator pumps are best suspended from a strong hook so that they do not come into contact with anything which might amplify the vibration. Many pumps are provided with a hole for this purpose, moulded into a rubber baseplate, but in use the rubber often splits.

If the pump is placed upon a smooth surface it may 'walk' about under the influence of its internal vibrations and some have been known to creep off shelves in this way!

Pumps must not be silenced by being shut up in boxes or very

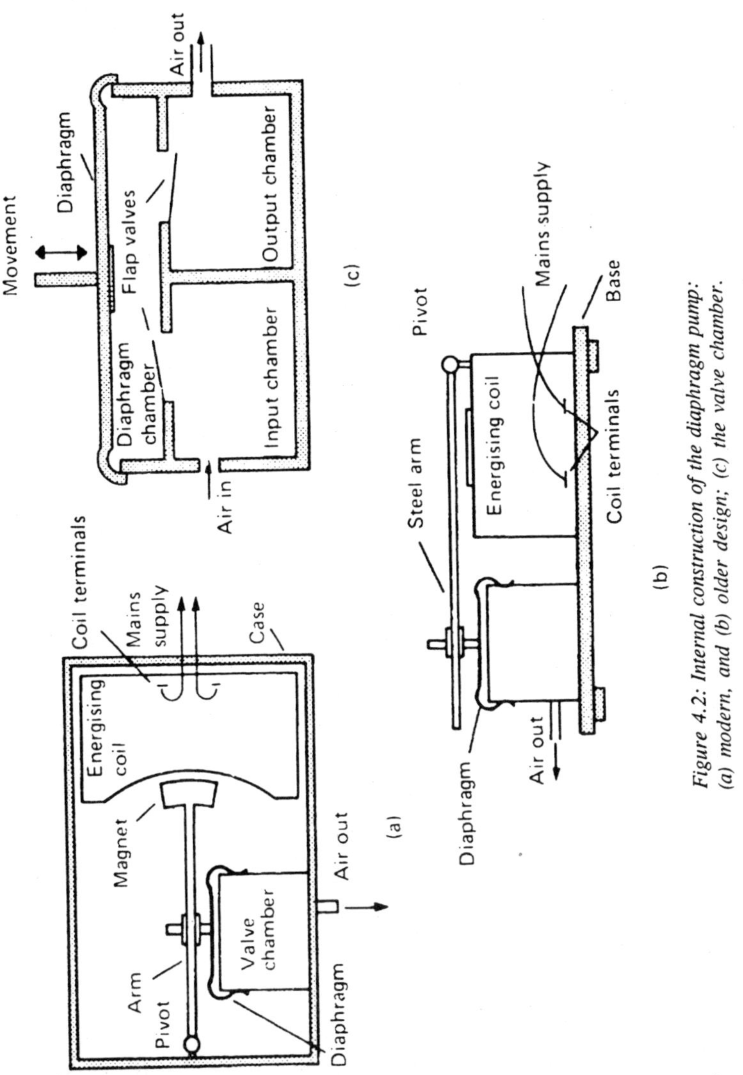

Figure 4.2: Internal construction of the diaphragm pump: (a) modern, and (b) older design; (c) the valve chamber.

small cupboards as they tend to overheat without adequate air circulation. If they are mounted level with, or below, the surface of the water in an aquarium, and particularly if stood on the floor below it, they must have a non-return valve fitted in the component which drives the piston has a very low torque or turning force and so the pump can easily be stopped by any small back pressure in either piston.

The pump must work at all times almost as though it were pumping

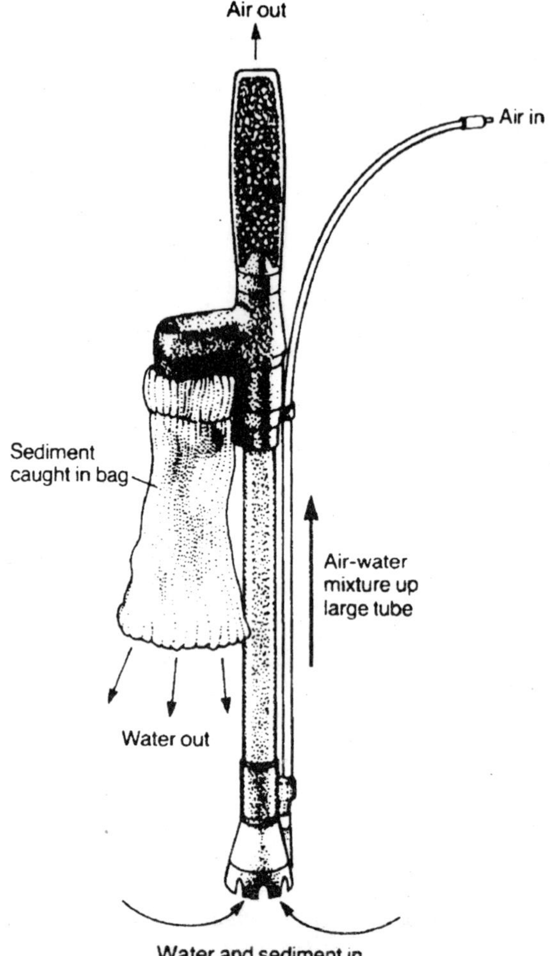

Figure 4.3: An air-operated water strainer and sediment remover, a useful cleaning tool.

straight into the atmosphere, and any excess air produced and not used by appliances must be bled away to the atmosphere.

This makes for constant attention. Air filters may be needed to exclude the pump's oil from the aquarium water, and large air reservoirs are advisable to smooth out the effects of the pulsations of the pistons.

The whole piping system should, if possible, be constructed in large-bore pipe in order to reduce back pressure, and will generally be more expensive and more complex to install than the equivalent system for a vibrator pump.

However, it must be said that any good piston pump is usually quieter and, if properly fitted up, can produce more air than a single, small vibrator. All air systems must be balanced so that the pumped air is not lost through the channel of least resistance.

Thus all appliances must be fitted with a regulator of some kind and these should be balanced when everything is running normally. For example, in the installation shown in Figure elsewhere in this chapter each air-lift may use as much as six times more air than the diffuser stone.

The resistance to air-flow present in the stone will tend to make all available air-flow through the air-lifts, so the regulators must be carefully adjusted more or less simultaneously to balance the system. Any change made in the air consumption of one appliance may affect at least some of the others and so balancing may be needed whenever a change in demand takes place.

Long-term changes, such as the gradual clogging up of diffuser stones, may necessitate compensating adjustments. For large fish houses, aquarium shops and so on an industrial type of air compressor is often used, fitted with a large reservoir and controlled by a pressure switch to maintain a steady working pressure in the reservoir.

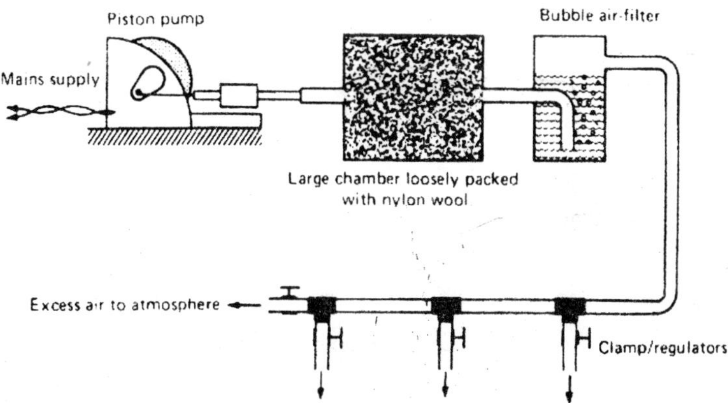

Figure 4.4: A typical air-supply system with a piston air pump. The pump should be mounted at least 12in above the water surface and should always be run at high speed, any slowdown indicating a blockage or back-pressure build-up, which should be dealt with either by clearance or by venting excess pressure to the atmosphere. If the system incorporates an ozoniser, the water filter should be replaced with a silica gel column.

Operation of the compressor motor is then intermittent but the supply taken from the reservoir is continuous. By keeping the pressure in the reservoir at, say, 10lb per sq in, pulsations from the pump section are eliminated and some reserve is provided for short-lived emergencies.

In terms of the consumption of electricity, intermittent pump operation proves to be more economical than releasing excess air to the atmosphere from a unit which runs continuously. To complete the supply system the compressor may need input and output air filters, depending on the type, and a safety blow-off valve (set higher than the reservoir pressure) should be fitted to cover any failure of the pressure switch.

The regulators fitted to the aquarium appliances should ideally be more reliable than the simple clamps normally used, since, if one of

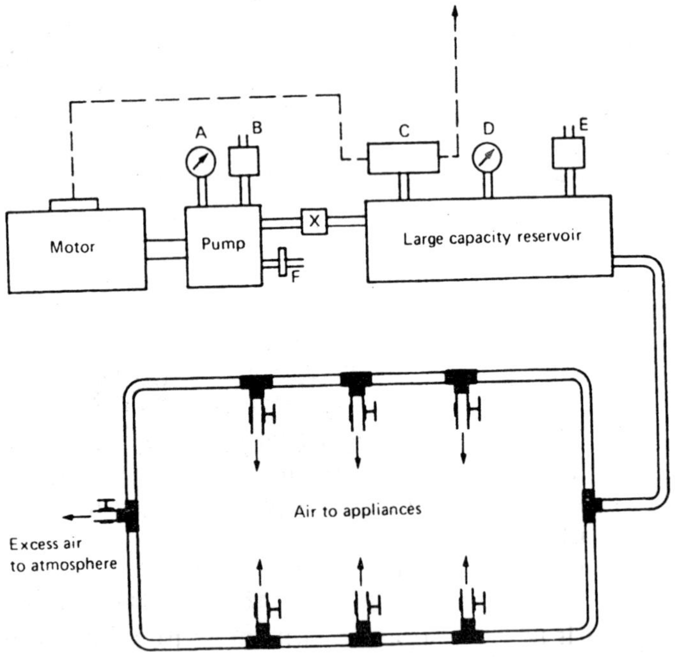

Figure 4.5: An air-supply system using a compressor. A proper unit designed for aquarium use should not produce any oil or other contaminant in the output pipe of the compressor, but if in doubt fit a filtering system at the point marked X. The unit should be mounted above the highest water level and will require firm support. The supply line and ring main can be assembled from 1½ in plastic piping with air-tight couplings. A: pump output pressure gauge; B: safety blow-off valve; C: pressure switch for controlling pump motor; D: reservoir pressure gauge; E: reservoir safety blow-off valve; F: input air filter.

these should fall off, the appliance concerned might receive a very high air input which could create problems in the environment through excess turbulence or supersaturation.

Most compressors are fairly noisy when operating and are best installed in a remote location, the air supply being fed through a large-bore ring distribution system. Balancing of individual appliances may be less important because of the air reserve in the reservoir.

The simplest air-operated appliance used in aquaria is the diffuser stone. This is a block of sintered material which is porous and breaks the air-stream up into a multitude of extremely small bubbles, so that the effect of the air column on the environment is increased by the larger total surface area of so many small bubbles.

Good diffusers are trouble free and last for many years. When blocked they can usually be cleared by holding under hot running water or by boiling. The basis of all air-operated appliances such as filters is the use of the air-lift principle.

If the unconnected air-lift assembly is placed inside the aquarium the water inside the pipe automatically levels with that outside. When air is then introduced at the base of the pipe, bubbles form and an airwater mixture is produced which is less dense than the water alone and therefore rises up the pipe.

Provided the air supply is maintained, this mixture leaves the pipe at the top in a continuous process and water is replaced naturally from below. Thus a circulation is set up through the lift pipe and if one end is in the aquarium and the other end in, say, an outside filter, water will be moved from one to the other.

The efficiency of an air-lift is best when at least 70 per cent of its total lifting distance is below the aquarium water surface level, and when the injected air bubbles are as small as possible. If the injected air supply is increased to improve the water-flow, a point will be reached at which it will be necessary to increase the internal diameter of the lift tube in order to allow the larger flow to pass through.

If this is not done the air will not mix properly with the water and the rate of circulation will not increase. Emergency air supplies can be generated by battery-operated pumps or by a temporary reservoir such as a large clean plastic bottle or an inflated car inner tube.

For multiple installations, which use more air, a gasometer-type system can be built with some time and trouble, although this is a rather large, permanent installation which might only be used very

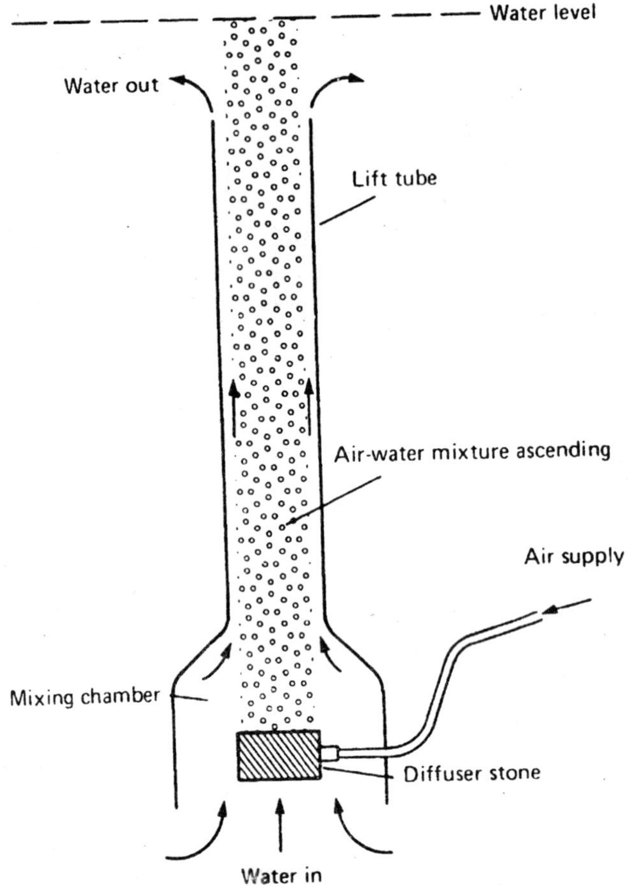

Figure 4.6: Function of the air-life mechanism.

occasionally. The gasometer is made from an airtight container such as an oil drum which has been thoroughly cleaned internally.

The bottom end is completely open and the drum is suspended over a water-filled hole of its own depth. The air trapped is forced out through a smaller hole in the top as the drum is gradually forced down into the water. Some sort of guiding framework is needed to keep the drum vertical and some means must be provided to lift it out of the hole again when all the air has been used.

The pressure produced at the outlet depends on the rate of descent of the drum and will influence the length of time for which the supply lasts. The outlet pressure should therefore be only slightly in excess of that required. If the rate of descent is very high the air inside the drum

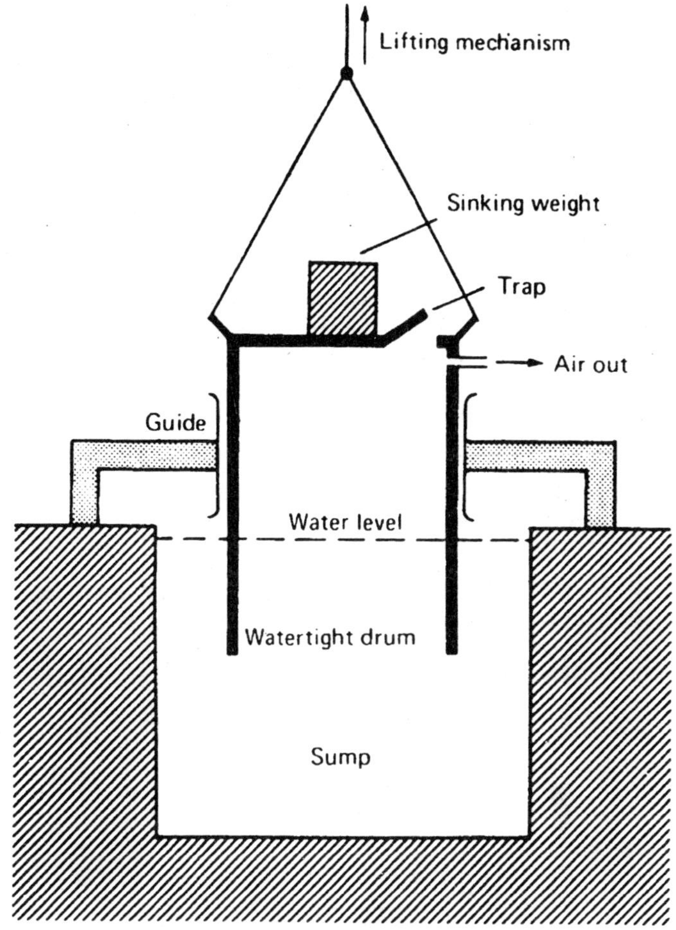

Figure 4.7: A homemade gasometer-type air compressor. The trap allows fast entry of air while lifting.

may become so pressurised that it breaks the water seal and leaks to the atmosphere.

The trick is to weight the drum just sufficiently so that it descends into the hole at a rate which just provides enough air to run the required appliances. Repositioning of the drum at the start position is easier if a large hole can be temporarily opened in the top to admit air quickly.

This system is admittedly rather unorthodox and troublesome to install, but if correctly used it can run a fair number of appliances with only daily recharging and it does demonstrate what a little thought and enterprise can achieve.

FILTERS

Filters for aquaria come in all sorts of shapes, types and sizes, but they all perform the same basic function, and that is to circulate the water through some form of straining or cleansing medium at such a rate that the water is kept clean and sweet.

There are various categories into which filters can be grouped, such as 'inside', 'outside' and 'sub-gravel', but the situation of the filter is not nearly as important as the way in which it operates.

Mechanical filters remove unwanted materials from the water by straining and/or the use of an absorbent material. Examples are shown in Figure elsewhere in this chapter. They are usually made in the form of a box to hold the filter material and may be fitted inside or outside the aquarium.

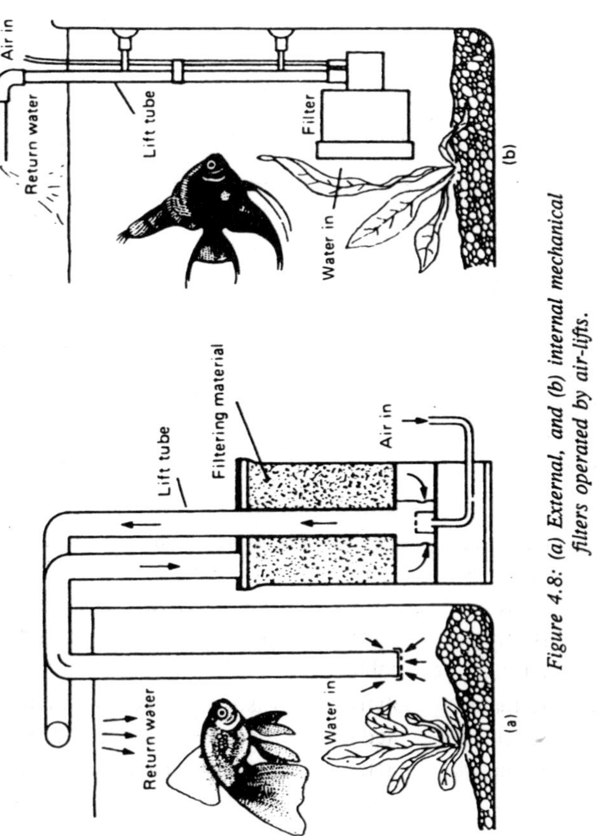

Figure 4.8: (a) External, and (b) internal mechanical filters operated by air-lifts.

Most mechanical filters are operated by an air-lift but some large ones, commonly called power filters, are operated by rotating water pumps. The most important characteristics of any mechanical filter are its capacity for holding cleaning materials and its circulation rate.

A common fault among aquarists is to buy only the cheapest small air pump and then to find that the filter is apparently useless because there is not enough air available to make it operate properly.

As can be seen from the earliest description of air-lift principles, good water circulation requires a good air supply and wide-bore pipes. All but the smallest mechanical filters are fitted outside the aquarium, either suspended from it or mounted close by, and these must ideally be arranged so that the water level in the filter, when the filtering medium is submerged, is level with the water surface in the aquarium.

A siphon is then fitted to maintain this condition automatically. Water can either be pumped from the aquarium to the filter, or vice versa, by the air-lift and the automatic siphon completes the circuit by continuously levelling the two surfaces.

All that remains then is to arrange that the water passes through the filtering medium during its passage through the filter. The air-lift should preferably operate so that water is moved from the filter to the aquarium rather than the other way around, in case the siphon should stop, in which event the filter box will flood, emptying the aquarium.

If the water moves from the filter to the aquarium only the filter will empty and its contents will run harmlessly into the aquarium. The filtering materials commonly used for straining include gravel, wools of various kinds and sponges.

Gravel is a good coarse filter but will not remove the smallest particles unless used in very deep layers. It is heavy and difficult to remove for cleaning without dismantling the filter. Nylon wool is a very useful material if packed into the filter correctly.

It should fill all spaces and corners so that it is not bypassed by the water current, but must not be squeezed in so tightly that the circulation rate is impeded. Glass-fibre materials should never be used in filters as they produce small sharp splinters which enter the gills of fish and cause serious problems.

Sponge material (polyfoam etc) is useful because it can be cut to fit the filter box exactly and can be removed, washed and reused many times. Like nylon wool it must not be so dense that it impedes circulation. Whichever material is used it should be cleaned before it becomes absolutely clogged up or the efficiency of the filter will decrease.

Commercial filters seldom have the capacity to cope with very large aquaria and aquarists are often better advised to build their own from a small aquarium or other similar container (Figure 28). It should be pointed out that a large mechanical filter which is left uncleaned may eventually take on a biological action if conditions are right for its population by nitrifying bacteria, and if its total bed surface area is big enough it can perform a useful service in this mode.

Activated charcoal (or carbon) is commonly used in mechanical filters to adsorb unwanted chemical compounds such as urine in freshwater environments. In addition, it may also remove many useful ingredients and in particular it will be found that the filter must be turned off whenever medicines are added.

The life of the charcoal filter is determined by how soon its adsorbent capacity is used up and this can be tested by putting a few drops of methylene blue into the filter box. The dye colour will disappear if the filter is still efficient.

Charcoal will of course also act as a mechanical filter and, if left uncleaned, also acquire a nitrifying potential. Since it is a very light material, easily moved by the water current, it is useful to sandwich the charcoal between two gravel or wool layers, or to waterlog

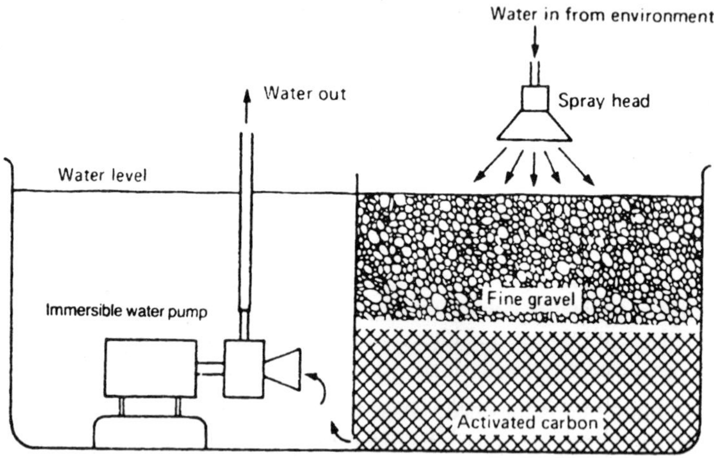

Figure 4.9: An efficient high-capacity mechanical and chemical filter. The water in the filter should be at the same level as that in the aquarium, so that if the pump stops the aquarium will not empty through the filter input syphon. If the filter is ever used in a lower position, the pump output flow must obviously be greater than the syphon input flow, but the difference must never be so great that the pump can empty the filter, as the pump will be damaged if operated out of water.

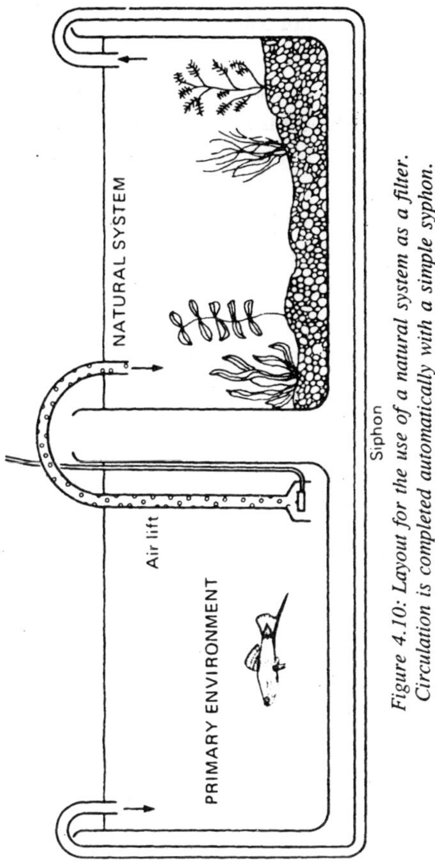

Figure 4.10: Layout for the use of a natural system as a filter. Circulation is completed automatically with a simple syphon.

it before use, thereby reducing the chances of its being swept into the aquarium.

A large mechanical filter with gravel and charcoal as its media can be maintained in two ways. Either it can be cleaned frequently and the charcoal replaced when fully loaded so that it performs its mechanical and chemical functions at top efficiency, or it can be left dirty and allowed to acquire a population of nitrifying bacteria, thus replacing the failing chemical action by an improving biological function.

The last argument, however, only holds good if the surface area is large enough and if aerobic conditions are maintained in the filter. A further system of some interest is that in which an aquarium populated by ancillary animals, such as snails and Daphnia (freshwater), or filter feeders (salt-water), can be used to clean the water of another aquarium containing fish which would not tolerate the presence of these animals if they were kept all together.

Water is circulated between the two aquaria and the system is, in fact, a complete natural aquarium in two parts. This method is worthy of more serious study than it has so far generally received, as there are many advantages in its use.

Medications which are necessary at times for the fish but which are harmful to other creatures can be isolated from the ancillary aquarium by temporarily stopping circulation and compensating with other methods of filtration.

If the ancillary creatures are also food animals (eg Daphnia) for the primary inhabitants they can be cultured in this system and the excess population transferred to the main container when available. Similarly, fish which do not tolerate plants in their environment can nevertheless enjoy the benefits of water from a planted aquarium.

Many other advantages result from this system, and of course, with good usage, one ancillary environment may well support more than one primary environment.

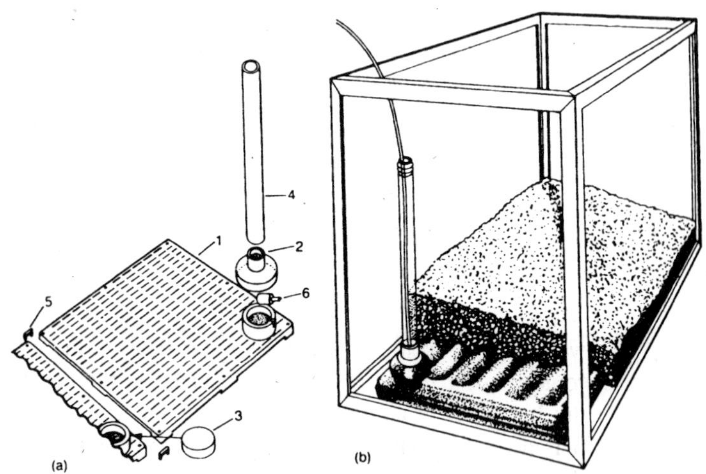

Figure 4.11: The sub-gravel filter. An air-lift draws water from beneath the filter plate, which is replaced by water from above. A filter bed (of gravel) is thereby provided with a steady circulation of oxygenated water, which facilitates the removal of toxic substances by aerobic bacteria. (a) An exploded diagram, showing how two or more filter plates can be joined and operated by one airlift: 1: filter plate; 2: mixing chamber; 3: blanking plug; 4: lift tube; 5: joining clip; 6: diffuser stone; (b) a sub-gravel filter in position (gravel cut away for illustration).

The principles of biological filtration have already been explained in other chapter of this book, but some consideration of the construction and installation of sub-gravel filters is worth while.

At present these are still being developed and this is one field in which the practical aquarist can often improve on commercial products and, indeed, is even obliged to in many cases because filter plates just cannot be bought ready-made to fit every size and shape of aquarium container.

Ideally the filter plate should cover the whole base area and should not allow water to flow past its edges and bypass the bed. It should have an efficient air-lift mechanism which will circulate water evenly over the whole bed area and the plate perforations should be such that gravel, mulm and so on are not drawn through to lie beneath the filter plate and thus impede circulation.

The plate must be rigidly constructed so as to take the weight of the gravel bed and any other heavy material above, such as decorative rocks, without sagging, and the junction between the air-lift mechanism and the filter plate must be sound. For added efficiency, the air-lift tube should preferably include space for a diffuser stone.

Material available to the home constructor are corrugated plastic sheeting, used normally for roofing, and small-bore plastic piping in various sizes as used in domestic waste water systems. Both must be made in non-toxic materials and plastics should be tested before use, especially when they are to be used in marine environments.

All cuts, holes and slots should be made smooth to eliminate small particles which could harm fish, and perforations in corrugated sheet should be in the troughs of the corrugations. Non-toxic joints can be made with silicone rubber sealant but tests should be made to see that it adheres properly to the particular material used.

To achieve the most even circulation of water through the whole bed area it would be best if the air-lift were situated in the centre of a circular plate; but as aquaria are usually anything but circular and a central air-lift is not very convenient there is inevitably some loss of performance for this reason.

However, this loss can be minimised if the other important points are attended to and enough air is provided. The main physical advantage of the sub-gravel filter over other types is that it is hidden inside the environment and does not detract from the overall appearance of the aquarium. Compared with externally mounted filters it allows rows of aquaria to be fitted up tightly side by side for economy of space. Its

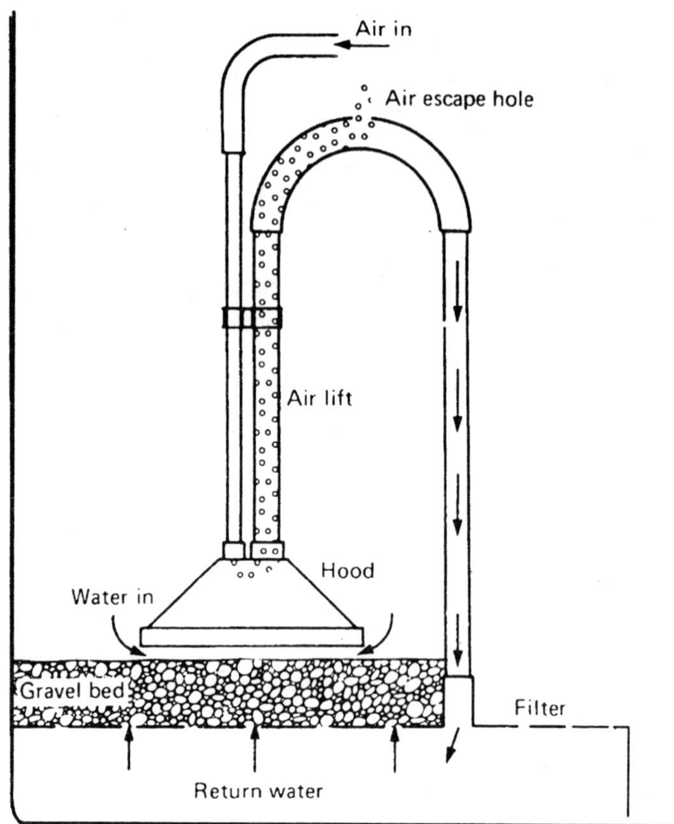

Figure 4.12: Illustration of the reverse-flow system which is used in some sub-gravel filters. The large area of the hood prevents gravel from being sucked up. In this arrangement, all debris is trapped under *the filter plate.*

main disadvantages are that it is not easily accessible should anything go wrong and its use demands a deep gravel bed which can spoil the look of a decorative aquarium unless the gravel showing above the bottom frame of the container is camouflaged in some way.

An interesting variation on the conventional sub-gravel filter is shown in Figure elsewhere in this chapter. A reverse-flow action causes all debris to be trapped underneath the filter plate, thereby providing a cleaner gravel surface.

Both mechanical and biological filters can, of course, be operated by a water pump and this will enable larger flow-rates to be used if needed. The pump is usually situated below the level of the aquarium water so that it can be primed by siphoning initially and then if switched on and off at any time the system should be self-primed due to the automatic levelling action present.

Of course, it must not leak or be opened while it is below the level of the aquarium, and its return or output pipe must always be above the water level to prevent the aquarium from being emptied through the pump.

Water pumps nowadays can be made non-toxic, may not require lubrication and can have their electrical components completely isolated from the water. Some pumps are designed to run while submerged, for use inside the aquarium underwater.

5

Power Supply

The basic principles which govern the role of light as a key factor in the aquatic environment have been discussed in other chapter of this book. This chapter considers the equipment required to produce artificial light and the techniques which enable it to be used efficiently.

Only electrical sources produce light of sufficient intensity for aquatic use. Domestic appliances, such as tungsten filament lamps or fluorescent tubes, are usually used, sometimes with minor modifications to suit them for use in aquaria.

Tungsten lamps have several serious disadvantages. Because they are relatively cheap to buy and easy to install they are often used with little thought, resulting in a short life for the lamps, inefficient use of their light and potentially dangerous situations.

Bulbs made for domestic use are often designed so that the filament is only properly supported internally when the bulb is hanging vertically, and they are not meant to be moved or knocked while switched on. Thus their installation horizontally in shallow hoods (unfortunately the only kind commercially available), which must be moved to gain access for feeding and cleaning, can result in a considerable rate of replacement.

Also, the usual type of domestic lampholder, which is often fitted in a metal hood, has poorly designed terminals which may collect condensation from the water surface below, thereby becoming dangerous. In addition, the lamps produce a lot of heat and this may overheat the surface water and cause distortion of any nearby plastic materials, often the hood itself.

Their advantages are that they produce a type of light similar in many respects to sunlight, so that plants will flourish, they are relatively

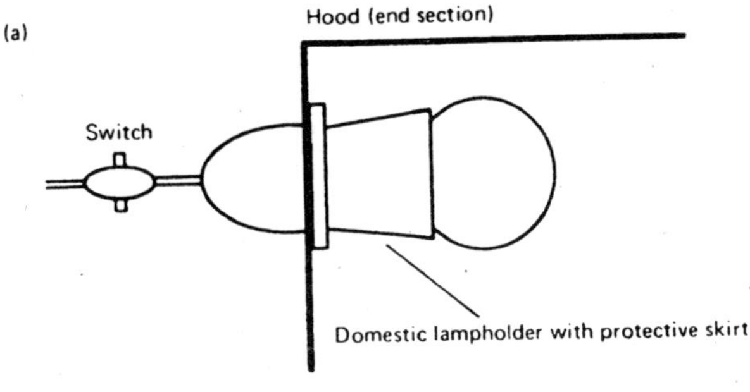

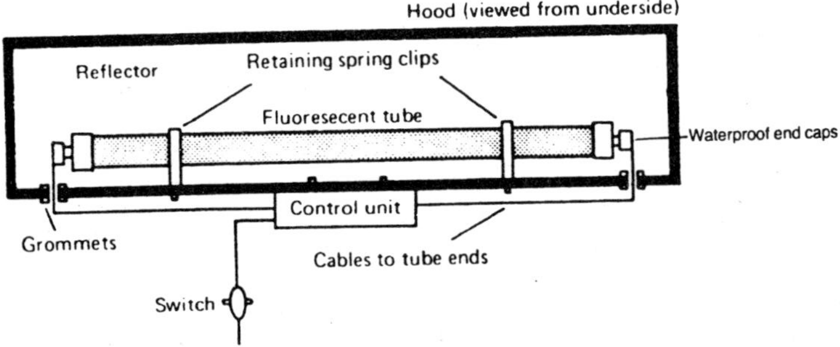

Figure 5.1: Typical light fittings for the aquarium: (a) tungsten filament lamp; (b) fluorescent tube.

small and are available in a convenient range of vab..s of light output and supply voltage. For best results, bulbs should be mounted vertically and provided with air circulation to remove excess heat, and the aquarium should have a cover glass to keep condensation away from the light fittings.

Industrial bulbs designed for horizontal use, known as 'rough service' lamps, can be used and have stronger filament supports. Reflectors or hoods for use with bulbs should be made so that the fish can be fed without disturbing the hood.

When the aquarium is being cleaned, the lamps should be switched off and allowed sufficient time to cool before the hood is removed. In most rectangular aquaria more than one lamp is needed to give an even spread of light over the whole area, but it is usually better to use, say, two powerful lamps rather than four weaker ones, as the absorption of light by the water is quite noticeable and low-powered lamps will adequately illuminate only the upper levels of the aquarium.

Table elsewhere in this chapter gives some idea of the light output of tungsten lamps. It should be remembered that where aquaria are

Table 5.1: Light output of tungstem filament lamps.

(All lamps have a rated life of 1000 hours)

Single coil- light output (lumens)			*Coiled coil- light Output at 240V*	
Watts	*110V*	*240V*	*Watts*	*Lumens*
25	200	200	40	390
40	400	325	60	665
60	695	575	100	1,260
100	1,280	1,160	150	2,075
150	2,090	1,960		
200	2,090	2,720		
300	4,700	4,300		
500	8,500	7,700		
750	13,800	12,400		
1,000	19,000	17,300		
1,500	—	27,500		

Table 5.2: Light output of fluorescent tubes.

	Length (in)								
Type	*standard*						*miniature*		
Length(in) 6	60	48	42	36	24	18	21	12	9
Wattage 4	65	40	40	30	20	15	13	8	6
White 100	4700	2800	2800	2150	1100	800	750	420	250
Warm white —	4600	2700	2700	2150	1100	800	750	420	250
Coolwhite —	4450	2650	—	2050	1050	750	700	360	240
Natural —	3400	2100	—	1600	800	600	—	—	—
North light! col match —	2700	1700	—	1250	700	500	—	—	—
Artificial daylight —	2100	1200	—	—	500	—	—	—	—

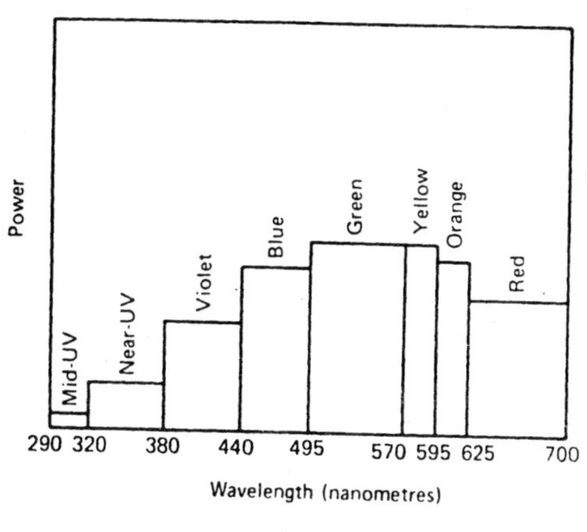

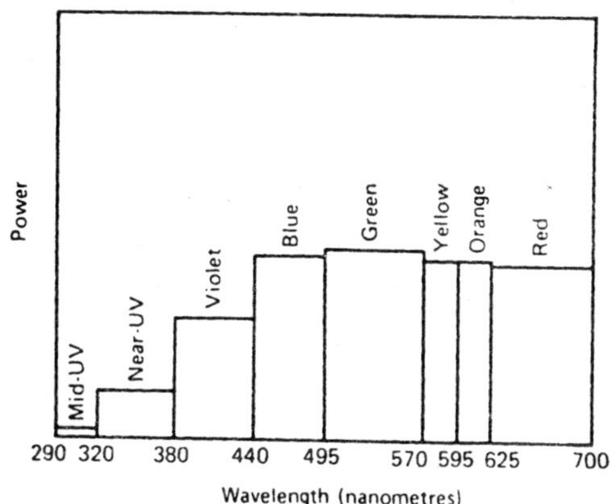

Figure 5.2: The remarkable similarity of the distribution of colours in natural light (below) and the fluorescent tube Tru-lite.

mounted one above another any tungsten lamps in the lower installations will tend to heat the upper containers by convection, unless some insulation is fitted.

Nowadays aquarists use fluorescent lighting because of its several advantages. Originally the types of tubes available did not give off a natural kind of light and were so deficient in certain areas of the light spectrum that plants would not flourish.

Better tubes are now available in the domestic range and, in addition, special types have been developed (eg Grolux, Tru-lite) which simulate natural light and encourage plant growth.

Grolux tubes are recommended even where plants are not grown, as they also emphasise the colours of the fish and other creatures,

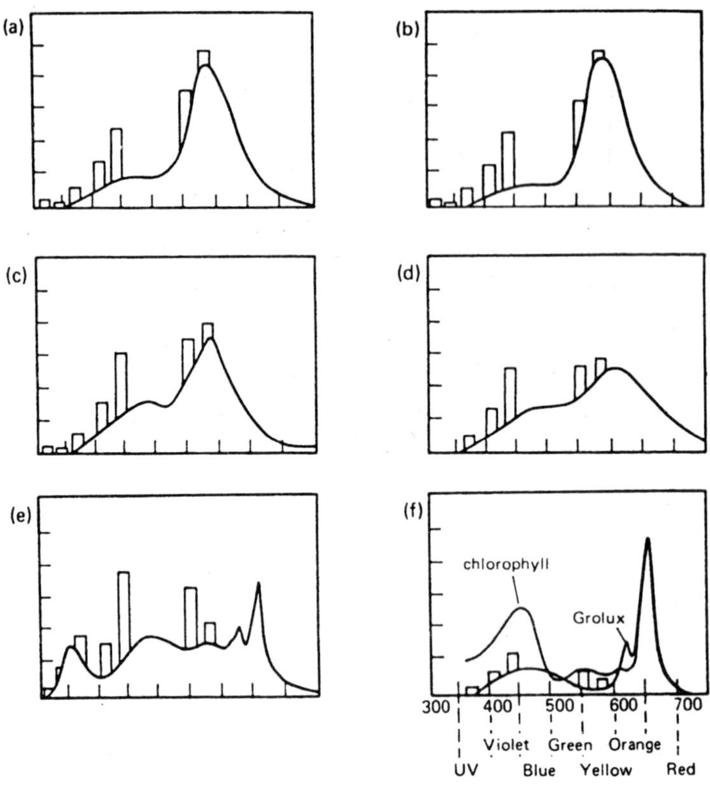

Figure 5.3: The distribution of colours in the light from a range of typical fluorescent tubes: (a) white; (b) warm white; (c) daylight; (d) natural; (e) artificial daylight; (f) Grolux with superimposition of the chlorophyl synthesis curve in plants.

particularly the reds and pinks. The wavelength distributions of a number of typical tubes are shown in Figure elsewhere in this chapter. Fluorescent lighting is not cheap to install but it is more efficient in use and the replacement rate is usually very low.

It produces unwanted heat at a much lower rate than tungsten lamps and generates more light per watt of power consumed by the tube. The tube gives a good dispersion of light, but the power is governed by the length of the tube and it is not possible, for instance, to have a 50W tube only 30cm (1ft) long or a 10W tube 120cm (4ft) long, and this must be taken into account in the design of the system.

Associated with the fluorescent tube are a choke and a starter which are essential to its performance, shown anywhere else in this book. These may be supplied in a common case with the tube holders or mounted separately.

Two fluorescent lighting circuits are shown in Figure elsewhere in this chapter. The auto-transformer system tends to eliminate flashing when the tube is first switched on and may also allow a long tube life.

The choke is heavy and allowance should be made for this when building or buying a reflector, and the starter needs to be accessible for easy substitution if a fault arises.

Some fittings may also have a capacitor in the circuit, as shown, but this is not usual in the low-powered lamps used in aquaria. Once the aquarist is certain there are no loose connections, all fault finding in fluorescent systems is most easily done by substitution with new parts.

The advice of a competent electrician is advisable in complicated installations. Switches for fluorescent lighting should be of a higher current rating than those used for tungsten lamps of the same power, as the choke produces a power surge at the instant of switching on.

For this reason multiple lighting systems should not be run from a common low-current switch but should be treated individually. It is recommended that each lamp installation should have a switch capable

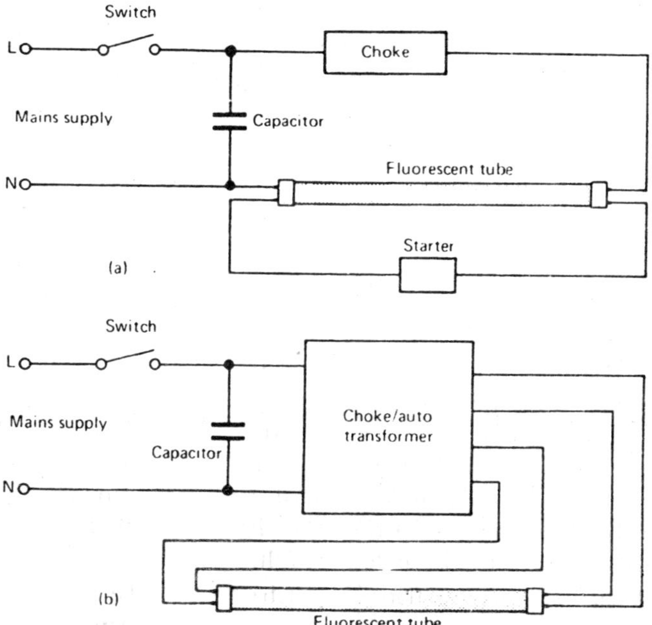

Figure 5.4: Circuits for fluorescent lighting systems using (a) an automatic starter, and (b) an auto transformer.

of carrying at least 5A current. Also, because of the influence of the choke, electric shocks received from this type of equipment are likely to be more severe than from some other sources and so every care should be taken to see that condensation, splashing or salt deposits from marine aquaria do not find their way on to or into the equipment.

In this respect there is a ready market waiting for a properly-designed aquarium hood, as a good one does not seem to be available. Combinations of tungsten and fluorescent lighting are often used to good effect.

It seems that there may still be some radiation missing from individual fluorescent lamps which plants can obtain in a combined system, and also the problem of applying higher powers of light to small areas is made easier.

If the installation conditions required for both types of lamp are met there are no technical difficulties in this kind of system. Two useful lighting accessories are the dimmer and the time switch. The dimmer enables the aquarist to vary the lighting smoothly to any value up to full brilliance, so that by experiment an optimum system can be arrived at without expensive substitution.

A time switch allows the period of illumination to be set automatically to suit the environment and also ensures day-to-day constancy. It is quite a simple thing to install and use; the type supplied for domestic appliances is most suitable and widely available.

Both these accessories can be used together if connected one after the other in the supply line and both must of course be able to carry the full current drawn by the lighting circuit at any time.

SAFETY

In this chapter it is hoped to explain enough about aquarium electrical installations to enable the aquarist to install equipment in a safe and reliable manner. Many sources of information evade this question by quite correctly advising the aquarist to consult a competent electrician, as has already been mentioned.

It is however a fact that when a person buys, say, a heater and a thermostat he does not often call in an electrician to wire up the circuit, but for various reasons does it himself. Having wired up a heater system which seems satisfactory, confidence is gained for more complex enterprises often with disastrous results.

It is therefore felt that it is better to explain some electrical theory in simple terms and to discuss some simple methods, rather than to

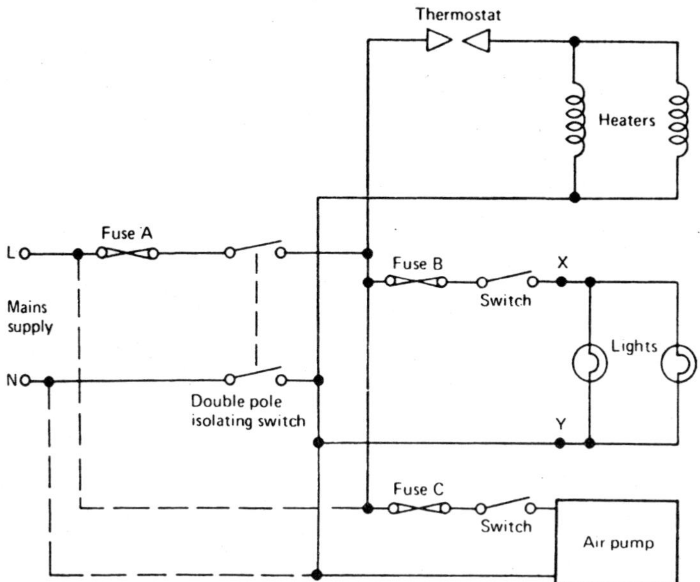

Figure 5.5: Electrical connections for a typical aquarium. Fuse A must be able to carry the whole current but B and C should be rated to match the lighting system and the air pump respectively. By this means, a fault which blows either fuse B or C does not affect the heating circuit. If there is a short circuit in the heating system, fuse A will blow and both the pump and the lights will fail. A fluorescent lamp can be substituted for the tungsten lamps by connecting at points X and Y. All switches and fuses must be rated to carry the required load. The dotted lines show an alternative arrangement in which a failure of the heating system does not affect the air pump, as will be necessary in a crowded aquarium.

dismiss the subject with advice which, although good, will probably not be heeded. As an introduction, Figure elsewhere in this chapter shows the electrical connections for a typical aquarium.

The normal mains electricity supply in the British Isles is 240V ac at 50 hertz. The letters 'ac' stand for 'alternating current' and show that the supply fluctuates in a cyclic fashion. A battery, for instance, supplies direct current (dc) which is continuous, and has a positive and negative terminal.

An ac supply alternates between positive and negative at its terminals, ie one terminal is positive at one instant, negative at the next, then positive again, and so on, and the other terminal is always in the opposite condition.

The speed at which this reversing process occurs is called the frequency of the supply and is measured in cycles per second, nowadays called hertz (Hz). The voltage of the supply, 240V in Britain, is the 'pressure' of the electricity which is available and waiting to push the electric current into any load placed on the supply system.

Thus the designation shows that the electricity available at the supply point is at 240V 'pressure' and cycling between positive and negative at a rate of 50 times per second.

The amount of electricity taken by a connected appliance is called the current and is measured in amperes, usually abbreviated to amps, and is determined by the power of that appliance, which is measured in watts.

Because the amount of current taken by a particular appliance or load will depend also on the pressure of voltage available to push it into the appliance there is a simple relationship between these three properties which is expressed as:

Power = current × voltage

or

Watts = amps × volts

(There are further complications to the above equation in more complex circuits than are used for aquarium apparatus and where extremely high current values are drawn, but these do not concern us here and can be ignored.)

Thus, if a heater is specified by the manufacturer as suitable for operation on a 240V supply and has a power of 100W the current it will draw can be calculated as follows:

Watts = amps × volts

Thus: amps - watts volts

= 100 - 240 = 0.417A

By approximating to a convenient round number it can be said that a 100W heater takes a current of just under half an amp. It may not seem important at first glance to know this fact, but the point is that electrical wiring, switches and other items through which the current flows on its way to any appliance are all designed to carry only a certain maximum current, and if this is exceeded either a fuse will blow to protect the circuit, or the wire or switch will overheat and be damaged, or a fire may start.

It follows that when electrical apparatus is installed it is important to know the maximum value of current needed and then to use materials which can carry all of this current safely. It can also be seen from the above that an appliance performs at its specified power only when it is connected to a supply system which provides the proper voltage.

Thus a 240V light bulb applied to a 12V supply would only glow feebly, if at all, and a 12V lamp applied to a 240V supply would burn out immediately and might even explode. Some items such as heaters and light bulbs can work equally well on ac or dc supplies, provided the voltage is correct, but others such as air pumps and fluorescent lamps will work only with an ac supply.

This last point is mentioned only as a matter of interest as there is no point in the aquarist considering the use of any other supply than the domestic one. Certain items can be bought, for instance some pumps for goldfish ponds, which operate at a lower voltage, but these are then supplied with a transformer which converts the normal mains voltage to that used by the appliance, and the whole apparatus is still plugged into the domestic supply system.

Installations of one or two average-sized aquaria in the home will not cause problems in electricity supply because their total current consumption will be low. For instance, two 3ft aquaria, each with two 75W heaters and two 40W lamps, have a power consumption of 460W.

Adding a little for an air pump gives a total of 480W and then by repeating the calculation used previously we can derive a current consumption of 2A. As modern domestic installations are wired for 13A, or 5 or 15A in older systems, this set-up can be plugged into any convenient wall socket. Connecting cable and switches should have a current rating of 5A to allow for some safety margin.

Larger installations using electrical heating systems can be treated in the same way but eventually a point may be reached where the total current demand of the installation is greater than that which can be supplied by a domestic wall socket.

This is where the competent electrician really must become involved because it will now be necessary to run a heavy duty cable from the main fuse box to wherever the aquaria are situated and to set up the necessary terminations and switches.

In order to allow domestic wall socket circuits to be run below their maximum, so as to cater for other appliances in the house, a good general rule is that an independent system should be fitted up as soon as the total current consumption for the aquarium facility is more than 5A (assuming a 13A wall socket system).

Connections and cables in multiple immersion-heated systems are often a terrible mess when installed by the aquarist and are frequently downright dangerous. Badly-kept fish houses in particular often have damp atmospheres with condensation running down the walls, and this

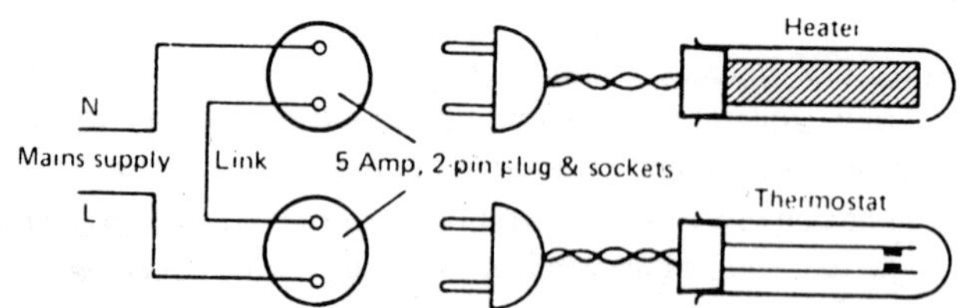

Figure 5.6: Connections for a single heater system using interlinked wall sockets.

must be eliminated and all wiring kept short and tidy to ensure safe working and reliability.

Lighting circuits should be fused and switched independently of heating circuits so that a fault in one system does not affect the other. Any small air pumps can be supplied from the lighting circuit or from their own separate line.

Amateur electricians frequently use insulation tape to separate twisted wire junctions from each other and this is not recommended as a reliable or safe method since damp can often get in and the tape deteriorates in time.

All connections should be made in enclosed boxes or by means of interlinked wall sockets, this last method having the advantage that components can be replaced without interfering with the rest of the installation.

The question of earthing has caused a lot of controversy amongst aquarists because it is very difficult to apply a suitable method to aquaria. The principle behind the idea of earthing electrical appliances is that if a fault develops which, for instance, results in the metal casing of an electric iron becoming live, then if that casing is effectively connected to the earth of the supply system a large current will flow from the live terminal to the earth with the result that the fuses blow out immediately to make everything safe.

Various difficulties are encountered in aquaria, and the problem is not really capable of solution; it is instructive to consider why this is so.

The usual aquarium construction, whereby the water is contained within glass, putty, plastics, glass-fibre and other materials which are all electrical insulators, means that should the water become live, for instance through a cracked heater tube, there is no conducting material in direct contact with the water to which an earth wire can be attached.

The only usable, efficient conducting materials are metals, usually copper, but even if an aquarium frame were made of copper it would still be insulated wholly or partially, from the water, by the glass and sealant.

Thus the only effective earth would be a terminal actually in the water, but this is not possible because of the toxic effects of submerged metals on small living creatures. It is well known, for instance, that particles from new copper water piping in extremely low concentrations will kill fish easily.

Figure 5.7: Earthing dangers: (a) without an earthing point, the aquarist will draw current from live water via his shoes, floor coverings etc, which will provide some limited protection; (b) when the frame of the container is earthed, the aquarist runs the risk of having a large current flow through his body from live water if he touches the frame.

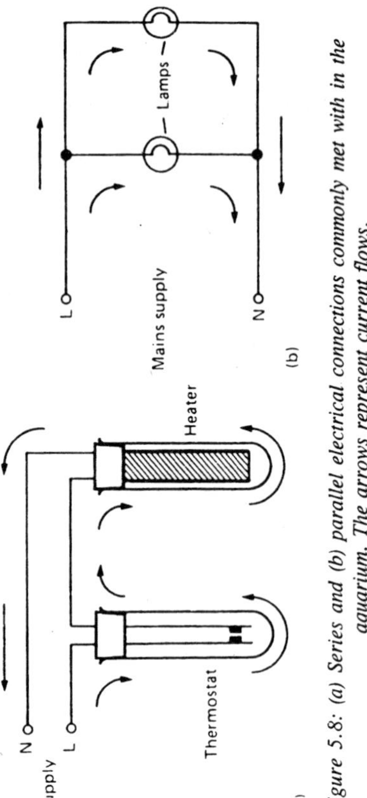

Figure 5.8: (a) Series and (b) parallel electrical connections commonly met with in the aquarium. The arrows represent current flows.

Fortunately water is not one of the best conductors of electricity and if the aquarist puts a hand into a live tank, and is suitably insulated by shoes, clothes and carpeting which are dry, he will not usually receive a shock which has the full capability of the supply behind it, although it will still be unpleasant.

However, if he has one hand immersed in a live aquarium and then touches an earth terminal, such as a metal tank frame connected to the supply earth but insulated from the live water by the glass and putty, then the full current available may flow through his body on its way to that earth, with probably fatal results.

It would therefore seem that the aquarist must risk any shocks which may come along and must minimise their possible effect by reliable installation and wiring and dry conditions.

It is better to do without ineffective earths, which if touched at the wrong time as explained above would in fact make things far worse.

Now that some metal-framed aquaria and their stands are being coated in plastic and nylon the temptation to earth these is less and this is probably a very good thing. All-glass aquaria do not have frames at all of course.

If sufficient water gains entry into an item of immersible equipment it may short out the live and neutral terminals directly and thus cause the fuses to blow, rendering everything safe.

Unfortunately it is often possible to get a shock from an aquarium long before this happens, and indeed it may never happen at all if for some reason only the live side of the appliance is in contact with the water.

Finally, two electrical terms with which the aquarist may meet are 'series' and 'parallel' which are used to describe connection configurations.

For instance, if a thermostat and heater are connected together as in Figure elsewhere in this chapter they are said to be in series with each other because the current has to flow through the thermostat to get to the heater. In a parallel connection, such as where two lamps use the same supply, the current flows through each one independently of the other, and one can be removed without affecting the other.

6

Feeding

Most non-aquatic animals can be fed quite easily but in fishkeeping feeding is an acquired skill calling for understanding and discipline on the part of the aquarist because the success of the whole environment will depend on the proper introduction of food.

Feeding is therefore as much a technique as a routine and food is a true factor in the environment. While food has the obvious property of keeping alive the inhabitants of the aquarium, it also has many other influences. Growth, health and general well-being are determined by proper feeding.

The ability of species to live together, their reproductive potential, their condition and decorative appearance, and many other characteristics, are all dependent on the feeding methods used. These same characteristics are, of course, also dependent on other environmental factors but the point is that, even if these other factors are perfect, bad feeding will spoil everything.

Aquatic creatures are very adaptable and will quite easily become accustomed to a variety of foods which are not found in their natural habitats. This fact is of immense benefit to the aquarist, who is thus able to use foods which are easily obtainable.

It does not mean, however, that a new 'unnatural' food can be used thoughtlessly because it may be that while it suits the creatures which eat it, it may have some property which has an extremely detrimental effect on the management of the environment as a whole.

Frequency of feeding is important. Most of the commonly kept fish are of the smaller shoaling kinds and in nature these will feed often or continually if conditions (especially temperature) are favourable.

In an artificial environment where constant favourable conditions are maintained the fish may take food frequently and therefore need to be fed quite often, particularly when they are young.

In order to avoid the consequences of overfeeding, aquarists are usually advised as a safety measure to feed infrequently, and because most people work away from home it is easy to settle into a routine of providing food only twice daily at the most. This practice goes against the needs of many fish and inhibits their development.

Fortunately, fish do absorb nutrients from the water through their body surfaces which allow them to exist for long periods without eating; but this does not mean that they will thrive when food is not available, and thus their development can be retarded.

Some fish and other creatures which are predatory feed only infrequently but in most aquaria these are the exception rather than the rule. All young fish and many adults should, if possible, be offered food of the right kind as often as they will take it.

If the aquarist is unable to supply food at frequent intervals then methods of feeding must be worked out which allow suitable foods to be available in the aquarium for long periods but which do not lead to any deterioration in environmental conditions as a result.

Overfeeding is a common fault amongst inexperienced and disinterested aquarists. The term 'overfeeding' applies to the environment, not to its inhabitants, and if it is viewed in this way it is easier to understand its implications.

A fish can hardly be overfed because it will simply refrain from eating when full, but the artificial environment can easily be overloaded with food in such amounts that its cleansing facilities cannot cope with the resulting deterioration and pollution.

When fish are fed heavily, say with a commercial dry food, they eat as much as possible until their initial hunger is sated. They then cruise about picking up odd bits, playing with them, swallowing some and rejecting others, and finally perhaps not feeding at all until after a period of digestion.

In the meantime the uneaten food settles in the gravel and other niches, absorbs water and begins to rot. When the fish are willing to feed again most of these uneaten remains are unavailable to them, and unpalatable anyway, and so are left untouched.

If the aquarist now administers another heavy feed the process is repeated so that a continuous build-up of uneaten food is generated, which completes a vicious circle because the resulting pollution eventually affects the inhabitants and causes them to go off their food due to ill-health and so the situation becomes even worse.

In effect, overfeeding prevents successful completion of the nitrogen cycle and an accumulation of toxic minerals occurs. The aquarist may reduce the effects of this by water changing or by constant, heavy filtration, but this does not solve the basic problem and only makes more work.

Many potentially good aquarists are lost from the hobby because they simply do not understand this problem and do not realise that the cause of much of the trouble they experience maintaining their aquaria may quite simply be a result of incorrect feeding.

The solution to the problem, then, is either to feed the fish often but with only as much food as will be completely consumed in a short while, or to use foods which stay alive until eaten or at least do not deteriorate quickly and do not become inaccessible.

The fish should be kept just slightly hungry so that they will search for food between feeds and will take the trouble to dig out odd pieces from crevices, thus generally helping to keep the environment clean. The environment's capacity for completing the nitrogen cycle is usually fully taken up in dealing with the fish's wastes and ideally should never be called on to deal with uneaten food.

Of course some food will always escape the fish, no matter how careful the aquarist may be, but this amount must be so small that its effects are negligible. Certainly many people put so much food into aquaria that more is left uneaten than is consumed, and this situation causes the greater proportion of all troubles encountered by the novice.

Children and visitors must never be allowed to feed the fish for amusement as they invariably are heavy-handed in the cause of well-meant generosity.

Aquaria in schools, hospitals and other such places inevitably suffer from uneducated feeding and then create the impression among the general public that fishkeeping is dirty and smelly and requires constant work—which, of course, is true if feeding practices are incorrect. Variety in the fish's diet is not always as important as some people, particularly advertisers, would have us believe.

As long as the diet of the fish meets all their requirements, and the aquarist's convenience as well, there is no need to go to too much trouble to provide other items 'for a change'. Variety in feeding is necessary only when it provides essential dietary requirements which may not all be present in one particular food.

The merits of the various foods available should be studied and a composite diet provided to meet the fish's specific requirements. There is no point in alternating a good food with one which is different but of far less benefit.

The main substances required to form a balanced diet for aquarium fish, and indeed all vertebrates, are proteins, carbohydrates, fats and oils, minerals and vitamins, and an understanding of their functions will prove useful.

Proteins are the foundation of the diet and its most essential component for they encourage growth and the replacement of body tissues. Proteins are, chemically, compounds of carbon, nitrogen, oxygen, hydrogen and various trace elements. They can be classified either as animal or vegetable depending on their origin and for aquarium use can be obtained from live creatures and plants.

Carbohydrates act as a fuel in that they provide energy and body heat, and are obtainable from starchy foods such as biscuit meal and oatmeal. Fats and oils similarly promote energy and warmth and nourish the nervous system.

The body can store these substances against times of shortage. They are best obtained as constituents of foods such as meat and fish. Minerals such as iron, calcium and phosphorus help to build the bones, teeth, muscles and circulatory system and are common in many foods as trace ingredients.

Vitamins are active organic compounds which provide protection against disease and generally facilitate the body functions. Vegetable foods, or creatures which feed directly on them, are the primary sources of vitamins in aquaria. Vitamin A, for example, is formed in the body from a compound called carotene which is found in plants and this is used by the fish to develop and intensify colouring.

Vitamin B is similarly obtained from plants and one of its properties is to assist in the correct functioning of the digestive organs. The importance of vegetable foods as suppliers of vitamins is paramount and many aquarists fail in this respect by not providing enough green food.

It is convenient to classify the various foods commonly used into four categories, namely: natural foods, cultured foods, table foods and prepared dry foods. These are dealt with below under their individual headings.

NATURAL FOODS

Natural foods are those which fish feed on in the wild state.

Some little trouble is involved in their collection but they do seem to provide something which other foods lack, and are especially good for rearing young fish and for bringing adults into breeding condition.

Some live foods can be bought but their condition cannot always be relied on as some types do not store well. Earthworms are one of the best foods for all fish, either whole for larger specimens or broken or mashed up for small fish.

A certain amount of dirt and slime comes with them and should be washed off before use. They must not be taken from ground which has been treated with weedkillers or fertilisers. They can be bred and encouraged to collect in compost heaps or holes filled with tea leaves and kitchen scraps.

They flourish best in dark, damp conditions and moderate temperatures. Earthworms are ideal for bringing the larger fish into breeding condition, but it may be found that the quantities eaten by very large fish makes their acquisition a demanding job.

They live for some time in water if left uneaten but will often burrow into the gravel before death occurs, so that removal of the bodies is usually impossible. Feeding should therefore be carried out carefully and sparingly. Small worms called brandlings, found in manure and some compost heaps, are not good for aquarium use as they exude a thick yellow fluid when damaged which will cause problems in a closed habitat.

Various small creatures under the general name of Daphnia are used by aquarists. As collected or purchased a quantity of Daphnia often contains a multitude of organisms, such as cyclops and rotifers, all of which are good fish foods.

Daphnia are crustaceans and have a hard exterior skeleton which provides needed roughage in the fish's diet. They are found in shallow water in farm ponds, ditches, canals, in fact in almost any still water containing even smaller organisms, such as Infusoria, on which they feed.

Cattle droppings or green water thus indirectly stimulate the development of Daphnia and their population level is apparently also dependent on weather conditions. There are several varieties of Daphnia, of different size and colour, and some of these seem to be seasonal.

Daphnia can be collected simply by netting with a fine mesh. They will not tolerate crowded conditions for long and do not transfer well to unmatured tap-water. They must be kept cool and if stored for any time should be maintained in well-aerated conditions.

Some larger creatures, such as beetles and various insect larvae, are often caught with Daphnia and these can be useful in the aquarium if they are eaten by larger fish. Generally, however, larger pond creatures should be removed as they may attack small fish.

The pond water acquired with the Daphnia can be put into the aquarium with them if it is clean and may be beneficial in providing many other microscopic organisms which the fish will also eat. Daphnia must of course never be collected from any body of water containing any kind of fish life.

All wild fish have parasites and these will usually fluorish in an aquarium, and, being small, are extremely difficult to eradicate. Daphnia can be introduced into freshwater environments in quite reasonable quantities as they live for some time and are useful where infrequent feeding is practised.

In salt water they die quickly and so must be used more carefully. Daphnia can be bred at home in shallow ponds fed with cow dung or kitchen scraps to produce thick Infusoria colonies, but the amount may not make the effort and inconvenience worth while. Young fish particularly benefit from large quantities of small Daphnia in their diet.

Tubifex worms are obtained commercially from mud in tidal estuaries, such as the Thames in London, and from sewer outlets and similar places. Collection is unpleasant and specialised, requiring a knowledge of local conditions and equipment such as sieves and waders. They can, however, be bought at most aquarists' suppliers at reasonable prices for small quantities and it would not benefit the average aquarist to collect his own.

They cannot be completely recommended because of various disadvantages. Due to the conditions existing in their natural habitat they require thorough washing and cleaning with a suitable commercial preparation before use, and will easily die unless kept in cold running water.

As bought they may or may not be clean and fresh, depending on the previous treatment received, and those which are unhealthy must not be fed to the fish. It is difficult to be sure what state they are in. Some varieties of tubifex are said to be parasitic and able to live inside, and later eat their way out of, fish which swallow them whole.

Any which settle in a gravel bed will quickly establish themselves so well that only certain fish can then make use of them. They live in the gravel for some time but die eventually, especially at tropical temperatures, and their resulting decomposition can cause pollution if they are present in large numbers. Boils, gill disorders and unexplained deaths are a feature of fish fed on this food, so the aquarist is advised against its use.

Glassworms, properly called gnat larvae, occur mainly in cold weather in waters containing decaying vegetable matter. They are small free-swimming creatures about half an inch long and have a transparent body which is usually horizontal in the water.

They are collected in the same way as Daphnia and are often found with them. They have the advantage that they can be crowded together for transport and storage, and make an excellent food for medium-sized and adult fish.

They are able to catch fish fry with a hooked appendage at their heads and so must not be put in with small fish.

Their food value seems excellent and they live in the aquarium for long periods if uneaten. Aquarium snails can be considered a natural food. When they achieve an excess population, instead of being thrown away, or killed with proprietary liquids, they can be crushed and fed to the fish.

Very large fish, such as Oscars, will crack the shells themselves, but they are too tough for most other fish. Snails are a good food that should be used at every opportunity and certainly not wasted.

CULTURED FOODS

Over many years, knowledgeable aquarists have developed methods of culturing and breeding satisfactorily several small food animals which are extremely useful, especially when rearing young fish. Most of them are available commercially in the form of 'starter' cultures, or even eggs, and they can fairly easily be propagated in quantity.

Table elsewhere in this chapter gives a summary of various cultured foods.

The smallest of these food animals are Infusoria, the collective name given to colonies of microscopic organisms occurring naturally in sunlit waters containing organic refuse.

They can be collected from ponds and water butts but if regularly required in reasonable quantities they should be cultured artificially. Infusoria are practically the only live food small enough, and capable of being produced in sufficient quantities, for the newly-hatched fry of many of the smaller fish.

It is imperative that aquarists wishing to breed any of the smaller egglaying fish develop a satisfactory method of culturing Infusoria in

Table 6.1: Cultured Foods—Summary of methods.

Type	*Culture medium*	*Temp range*	*Food*	*Develop-menttime*	*Culture lifetime*
Infusoria	Decaying vegetable matter in water	65-70°F	Bacteria in culture	10-20 days	Used all at once
Microworm	Wet cooked oatmeal	70-80°F	Oatmeal	3-5 days	Approx 14 days
Brine Shrimp	Salt solution	75-80°F	None	Hatch in 24 hours at 80°F	Use as soon as possible
Grindaf worm	2:1 peat/ sand mixture kept damp	65-75°F	Oatmeal paste	14 days	Indefinite if properly cared for
Whiteworm		55-70°F	Wet bread		

quantity. There are several old-fashioned methods commonly recommended but those which involve standing containers of culture medium outdoors in the sun are not sufficiently reliable for consistent production, as fluctuations of temperature and light cannot be controlled.

The Infusoria culture is produced by placing crushed lettuce, banana skins or other vegetable matter in a container and then pouring boiling water over it to initiate its breakdown and subsequent rotting.

After a little time, say twenty-four hours, the bulk of the culture can be made up with cold water to fill the container, but this must not contain live organisms which might eat the Infusoria.

The Infusoria find their way into the culture by means of air-borne spores and the initial population should be acquired automatically. It is vital to keep the culture at a minimum temperature of 65°F (18.5°C).

After a few days the culture becomes turbid and at this time may not be very pleasant. Many aquarists mistake this for the completed culture but at this stage it has no value as a fish food.

It is, in fact, a bacterial culture and the Infusoria multiply by consuming the bacteria, so that after about a week and a half the turbidity clears and the culture becomes transparent and practically odourless.

Gentle aeration is useful to maintain aerobic conditions, otherwise it may need frequent stirring by hand. After three weeks the culture should be really thick and the Infusoria can be seen collectively as a shimmering mass when the container is viewed against the light.

If it is desired to use one culture per day a rotation system of about twenty containers (eg large sweet jars) must be set up such that as one is used another is started. This of course requires space and some artificial heating may be needed to maintain the minimum temperature, as well as illumination.

If a continuous supply is not needed the culture should be started three weeks before it will be required. To feed the fish, the liquid culture is simply poured into the aquarium. It should be noted that Infusoria consume oxygen, so any overfeeding may cause problems in crowded environments.

For the young of the common livebearers and the larger egglayers the ideal first food is the Brine Shrimp *(Artemia sauna)*. This is a small salt-water organism whose eggs are collected commercially and, as they are storable, can be hatched out as required.

There is some controversy as to whether they should be used for freshwater fish for long periods because of the salt content in their bodies, but certainly for the initial period, until the fry can take larger foods, they are excellent. A salt environment is necessary for hatching the eggs but this need not be as perfect as that used for keeping marine fish.

The artificial salt-water mixes sold for marine fishkeeping do give a better hatching of the eggs, but as the water used is generally spoilt after a few hatches this might be considered expensive. A good general method is to use a plastic bucket containing a solution of ordinary block salt, or 'aquarium salt' as sold in shops, made up to a density of 1.025.

The temperature of the solution will determine the hatching time and usually at 80°F (27°C) the shrimps appear after about twenty-four hours. A heater and thermostat can be included to maintain this temperature. The young shrimps also benefit from turbulence and aerobic conditions, so aeration can be applied to advantage. A more sophisticated method is illustrated in Figure elsewhere in this chapter.

A triangular or funnelshaped container with an airstone fitted at the inverted apex ensures that the eggs cannot settle anywhere and are thus always properly exposed to the brine solution. The best results are obtained if the unit is big enough to hold its own heating system

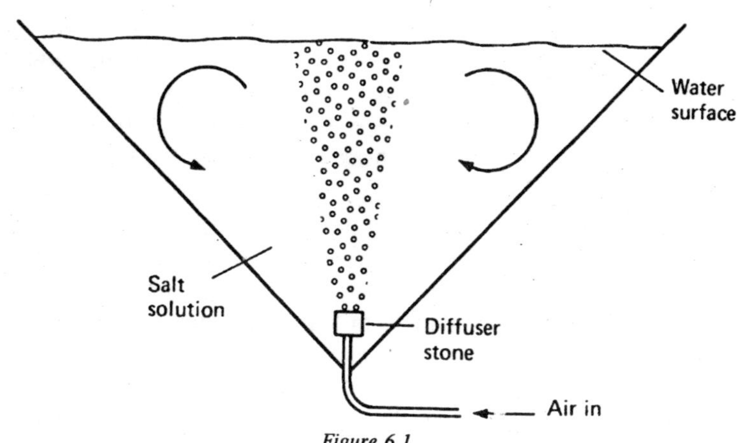

Figure 6.1.

for constant temperature control. Tubes for drainage and shrimp collecting can be fitted if required. The culture technique described above makes use of a warm salt-water environment of a very simple kind which is easy to set up but will only hatch a certain number of eggs before becoming spoilt.

Therefore for continuous production a rotation system is again needed, but because the hatching time is quite fast not so many containers will be required as for Infusoria, three usu ally being sufficient.

The individual baby shrimps are just discernable to the eye and in quantity are seen as a bright orange cloud in the water. When they are about to be removed for feeding, aeration should be stopped and time allowed for the water to settle, when it will be seen that the empty eggshells will either float or sink and the live shrimps will swim in mid-water, from where they can easily be siphoned off into a fine net.

They are light-sensitive and collect together if a small bulb is placed near a convenient point. Some aquarists like to wash the shrimps to remove any salt before they are fed to the fish, but this is a minor point, especially where the fry receive shrimps for perhaps only two weeks.

The shrimps do not live long in freshwater aquaria, so must be used carefully, but they will live and grow in marine environments if uneaten. Many marine aquarists simply put the eggs into their aquaria and allow them to hatch there. This method is extremely convenient but after a time the accretion of empty shells may detract from the decorative appearance of the aquarium.

Brine Shrimp can be reared easily to the adult stage if they are kept in a more stable environment and fed on Infusoria (and one another). They are interesting aquatically as well as being good food for larger fish, but the process is as troublesome as rearing the fish themselves, so is not often practised. Marine fishkeepers can do it in any old water which is not polluted.

Microworms are another small food easily accepted by small fish. They are cultured in trays containing a thick paste of cooked oatmeal, kept at a temperature of about 75°F (24°C). A small quantity of microworms are needed initially to start the culture and these then multiply rapidly to the point where many of them leave the medium and move on to the sides of the tray.

They can then be collected from there with a fine brush and fed directly to the fish. A culture usually lasts about a fortnight before becoming foul, when it can be replaced with a new one seeded from the original. The system is quite simple and, provided the temperature is maintained and the culture is not allowed to dry out, there should be no problems.

As with the previous cultures, if a good continuous supply is required r rotation system of replacement can be used. Grindal worms are larger and are bred in shallow boxes containing a mixture of two parts peat to one part fine sand (building sand is ideal). The culture is kept warm and damp and again a starter culture is used initially.

The worms are fed on oatmeal paste which is placed on top of the peat under a cover glass. When the worms have developed in sufficient quantity many of them will move on to the underside of the glass and can readily be removed from there.

The peat should be dug over periodically to prevent caking and eventually replaced with fresh material if the culture goes sour. The size of the grindal worm makes it a very acceptable second food for young fish and it can be a beneficial permanent part of the diet of any of the smaller fish at the adult stage.

The whole point about Grindal and also Whiteworm cultures (see below) is that the aquarist must not take away the worms faster than they can be replaced otherwise the supply will obviously decline.

Whiteworms are larger than Grindal but otherwise similar, and often a culture may contain both types together. They are bred in peat cultures in the same way although larger containers are recommended, such as plastic seed-trays.

The cultures should be kept in a warm but not hot place, which should be damp and dark. The most convenient food is simply a piece of wet bread and if other conditions are correct this will be all that is needed.

Many aquarists use porridge, custard and all manner of things as food for their cultures, but there is no point in such complications if a simpler method will produce the same results.

Every aquarist can benefit from a healthy supply of whiteworm whatever his aquatic interests, as it is relished by all adult fish, including marines, and is excellent for bringing adults into breeding condition. At least one culture should be kept for use when other live foods are not available.

One point with peat cultures is that they tend to become populated with other creatures as well as the worms for which they are intended. These 'nits', 'fleas' and so on do not particularly affect the worms or harm aquarium inhabitants but they do make it advisable to keep the cultures out of the house in a shed or garage.

If these other inhabitants become too troublesome the culture is best renewed with fresh peat, or carefully cleared with a vacuum cleaner. Drosophila, a genus of small wingless fruit-fly developed by scientists for experimental use, is a very good food for fish and can be cultured in glass bottles containing a warm fermenting fruit mash.

Initial supplies may be obtained from a biological or school supplier, and will contain complete culturing instructions, but the general use of Drosophila as food is not recommended due to the trouble and inconvenience involved and the poor yield resulting by comparison with, say, a good whiteworm culture.

Some problem fish which eat only insects might benefit from the use of Drosophila but generally its culture is hardly worth while.

TABLE FOODS

Almost anything which we eat ourselves can be fed with advantage to fish, providing it can be supplied in a suitable form and does not lead to pollution in the aquarium.

It is obviously not possible to throw the leftovers into the fish tank instead of into the dog's dish but with care use can be made of a good selection of normal domestic foods. First and foremost come cooked peas. Fish invariably do not get enough green food and peas are the simplest means of rectifying this.

After cooking, the transparent shell should be removed and the whole pea dropped into the water in one lump to avoid clouding. All sorts of meat and fish products are very welcome provided they are not too tough or greasy and do not disperse easily in the water. Foods which remain in lumps are best as the fish will break them up as they need them and if the food remains uneaten the lump form retards deterioration.

Large unwanted pieces can also be removed more easily. Examples include boiled liver, bacon, roe, fish, lettuce, spinach and occasionally cheese. New foods may not be taken eagerly on introduction so it is wise to feed very carefully until the fish become used to them. It may pay to introduce a little with a more familiar food at first.

Commercial pet foods which are not too soft or greasy, such as cat biscuits and the drier dog meats, go a lot further for the same cost than commercial fish foods. Large fish such as Oscars are often kept in relatively small containers.

A 10in fish in a 3ft aquarium is rather like a goldfish in a glass bowl and must be fed extremely carefully if pollution is to be avoided. Most fish of this kind have teeth in their throats and when, for instance, they eat lumps of meat many fine particles are expelled through their gills and into the water, with obvious disadvantages.

Experiments have shown that the way to overcome this difficulty is to use a food which the fish cannot chew easily and therefore swallow whole. Uncooked lean bacon performs this function nicely and keeps the environment clean even though the fish is receiving large quantities of food daily.

The absence of mastication does not seem to have any ill effect as long as sensibly sized pieces are provided.

DRY FOODS

Commercially packed dry fish foods are on the whole wellprepared and quite suitable for use if several points are understood. Their most damaging quality is the ease with which they can pollute the environment when used incorrectly.

Due to the methods of preparation most are sensitive to water and quickly rot away if left uneaten in the aquarium. As mentioned repeatedly in this book, large quantities of uneaten food will ruin any environment and much care must therefore be taken.

It is recommended that fish living mainly on dry foods be fed four or five times daily so that only a little food need be given at any one time. Even then, in inexperienced hands this will often be too much, particularly in partially-populated aquaria.

Dry foods are extremely expensive compared to other commodities.

Even in the small quantities sold to aquarists the cost can be prohibitive if a large number of fish are kept.

It is doubtful whether any commercial fisheries or public aquaria use fishfood as the aquarist buys it, even though it can be bought in bulk more cheaply. The aquarist's best approach is to regard all commercial dry foods as stop-gaps for emergency use and perhaps as a provider of roughage to assist the fish's digestive processes if other foods which perform this function, such as Daphnia, are not available.

Certainly any good aquarist should never need to use dry foods as the basis of the fish's diet. Many prepared foods are sold as being especially for coldwater, or tropical, or marine, fish. While there may be some slight benefit to be gained by a particular type of fish from one particular formula, most formulae will be eaten by any fish which takes dry food.

The thrifty aquarist can economise for instance by using goldfish foods for other fish, as these are usually cheaper, although it must be said that the commonly sold biscuit meal is not even recommended for goldfish.

Many fish of course will simply not take prepared food in any form at all and these must be fed in other ways even at some inconvenience to the aquarist. Some of them can be trained to take fresh meat but many will eat only live creatures.

It must never be imagined that when a fish eats dry foods because nothing else is ever offered to it that this food is adequate for its needs. Many people who keep community aquaria provide only one brand of dry food and feed only this to every fish in their care, regardless of species or size or any other factor. This attitude is only to be deplored and shows either ignorance or a complete lack of consideration for the requirements of the fish.

7

BREEDING

Sooner or later most aquarists become involved in one way or another in breeding fish. The first baby livebearer born usually sets up a reaction which invariably stimulates interest and participation in the subject. Methods for breeding various species of fish have a number of factors in common, and this chapter will principally be concerned with these important generalities.

It is not within the scope of this book to give details of the particular requirements of individual species, but the aquarist requiring specialised information on certain fish will find that the relevant publications are widely available.

Each case should be treated systematically as a separate exercise until full knowledge and reliable methods are evolved for that species. Communication between serious aquarists is usually good and our system of societies and associations makes for the free exchange of much hard-won information.

The beginner should never be afraid to ask, or reluctant to discuss personal experiences, because there is so much to learn that the pooling of data and ideas is essential. Before discussing the techniques involved, the ethics of the situation must be considered.

Fish must never be treated as mere playthings and if a species is to be encouraged to reproduce it must be provided with the best possible chances of success, Breeding does not end with the production of live fry but rather with a properly-reared group of young adults. It is quite easy to obtain numerous fry from very many species with only a minimum of trouble.

The secret is to rear them to be true representatives of their species. The aquarist must realise that buying or breeding a fish means taking on an obligation to ensure that the creature has the best habitat that can be provided. There is no point in breeding fish to be eaten by others or to be permanently stunted by overcrowding and bad feeding. The common practice of culling healthy fry to provide space for a selected few is ethically wrong and unless the aquarist can hope to raise and care for the whole number of fry produced at a spawning the exercise should not be initiated.

In community environments, or where the aquarist has only one aquarium, it is very difficult to take note of ethical factors. Livebearers will reproduce frequently and egglayers may spawn quite often. These fry and eggs will be eaten by the other inhabitants almost immediately and there is little the aquarist can do about it, except to keep only fish of a single sex in any particular species.

This is hardly ever practised and indeed a lot of interest and enjoyment would be lost if it were, because the whole idea of studying the fish's habits and way of life argues for the presence of both sexes. It would seem then that we must accept the losses involved in this situation as inevitable.

The loss of the spawn of egglayers is not perhaps so important but to see young livebearers gobbled up can be distressing and could be avoided if only one sex of these were kept in mixed aquaria. To avoid the loss of fry in this way many aquarists attempt to retain them by the use of small containers, so-called 'breeding traps', or by dividing off a small portion of the aquarium.

This practice is suitable only for a very small number of certain hardy species and must be recognised as such. It is no good putting, say, thirty baby guppies in a container which holds only two pints of water and then expecting them to grow and live normally. It is better not to breed them at all than to subject them to this treatment.

It can be argued of course that in nature young fry provide an item in the diet of many adult fish and other creatures and are in fact produced so prolifically because of this; but the aquarist must not fall into the trap of excusing callous actions with this argument because once safe, reasonable living conditions have been provided for the adults, it is hypocritical to ignore the obligations to the fry and to consider them expendable.

Nature is cruel, but there are no similar requirements for the aquarist. Let us assume that the serious aquarist wishes to breed a few fish to gain further knowledge and enjoyment of the hobby and is willing to provide the extra facilities needed and to carry out the work involved so that the resulting fish are a worthwhile acquisition. How should the exercise be approached?

Fish can be categorised into those which produce live young (livebearers) and those which produce spawn (egglayers). Furthermore, the overall breeding process can conveniently be divided into three stages, ie preparation, the breeding act, and rearing the fry.

The subject of preparation and rearing are fairly similar for both livebearers and egglayers so can be treated in common; but for the breeding act itself a distinction can be made between the two types of fish and indeed the egglayers can be sub-divided even further as will be seen.

The question of the use of suitable breeding stock is a thorny one. Most aquarists who are breeding for the first time will tend to use whatever parents are at hand, without going to a lot of trouble to find the best available specimens; this may prove satisfactory or it may not.

There are two basic types of fish bred by aquarists, those which are either wild or retain all the characteristics of the wild species although bred in captivity, and those which are a cultivated variety of a wild species and differ considerably from the natural fish. These two types require different methods of breeding and selection of breeding stock.

Those fish which have been bred in captivity for many generations and yet still closely resemble the wild type are in fact a pure strain developed and fixed by nature. On the other hand, cultivated fish such as the fancy goldfish, Guppies and Siamese Fighters have all resulted from attempts by man to alter nature's pure strains.

Once obtained, the new strain is maintained through generations of selective breeding in an effort to accentuate any new characteristics still further and, having reached the desired level of accentuation, to fix it in the new strain.

Such accentuations may be considered beautiful or otherwise, but as far as nature is concerned these 'altered' fish are undesirable freaks which can only weaken the naturally fixed pure strain. Therefore there is always the certainty present that if the cultivated fish are allowed to breed indiscriminately they will eventually revert back to the pattern of the natural strain.

It is thus essential to practise careful selective breeding in order to keep the strain in its altered state. With natural fish, however, indiscriminate breeding can be practised since there can be no reversion to a wild form. Indiscriminate breeding is in fact essential to maintain the strain at its best.

While a natural strain may appear to be improved a little in captivity in such characteristics as size and intensity of colour, these are not necessarily alterations to the strain itself but may only be improvements to the individual fish caused by better living conditions and the removal of many of the hazards which occur in nature.

It follows therefore that the selection of breeding stock for a natural strain is considerably easier than for a cultivated strain because we are not trying to alter nature's pattern. From time to time freak fish will be produced from a natural strain, for instance Tiger Barbs which have part of one of the black bars missing.

These fish must not be used as breeding stock since the fault will probably be reproduced in their offspring, either immediately or in a later generation. From this then it can be seen that to keep a natural strain at its best, close inbreeding must be avoided at all costs.

To breed a natural species, the aquarist must start off by obtaining male and female breeding stocks which are not closely related. Enough fish should be obtained to make up as many breeding pairs as can be managed thus allowing the adults to pair up indiscriminately and ensuring that the fry in one batch are not closely related to other batches.

If it is difficult to obtain unrelated breeding stock, as may be the case with some of the rarer species, the aquarist may be forced to start off with close inbreeding. Provided the initial pair are true representatives of the natural strain a little close inbreeding can be tolerated if circumstances make this unavoidable but, unless the strain is to deteriorate, fresh unrelated blood must be brought in as soon as possible.

As well as amplifying freak characteristics, close inbreeding will introduce defects such as lack of vitality and delicate health if carried on indefinitely. This is why cultivated fish are often much harder to keep than their wild counterparts.

Indiscriminate breeding of a natural strain is made easier in many cases by the fact that many species spawn as a shoal. This is termed 'flock breeding'. The danios and most of the barbs are good examples of such species. Several pairs can be placed together and will freely interbreed. Wherever possible, flock breeding should be encouraged as this is nature's own way of avoiding close inbreeding.

The propagation of a cultivated fish strain is far more challenging to the serious breeder and demands a lot more effort and experience. As explained above, nature considers these fish to be abnormal and any mistakes by the breeder in the selection of breeding stock will result in the strains starting to revert to the wild form.

If breeding stock is used which has partly reverted then the rate of reversion will be accelerated. Furthermore, while the breeder is trying to produce in a strain those altered characteristics which are considered desirable, other traits will probably be encountered which may be undesirable and even detrimental.

Even more intensive selective breeding may then be necessary to eliminate these undesired alterations without in the process losing the original requirements. Let us suppose that an aquarist has a good natural strain of fish and in one of the batches of young there appears a freak fish which is different in some characteristic.

Let us further suppose that this new feature is so attractive that the aquarist decides to attempt to establish a cultivated strain of fish which will eventually breed true in this altered form. The first step will be to give the freak fish the best food available and to attend to its environmental conditions with the utmost care so as to bring it to maturity in as good a condition as possible.

This fish is then backcrossed either to its father or mother, depending on its sex, or, if this is not possible for some reason, to its brother or sister. Unless the brother or sister exhibits the same freak characteristic, however, this method is not so reliable. All the young from the first backcrossing are then kept and reared to maturity in the best possible conditions.

It may be found that the important characteristic does not appear in the first generation at all. This does not mean that it is lost but that it is only 'covered up' by more dominant characteristics which still exist in the strain.

The way to uncover the freak characteristic is to mate the original fish with all the fish of the opposite sex in the first generation, when the characteristic should appear in a reasonable proportion in the second generation.

If the second generation fish which show the alteration are now backcrossed to the original fish, which is actually their grandparent, the characteristic will become fairly well established in the strain.

When initial breeding stock has been obtained in this way the breeder can then proceed to concentrate on developing the freak condition into a fixed, altered characteristic and also, of course, concentrate on removing any undesirable side effects such as small size or poor health.

Development of the new strain to a pure state may take many generations of careful and exacting work, but finally the aquarist may reach a point where all of the fish bred show the altered characteristic. At this point the strain can be tested for purity by flock breeding and if this proves successful the strain can be considered pure.

There are many complications to overcome in some particular cases but others may be exceptionally easy. It all depends on the nature of the required alteration. Some characteristics may be sex-linked, ie the hereditary factor may be carried only by the male or female fish but never both, or the characteristic may become so entangled with some other undesirable factor, perhaps a result of the particular inbreeding methods used, that it may become impossible or extremely difficult to continue the strain at all.

All these problems are a challenge to the aquarist and this is of course what makes the cultivation of a new strain so interesting.

BREEDING TECHNIQUES

Many of our common fish will breed quite easily without any help at all if their age and the environmental conditions are correct. This is indeed the reason why some species are so common and obviously the ease with which a species can be reproduced is a major factor in determining its price and availability in commercial aquatic establishments.

The serious breeder should, however, take a certain amount of trouble, even with the easiest species, otherwise stunted and unhealthy fish may be produced or the young (or eggs) may be eaten at birth.

Fish which breed in a community aquarium will hardly ever be successful because the young or spawn will be eaten. Some young livebearers may survive if they can shelter quickly after birth.

Also, egglayer fry which are protected by their parents may survive if the demands on the parents are not too great during the protection period and if they are large enough at the end of this period to survive on their own; but these possibilities cannot be depended on.

It is far better for the aquarist to provide proper breeding facilities and to carry out the exercise thoroughly. During the earlier discussion of environmental conditions in other chapter of this book, use was made of the springtime-summertime analogy and it was shown that definite conditions may be required by the fish to induce them to reproduce in captivity. The selected breeding stock must therefore be kept in environments where these conditions exist. For instance, most shoaling egglayers will come into readiness if the water temperature is increased to 80°F (27°C) and richer foods are given.

These are not necessarily the conditions in which the species will actually breed but rather those which bring the prospective parents into good breeding condition.

Some fish, such as the livebearers and the protective egglayers, can be conditioned and bred in the same environment and there is little point in any other method, but the majority of the common egglayers, which do not protect their eggs, will need more careful handling both to protect the eggs from the parents' appetites and from fungal growths.

It will also be necessary to ensure that the female has enough eggs ready to produce a good batch of young.

Livebearers

These very common and popular fish are among the easiest to breed because they bear their young alive and fully formed. Most aquarists start breeding with livebearers, and for young aquarists especially the lessons learned and the experience gained are invaluable.

Almost all our common livebearers (guppies, platies, mollies and swordtails) are so easy to breed that fry are produced regularly without any special involvement on the part of the aquarist.

Unfortunately, as a result of careless breeding by inexperienced aquarists, this proclivity has led to a weakening of some strains of these species over the years. At present there seems to be a shortage of really good livebearers and those generally available are often smaller, less hardy or not as representative of their species as they ought to be.

The situation today is such that it is very difficult for an aquarist to acquire top-class unspoilt breeding stock in any particular strain. On the other hand, because of the ease of reproduction of these fish and the numbers of generations which can be produced in a remarkably short time, all of the common livebearers found in aquaria are now definite cultivated strains.

This situation has been brought about by deliberate action by skilled breeders who have given us the wonderful colours and fin extensions now available in many of these fish. Livebearers intended as parents are best kept away from egglaying fish and other livebearers of greatly differing size, otherwise bullying and fin-biting may occur.

They are generally more vegetarian than most egglayers, so planted aquaria with soft algal growths are ideal. The young are born in cycles of about four weeks and the females are usually permanently pregnant from a very early age until old age. Even if the males are removed the females have an unusual ability to store sperm so that several subsequent broods can be produced from one mating.

The males seem to be continuously sexually active when in good health so it is better to have at least twice as many females present as males (except where very strict selective breeding is practised, of course) so as to give individual females some chance of avoiding the constant attentions of the males.

Certainly one female should never be kept with a group of males as this must impose a considerable strain. It must also be remembered that it is possible for some livebearing species to interbreed, for instance platies x swordtails, so they should be kept separate.

Furthermore, the water in environments containing male fish often contain live sperm which might easily be transferred to other environments, so some care is required with general cleanliness when working with a number of aquaria.

As a breeding example, let us discuss a trio of platies—two females and one male—whose offspring are required to be representative of the parents and the type generally but are not part of any complicated selective breeding system.

The first requirement is that the adults should not be closely related as we are making the assumption that the strain is a fixed, although probably unnatural one, and there is thus no advantage in inbreeding. If the females are young and virgin then a period of growth separate from the male may be beneficial, but usually they will be pregnant when obtained and also holding stored sperm so a period for 'emptying out' may be advisable.

Once a trio of mature adults with 'clean' females has been obtained they can then be put together in a suitable environment. Fry will be produced regularly and will not usually all be eaten at birth if the adults are properly fed. The newborn fry do not have complete control of their movement for a short period after birth and this is when they are most easily caught and eaten by adults.

If they survive this period they then need cover of some kind and usually spend their first few days among surface vegetation, so the environment should be shallow and contain floating plants or other surface cover.

The young are born without any appreciable yolk-sac and feed almost immediately. Most livebearers can accept baby Brine Shrimp at once but will still benefit from Infusoria if given.

Whatever the food used there must be plenty available so that the fish can feed at any time and in fact continuously if they wish. The first days are very important and any potential growth lost here is difficult to recover later.

Most female livebearers have anything between 20 and 200 young at a time, depending on their age and size, but an average of about 40 is reasonable. They can be left in the environment where they were born for about two weeks, with or without parents, but eventually must be moved to more spacious quarters for successful development.

Some aquarists move the young to other quarters as soon as they are born and there is some argument as to which method is best, but certainly they must be moved some time during their early development, otherwise they will become stunted through lack of space in the original container, unless this is unusually large.

The cause of this concern over the moving of the fry is that the operation may temporarily put them off their food and thus slow their rate of growth. If we also consider that newborn fry are probably more susceptible to damage by netting and handling, it might be thought better to leave the resettlement until as late as possible.

There is also the fact that heavy feeding with fine foods during the first couple of weeks after birth might foul the original environment and this can be cleaned out for use again if the fish are moved after this period.

The larger, rearing container must of course reproduce the environment conditions which existed in the previous one, so that the move imposes as little shock to the fry as possible. Again heavy feeding will be needed so some thought must be given to the type of environment used.

If some green food, such as garden peas, can be included in the diet as a substitute for natural plant and algal growth, a biological system can be utilised with consequent advantages from its large nitrifying potential. It is usual for experienced aquarists to rear about 100 fry to the young adult stage in a 20-gallon (90-litre) aquarium, but individual skill and technique may increase this figure surprisingly.

If the parent trio have been left in the original environment they will of course be producing more young even perhaps before the first batch has been moved out. This presents some difficulty for those aquarists operating on a limited scale and in these cases it may be better to use only one female and to remove the male elsewhere after mating.

As mentioned before, it is pointless to breed more fish than can be reared to the adult stage satisfactorily, if only because the overcrowding which results will be to the disadvantage of all the young produced. Female livebearers are notoriously adverse to being moved about from one environment to another while pregnant.

They are similarly harmed by enclosure in small containers such as breeding traps and jars. Female mollies in particular are extremely sensitive and often do not give birth at all if disturbed during pregnancy. They appear to absorb the young internally, or in some cases all may be stillborn.

Shoaling Egglayers

Egglaying fish can be divided for breeding purposes into two types: those which protect and care for their eggs and young, and those which do not. The latter can be labelled for convenience as shoaling egglayers because most fish of this category live, and breed, in shoals in the natural state.

The shoaling egglayers include a great many of the popular aquarium fish such as the barbs, danios and tetras. These species are generally all representative of their wild counterparts and so inbreeding should not be encouraged.

They are also suited to commercial quantity-production methods and hardly any of them have been altered by selective breeding. The behavioural intelligence of these fish is low and their breeding seems to be particularly dependent on instinctive actions triggered by environmental conditions, such as higher temperature and increased light intensity.

Their eggs are simply scattered about during mating and may fall to the bottom or may adhere to plants in the vicinity. That is all the protection they receive and so they are a popular food with other fish and the parents themselves. To compensate for this the eggs are laid in hundreds and often thousands at a time.

This creates a peculiar situation for the aquarist who wishes to breed these fish. Environmental triggers must be provided to induce the parents to spawn, the eggs must be guarded from the parents and other natural enemies including bacteria (intense light is also harmful to the eggs), and the resulting fry must be properly fed and then, when all this has been done, there will possibly be so many young fish that it will be difficult to raise them all satisfactorily.

This kind of fish breeding is easily the most demanding because the aquarist gets no help from the fish themselves and is hindered by their presence once the actual spawning is finished, but it can also be extremely rewarding especially when one of the more difficult species has been bred successfully.

The main difficulty in breeding all egglayers is encountered during the period of two to five days when the eggs are hatching. At this time they are extremely prone to attack by fungus and once this is established the eggs affected are invariably lost and the fungus may spread to the others as well. Protective fish clean

their eggs to prevent fungal attack but in other species the responsibility for protection is the aquarist's, and this task is very important. After the eggs have hatched the fry are still not fish in the true sense as they have an attached yolk-sac which they absorb before becoming free-swimming.

During this time they do not feed and cannot swim about, but are relatively safe if properly looked after. The hatching period is definitely crucial and the aquarist must be prepared to devote all necessary attention to the eggs during this time.

Spawning environments required by various species vary but, in general, the common barbs and tetras spawn in clumps of fine plant or some substitute, while danios spawn over gravel or pebble beds. The barbs and tetras will be discussed together as an example of a typical situation and the danios will be considered later.

The normal mating procedure for a pair of typical plantspawners is that the male fertilises the female's eggs while in very close contact with her and while lying in or pushing through a dense clump of fine plant.

The spawning is preceded by chasing, butting and humping and demonstrations of finspreading and colour intensity changes and other courtship displays. The spawning is usually followed by an avid egg-hunt unless the pair are removed promptly.

The spawning environment for these fish should consist of a small aquarium of about 10 gallons (45 litres) capacity which has previously been thoroughly cleaned internally. Everything used must be scrupulously clean to impede fungal attack of the eggs and nothing should be included which is not essential.

Nylon knitting wool can be tangled into loose clumps as a substitute for plants and should be sterilised by boiling. The outside of the bottom glass of the aquarium can be painted so that gravel is not required (fish are unsettled over a transparent base) and a properly fitting cover glass to exclude dust and other atmospheric influences can be used. Water conditions (usually soft and acid), temperature, light and other factors should be set up for the species concerned and the water allowed to age for a little time.

The breeding pair, which will have been conditioned separately elsewhere, can then be introduced in the evening and will usually spawn the next morning if all conditions are satisfactory. Sometimes a pair will not spawn until later in the day or even the day after and when these delays are met the dange, of fungal attack is increased.

The fish should be made to jurny or be dropped from the net into the water on introduction into the spawning environment so as to transfer as little as possible of the water and other constituents of the conditioning environment.

If carried out sensibly, healthy fish will not be at all affected by this treatment and it is preferable for hygenic reasons to the alternative of dipping a possibly contaminated net in the water.

After spawning the pair must be removed as soon as possible. The net used for this purpose should be spotlessly clean and the operation must be carried out quickly and efficiently without disturbing the eggs more than is necessary.

The aquarium should then be covered completely to exclude all light, and fungus preventative can be added at this stage. This is usually a 5 per cent aqueous solution of methylene blue, administered at two drops to the gallon, but one of the commercial substitutes can be used. There is now nothing for the aquarist to do for the time being unless the eggs show signs of fungus.

Any affected eggs should be removed without creating a major disturbance, if this can be done, but no attempt should be made to touch or move healthy eggs as any bruising will encourage the growth of fungus.

The crucial hatching period can, within limits, be shortened by increasing the temperature, so there is some advantage in keeping this as high as the eggs will tolerate.

Danios and other similar fish pose the same problems in somewhat different ways. These fish spawn while travelling together at some speed over a gravel bed. The eggs are not adhesive and simply fall to the bottom. The main problem encountered is that the fish often do not wait to finish spawning before eating their eggs.

They will usually eat any eggs with which they come into contact while swimming about and due to their speed and mobility they often meet the eggs before they have reached the bottom. This means that some trouble must be taken to save the eggs if a reasonable yield is to be obtained.

The popular method is to provide a long shallow container so that the fish are encouraged to swim up and down in more or less straight lines in the hope that by the time they are on their way back the eggs previously released will have reached the comparative safety of the gravel bed.

Another method is to substitute a double layer of smooth round pebbles or glass marbles for the gravel so that the eggs fall between them to safety. The same recommendations for the cleanliness of the spawning environments apply here.

Selection and conditioning of breeding stock is usually carried out in groups and the fish are best spawned together in ratios of three or four males to two females.

The reason for this is that the eggs are released by the female in full flight and the presence of a large number of males helps to ensure that all the eggs are fertilised satisfactorily. There is not a great deal of prespawning activity and not so much body contact as with the barbs and tetras, although there is often some butting and bumping.

If the pebble method described above is utilised there is no great urgency to remove the adult fish immediately after spawning ends as the eggs should by then be quite safe. This can be an advantage as fish of this type will often spawn again after a short rest period, particularly if the females are in really good condition.

One point which requires special attention is that the fry of most shoaling egglayers kept in aquaria are so small that they initially require extremely fine foods. Some aquarists make do with the yolk from hard-boiled eggs or similar fine dry foods but for best results Infusoria must be used.

Protective Egglayers

Cichlids and gouramies are examples of protective egglayers of which one or both of the parents always cares for the eggs through the difficult hatching period and then brings up the fry to the stage where they are reasonably capable of fending for themselves.

By and large this behaviour of the parents is advantageous to the aquarist, although it does not make the process by any means easy. Most of these fish are more 'intelligent' and more individualistic than the shoaling types and often show themselves to be quite discriminating with respect to their choice of spawning partner and their required environmental conditions.

They will not often tolerate interference from the aquarist in the breeding process or from any other inhabitants of the environment. One point which is sometimes not understood is that these fish are protective of their eggs or young only up to certain limits. It must never be thought that because they have produced viable spawn, success is ensured.

If the environmental conditions are not right for the growth of the young, or if they are in great danger, they will be promptly eaten by their parents. Both of these factors are under the direct control of the aquarist who must therefore make every effort to help the parents in these matters, particularly by not allowing them to be frightened by unfamiliar human activities.

In addition, when the fry have reached a certain size, a time comes when in the wild state they would naturally leave the parents to live their own lives. At this point the parental urge disappears and the parents see the young as just small fish, in other words as potential food.

The aquarist must therefore split the family before this happens. Similarly, where only one parent guards the fry, the other fish, which in the wild would go away, must be removed after spawning as it will now be considered a potential danger to the fry by the guarding parent and may be killed or at least bullied.

Given the above limitations, most of these fish make excellent parents and some of the aquarist's happiest times will be spent watching them carry out their parental duties.

The means used by the fish to overcome the tendency of the eggs to be attacked by fungus are varied in the extreme and some methods, such as bubble-nesting and mouth-breeding, are so fantastic as to be unbelievable to the novice, but whichever method is employed the results are the same and the recommendations for success are more or less similar.

Many of these fish grow to a relatively large size by maturity and some are among the largest fish kept in aquaria, so their spawning environment may have to be somewhat larger than those used for other groups. Furthermore, because the young may stay with the parents for as long as six weeks before the urge to disperse appears, the environment may need to be set up in a more permanent fashion.

Some essential differences in method must be made between those types which have complete parental care and those which involve only one parent.

Most of the fish are natural strains and should be treated as such with regard to the selection of breeding stock, but there are some important exceptions, which are classic examples of cultivated strains, such as the Siamese Fighting Fish and the fancy angelfish.

The gouramies and other anabantids practise single-parent protection and also construct a bubble-nest just beneath the surface of the water. Since the male is usually the active partner, there is some considerable danger to the female in the confines of the aquarium and the aquarist must be very careful of the way in which the inactive parent is employed.

A male in full breeding condition will often tolerate the female's presence only during the actual courtship and spawning and may kill or harm her afterwards. Furthermore, if she is not in breeding condition or is not receptive to that particular male then she must be removed to prevent injury from his repeatedly frustrated attempts to breed.

In the wild, of course, the female would either go away or be driven away from the vicinity of the male, but she cannot do this in a small aquarium. The bubble-nest is usually built by the male, who requires a clean water surface free of draughts and dust.

The preliminary courtship is often involved and long-winded but extremely interesting. Spawning takes place beneath the nest and the female is usually driven away afterwards. She can be carefully removed at this point but this must be done without breaking up or disturbing the bubble-nest.

If left alone and not threatened the male will generally hatch the eggs and care for the young satisfactorily. He will become aggressive towards any interference by the aquarist and may not feed much during this period.

The spawning environment need only be normally clean and not virtually sterile as for shoaling egglayers as the guarding fish will continually clean the eggs to keep fungus at bay. The one point of some importance is the condition of the water surface.

This must be clean and the young fish must not be exposed to draughty conditions when using their labyrinth organs to take in atmospheric air. Some anabantid fry are extremely small and so must have Infusoria for their first food, while a few species are large enough to use brine shrimps immediately.

The cichlid family are the most apparently intelligent of all aquarium fish and usually exercise devoted parental care. Often both sexes take an equal part in raising the fry and frequently the two fish will mate for life and show no interest in other fish of the opposite sex. Many members of this group, for instance angelfish, do not show sexual characteristics until they reach maturity.

They are therefore best raised together in a group of at least six so that breeding couples can pair off naturally. An established pair can then be separated from the rest and installed in a permanent environment in which they can breed and raise their young without disturbance.

There are many patterns of spawning behaviour, all of which involve different ways of protecting the eggs and young against fungus and other enemies. Some cichlids use caves, or flower pots if provided, some dig pits in the gravel bed, some spawn on plant leaves or the sides of the aquarium and, of course, the mouth-breeders have their own characteristic methods.

The cichlids are generally very easy to breed if their needs are understood. The parent fish must be truly adult and well fed at all times with meaty foods, preferably earthworms, as most of them are naturally carnivorous.

They will not tolerate other inhabitants in the spawning environment and many will not even tolerate plants. Environmental conditions must be adjusted to their liking and if seriously frightened they will eat the eggs or fry.

The parents usually take turns to care for and clean their offspring and during this time the other parent will often take up a guarding posture at a fixed distance, presumably as a front-line defence against natural enemies.

The most interesting part of the exercise for the aquarist comes after the fry are free-swimming. Up to this time the parents' jobs are fairly straightforward and in the artificial environment are mainly concerned with cleanliness; but once the fry start to swim properly they have a tendency to wander and a lot of time is then spent in catching strays and generally keeping the fry in a tight shoal.

Relationships between the parents during this time are almost always good and there is a fair division of labour and responsibility. Finally of course, the dispersion point is reached and then the young must be removed if they are not to be eaten, although with some cichlids this may not occur if the parents are kept well fed.

The young should still be removed, however, if overcrowding is likely, and in any event, should the parents spawn again, the original fry would be a serious nuisance. Spawnings generally produce about 400 fry and the young are quite large at hatching and grow quickly if properly fed. They need meaty foods such as boiled, crumbled liver and also thrive on small Daphnia, newly-hatched Brine Shrimp and chopped Whiteworm.

Other Egglayers

There are, of course, many egglaying fish kept in aquaria other than those groups mentioned above. Some of these breed in a somewhat similar fashion, while others breed in widely different ways. A great many common fish have never been bred at all in aquaria and others which have produced young have not yet been observed during the actual spawning.

All this makes for interest for the aquarist and leaves much experimental work to be done by the more seriously minded person.

The rules behind all fishbreeding are basically the same, however, and can be summarised as follows:

1. The chosen parents should be properly adult and in good breeding condition. They should not be related unless deliberate inbreeding is intended.
2. The conditioning process and the spawning environment must favour the species concerned in every possible way.
3. The hatching period of the eggs must be attended by the utmost care and attention to prevent fungal attack, except where the parents exercise complete protection.
4. Parents which eat eggs or young must be removed as soon as possible, or protective cover must be established.
5. Newborn fry must be provided with small-sized foods frequently enough and in sufficient quantities to achieve their full growth-rate potential.
6. Growing fry must have space enough to prevent overcrowding, and other environmental conditions such as temperature must be correct.
7. Separation of the young from the parents must be carried out before the fish's instinctive dispersal time occurs.

QUANTITY PRODUCTION

Many aquarists will eventually develop an interest in producing fish on an efficient commercial or semi-commercial basis. This is quite a feasible ambition, although the profitability of the enterprise will depend on the abilities of the individual.

The breeding and raising techniques involved will be as described above but attention must also be focused on the quantity and regularity of production of sizeable batches of young fish.

To take a hypothetical situation as an example, suppose an aquarist wishes to have available for sale every week 100 fish of reasonable size of one of the easily-spawned species of shoaling egglayers. The first consideration is the volume of water required to cater for such a quantity.

The three stages involved in the breeding programme are conditioning, spawning and development, and there must be available aquaria in which to carry out all of these. During conditioning, small to mediumsized adult fish can be accommodated in two aquaria, one for males and the other for females.

Two 15-gal (68-litre) aquaria will be suitable. The number of adults required to ensure weekly spawnings, and to allow a spare well-conditioned pair, is about four pairs, but six is better and gives the fish more of a rest between spawnings and plenty of chance to get into good condition again.

The spawning aquarium should have a capacity from 5—10 gallons (22-45 litres) depending on the species, but should not be larger than necessary if problems of hygiene are to be avoided. The young fry will usually live in these environments for at least the first two weeks after spawning, so a minimum number of three spawning aquaria will be required for weekly rotation.

The rearing aquaria can have a capacity of 20 gallons (90 litres) or more so that at least 100 fry can be accommodated in each. Assuming that a good aquarist can rear the fry to a reasonable 'selling size' in, say, ten weeks, then eight of these rearing aquaria at least would be required after allowing for the first two weeks in the spawning aquaria.

This brings the minimum total to three small, two medium and eight large aquaria, if each spawning produces about 100 fry. If more are produced then further rearing aquaria can be utilised, and if less are produced then further spawning environments can be set up and additional breeding pairs used so that the system can be run at full capacity.

Such a system will use not less than 200 gallons (900 litres) of water and on average at any one time there will be about 1,000 fish to look after. Electrical power consumption to provide normal tropical temperatures will be around 1kW if all the thermostats switch on at the same time, and a fair amount of pumped air will be needed to supply all the various appliances. It can therefore be seen that fish production in even reasonable quantities is not an easy matter and requires quite complex set-ups.

One hundred fish produced per week may seem a lot at first, but this will not produce any appreciable income, after expenses, unless the species concerned is some valuable variety. A target of 500 or more fish per week would seem reasonable to provide a worthwhile income and it can be seen just what would be involved in attaining this figure.

In spite of all this complexity, however, many aquarists do breed fish in saleable quantities, if only to pay for the upkeep of other non-productive fish, and these home-bred fish are usually healthier, larger and better coloured than their imported counterparts and can be purchased with confidence.

Breeders disposing of home-produced fish in large quantities will usually be doing so through a commercial wholesaler or retailer and must realise that they can expect to be paid at most 50 per cent of whatever price the fish will finally fetch.

Their economics must be based on this figure and not on the shopkeeper's selling price. The daily food requirements of several hundred young fish are quite substantial and this is the point on which many would be quantity producers fail. The fry must be fed properly and often, which can be costly and time-consuming.

Two or three feeds a day are not really enough, so the amateur aquarist who is away at work will probably depend on other members of the family for help. If he buys commercial fish foods at today's retail prices it is unlikely that he will ever cover his costs.

Luckily many of the better foods such as Infusoria and Whiteworm can readily be cultured after some practice, and Brine Shrimp eggs for hatching can be bought in bulk at reasonable prices.

Daphnia can be collected in most localities and earthworms obtained from the garden. Commercial dry flake and powder foods can be ignored and dry cat and dog foods used in their place.

Inevitably, the difficulties of consistently obtaining large quantities of any of the above foods will ensure that a varied diet is provided, and this is good for the fish. Cooked peas, liver and fish roe and other table foods should also be used.

From time to time all aquarists will encounter epidemics of white spot, velvet or other contagious diseases. The aquarist with hundreds of fish must be on guard at all times to avoid disease and the resulting complications in breeding schedules, which may be very severe.

Each aquarium should have its own thermometer. The common practice of having only one or two thermometers and moving these about as needed does not encourage frequent temperature checks.

Similarly, it is better if each aquarium has its own thermostat. Nets, scrapers and other accessories should be cleaned between immersions in different aquaria and there is a good argument for each aquarium having its own tool-kit. When a disease does strike every possible precaution must be taken immediately and priority must be given to eliminating the trouble.

Most common diseases can be cured nowadays with the appropriate proprietary products if the treatment is started soon enough, so a stock of these medicines should be kept. Sick or convalescing fish should not be sold until they are completely recovered and have gone through a proving period of at least a month.

Some spare aquarium capacity is advisable for this purpose. Inevitably, those who keep numerous fish are likely to have to kill very sick, injured or badly deformed specimens from time to time and a method should be developed to do this as humanely as possible.

Mistakes during inbreeding may produce deformities such as the hump-backed guppies often seen and while these should not be produced if breeding stock is properly selected, nothing is perfect. The kindest way to kill small fish is probably to feed them quickly to some larger hungry fish which will immediately swallow them whole.

Sick fish which cannot be disposed of in this way should be dropped into boiling water. They should not be allowed to swim about in a frightened state with a fish which may or may not eat them, and nor should they be fed to a fish which will bite or tear them before death occurs.

The practice of flushing unwanted fish down the toilet is cruel as they may not die for a long while. Strains of breeding stock which produce unhealthy or deformed fish should not be used again and no species should be bred unless the correct environment and foods are available; poor conditions will encourage the accumulation of imperfect fish.

It will be found that in the rearing environments used in any quantity breeding system some compromise must be reached between ease of maintenance and convenience of feeding. Theoretically the biological system should be the answer, there being no decorative requirements and no need for plant growth, but it may be found that even a good biological system may not cope with pollutants if the fish are fed only infrequently and hence with rather large quantities at one time, or if the environment is on the point of being overcrowded.

In these cases it will probably be necessary to organise a programme of water-changing to ensure regular dilution of toxic substances and urine. Some foods such as whiteworm may be lost in gravel beds when fed in quantity so some thought must also be given to this problem.

A further point is that when young fish find themselves crowded together in a small volume of water they exude biological substances (pheromones) into the water which inhibit the development of the weaker members of the shoal, presumably for reasons of natural selection.

It is assumed that only water-changing can combat the effects of this situation, although the use of adsorbent filter materials might prove effective.

A useful idea for making it easier to keep environments clean is shown in Figure elsewhere in this chapter. The aquarium is provided with a bare area on which all sinking food is placed, thus making it very easy to remove uneaten remains.

Meanwhile the gravel bed section of the base will be functioning as a normal biological system and when mature will still have sufficient nitrifying potential to justify its inclusion. This method works well in practice and it is found that a change of about one bucket of water weekly in a 20-gallon (90-litre) aquarium gives good results.

An airstone can be added at the bare end and the ascending column of bubbles will produce the protein skimmer cleansing action described anywhere else in this book.

It will be found that the fish find the food quickly on the bare base area and that foods such as whiteworm which live for some little time after submergence can be fed in largish quantities without worry.

When protective egglayers are bred for quantity it is a common practice to remove the eggs from the parents as soon as possible. This does not seem to worry the parents overmuch and they will often spawn again after a few days if they are in condition.

If possible, removal of the eggs should be done without exposing them to the air and they should not be handled directly but should be removed on the leaf or stone on which they were laid, or siphoned off through a wide pipe if loose in a pit.

Anabantid eggs can be sucked into a wide-necked jar complete with bubble-nest. Eggs laid on the container walls or on very large rocks cannot be moved successfully and so must be left to the parents.

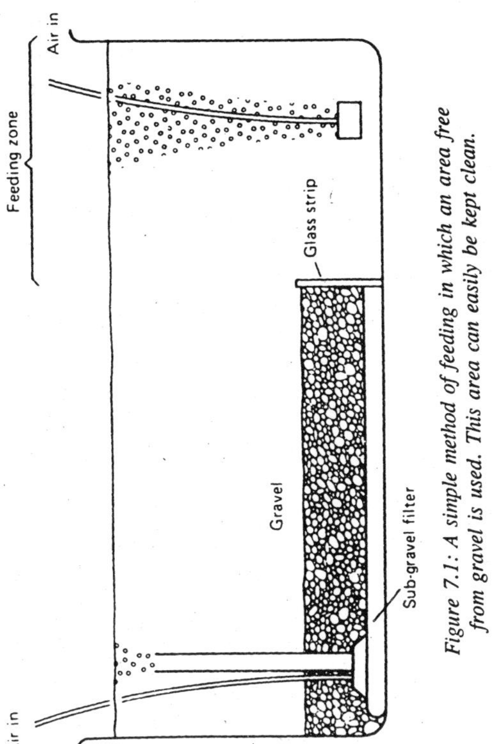

Figure 7.1: A simple method of feeding in which an area free from gravel is used. This area can easily be kept clean.

The eggs should be placed in a small, dark, sterile environment with medication against fungus and aeration to stimulate water movement around them. They are then treated in the same way as the eggs of the shoaling egglayers.

Exceptions to this are the Discus fish, whose young must feed initially on the mucus from the bodies of their parents and do not often survive without it, and the mouth-breeders, whose eggs will most likely be unobtainable.

By removing the eggs in this way it is possible to produce numerous frequent spawnings from one good pair of adults, although it would seem that this must eventually impose some unnatural strain on their bodies. A pair of Angelfish, for instance, have been known to spawn every week for eighteen months.

Some fish, such as the white cloud mountain minnows and corydoras catfish, take no notice of their eggs after spawning if properly fed and can be quite safely left with them. This fact lends itself to a very simple method. A large natural system, suited to the specific needs of the fish, is set up, the breeding stock is installed, and from time to time batches of young can be removed.

Snails, which are avid egg-eaters, must be completely excluded along with any other harmful creatures, and the approximate population of the environment must be known at all times so that the correct amount and variety of foods can be given, but otherwise the system is very easy to administer.

Fish which are easily bred in this way can be used to fill in gaps in other rearing schedules or can simply be held back in their own aquarium when others are plentiful.

8

Culture of the Common Carp

Of all the species of fish utilized by man the common carp (*Cyprinus carpio*) has the longest history of culture. As early as 475 B.c. spawning of captive carp in China was described and advocated as a profitable business by Fan Li in the first known treatise on aquaculture. Some authors believe the practice dates back as far as 2000 B.C. Aristotle mentions carp and it is likely that both the Greeks and Romans fattened carp in ponds.

Further introductions in Europe may have taken place around 1150. The history of carp culture in Austria goes back to 1227, and by 1860 the species was raised in most, if not all, the countries of Europe. Carp were first introduced into North America in the mid-nineteenth century and subsequently became widespread in streams and lakes there, although carp culture remained unimportant.

The countries of southeast Asia have many similar native cyprinids which are used in aquaculture, but common carp were introduced to every southeast Asian country between 1914 and 1957 and are now cultured throughout the region.

They were also introduced to Australia at an unknown date. In recent times carp have been widely introduced in Africa and Latin America for aquacultural purposes, but to date they do not play an important role in fish culture in Africa and among the Latin American countries only Guatemala and Haiti support significant carp-raising enterprises.

SUITABILITY OF COMMON CARP FOR CULTURE

The culture of carp has been a remarkably successful and widespread method of producing protein for human consumption. In 1965, carp were estimated to have contributed 210,000 tons to the world fish supply. This estimate did not include the carp production of mainland China, which exceeds that of all other countries combined; 1.5 million tons of common and Chinese carp were grown there in 1965.

Furthermore, these figures are based on market statistics which are notoriously inaccurate in developing countries where 50⁰/,, or more of the production is not offered for sale and therefore not counted.

The total world production of carp and similar cyprinids may well approach 2 million metric tons with perhaps half of this figure derived from waters under intensive culture.

If one assumes a per hectare yield of carp of 500 kg, which corresponds to the average in Israel for unfed fish in unfertilized ponds (2000 kg or more per hectare are attained with fertilization and feeding), 2 million hectares of water surface would be necessary to produce the estimated tonnage of cultured carp.

This area is less than 1% of the total estimated freshwater area of the globe, including brackish lagoons, and certainly a small fraction of the water areas that eventually could be made usable for this type of fish culture.

The success of carp culture is due largely to the relative ease with which carp can be made to spawn in captivity and the hardiness of the species at all life stages from egg to adult. Carp adapt themselves to both acid and alkaline waters and easily tolerate salinities of up to Israel, carp are raised at salinities of up to 30c,4,.

Although production at such high salinities is low, selective breeding is being carried out with the aim of developing a strain of carp which will thrive under such conditions. Carp are naturally tolerant of a wide range of temperatures, and selective breeding has enhanced this advantage by producing strains adapted to a wide variety of temperature regimes.

Thus carp are now profitably raised from the tropics to the northern limits of the north temperate zone. Unlike most fish species, carp do well under conditions of high turbidity. Complementing the general hardiness of carp are their catholic food habits.

The natural food of young carp is zooplankton. Later in life they feed chiefly on bottom invertebrates. Both of these animal groups respond by an increase in their biomass to fertilization of the water, which considerably simplifies the aquaculturists' feeding chores.

Other foods consumed in nature include algae, small fish, earthworms and other terrestrial invertebrates, and various kinds of detritus, particularly decaying plant matter. As might be expected, in captivity carp quickly learn to accept a wide variety of live and prepared foods.

The significance to the aquaculturist of the carp's remarkable hardiness is that, according to S. Tat, Director of the Inland Fisheries, Ministry of Agriculture, Tel Aviv, Israel, no other fish has yet been found that can be as easily managed for high yields per unit surface or volume of water, nor are there many other species that are as economical to raise.

The carp's adaptability is expressed not only in its wide distribution and long history as a cultured fish and in the enormous production of carp flesh throughout the world, but also by the wide variety of techniques employed in carp culture.

COLLECTION OF WILD CARP FOR USE IN CULTURE

Although the carp is notable for the ease with which it is bred in captivity, in some localities low-intensity methods, which do not involve reproduction in captivity, are still employed. In the Soviet Union many carp of various ages as well as other fishes are stranded in shallow pools when spring flood waters of the larger rivers recede.

It is common practice to rescue such fish for stocking in other waters. In some years as many as 1½ to 2 million carp are thus rescued. Collection of stocks of naturally spawned fish in mainland China is a somewhat more sophisticated operation. Eggs and fry, rather than adult fish, are collected from the larger rivers to be raised in ponds.

Common carp are not as highly valued in China as the various Chinese carps, but some are inevitably collected due to the nonselective methods of obtaining eggs and fry. (For a description of these methods see the following section on Chinese carp culture.)

Some of these fish are raised, either alone or in polyculture with the Chinese carps, so that common carp accounts for about 5% of the weight of cyprinid fishes cultured in mainland China and Taiwan.

BREEDING

Seminatural Breeding

Since the carp is so easily spawned in captivity, most cultured carp are many generations removed from wild stock. Breeding in captivity has the advantage of stabilizing the supply of carp available for culture.

More important, it permits selection for various desirable traits. The classical methods of breeding carp are many, but all are adaptations of the spawning habits of carp in nature. In nature, carp spawn seasonally in temperate climates and year round in the tropics.

The stimulus for spawning is a rise in water temperature, often accompanied by flooding. The adhesive eggs are laid near the surface on rooted aquatic plants, on floating plants, or on submerged terrestrial vegetation.

The aquaculturist simulates these conditions by bringing spawners together in freshwater slightly warmer than that in his holding areas and providing real or artificial plants for attachment of the eggs. Perhaps the oldest variation of this technique is the Dubisch method, which is still practiced in some parts of Europe and in Indonesia.

In this method, grass is grown on the bottom of a dry spawning pond to a height of 40 cm and the pond is filled until the water just reaches the top of the grass.

Eggs are deposited on the grass. A trench 0.75 m deep may be dug around the perimeter of the pond to prevent spawning on overhanging terrestrial plants. When spawning is completed the carp are removed and the eggs allowed to hatch in the spawning pond.

The classical Chinese method is identical except that filamentous floating plants such as *Ceratophyllum, Myriophyllum,* or water hyacinth are used as egg collectors. These should be thoroughly washed to remove potential egg predators.

In Europe, piles of brush are used in place of aquatic plants in the similar Hofer method of carp culture. Today most carp culturists rely on transporting the eggs to hatching ponds rather than removing the spawners. If the eggs are carefully handled this results in less disturbance than would be caused by netting out the adult carp.

The simplest way of accomplishing this is to introduce floating plants confined within a floating frame into carp stock ponds at spawning time and let the carp spawn naturally. When spawning has been completed, the egg-laden plants are removed.

Greater ease of handling may be effected by attaching the plants to bamboo poles fixed at regular intervals in the pond. Spawning carp in stock ponds has the advantage of minimizing handling operations and cutting down on the number of ponds required; however, it precludes selection of individual spawners, thus careful primary selection of spawning stock is imperative. Space, labor, and water supply permitting, it is better to provide separate enclosures for each phase of culture.

Spawning enclosures, particularly those used for small breeders, need not be nearly as large as ponds used in other carp culture operations. In India cement cisterns 10 m × 9 m × 1 m are used in commercial breeding.

When the fish are ready for spawning, water from a pond heavily populated by carp is pumped into a depth of 0.5m; 15 or 20 kg of thoroughly washed aquatic plants such as *Hydrilla* or *Naias* are used to collect the eggs.

In the evening 5 or 6 selected ripe females weighing about 20 kg each and 10 to 15 oozing males of the same weight are introduced. By morning, all or most of the fish will have spawned and the eggs can be removed to hatching tanks.

Containers placed in shallow areas of stock ponds may also be used for spawning. The best known device of this sort is. the Indian hapa, a rectangular cloth tank about 1 m in depth, stretched and fixed by bamboo poles.

The sizes of male and female carp and the amount of plants used are limited by the size of the hapa. Table elsewhere in this chapter is a guide to the approximate amounts of fish and plants used.

In the evening the spawners are introduced and the hapa is covered to prevent the fish jumping out. Most of the fish will spawn by the next morning, but to insure complete spawning 30 hours may be allowed before the plants and eggs are removed and transferred to the hatching area.

After spawning, the carp are returned to the stock pond. The females are weighed before and after spawning. The difference in weight in grams multiplied by the average number of ovarian eggs per gram weight of ovary is used as an estimate of the total number of eggs laid.

Table 8.1: Amounts of plants and fish to be stocked in Hapas for spawning common carp in India.

Dimensions of HAPA (M)	*No. ♀♀*	*Weight of ♀ (Kg)*	*No. ♂♂*	*Total Weight of ♂♂ (Kg)*	*Weight of Plants (KG)*
2 × 1	1	1 or less	2-3	1 or less	2
3 × 1½	1	3-4	2-3	3-4	5
4 × 2	1	5-6	2-3	5-6	7

In Indonesia, carp are spawned in ponds as small as 5 m^2. In such small ponds freshly cut grass or bunches of the dark, horsehairlike fibers of the indjuk plant (*Arenga pinnata* and *A. saccharifera*) are floated on the water surface to serve as egg collectors. However, most carp spawning in Indonesia is carried out in ponds 20 to 30 m^2.

For such ponds a more easily handled egg collecting device known

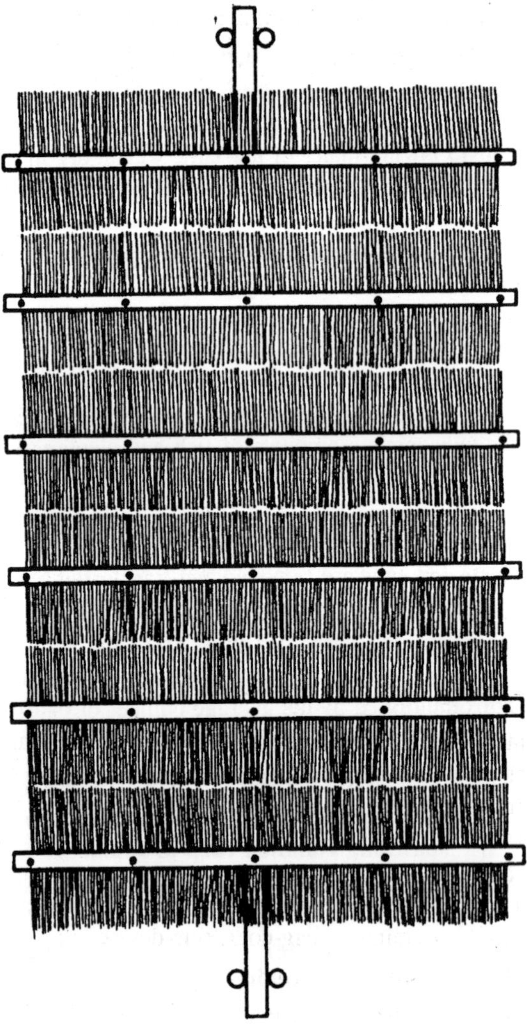

Figure 8.1: ArraDgement of kakabans in an Indonesian carp spawning pond.

as a kakaban or egg mat has been developed. Kakabans are made of indjuk fibers which have been strengthened by soaking them in water for about 5 days. A thin layer of fibers 1.2 to 1.5 m long is pressed longitudinally between two bamboo lathes 4 to 5 cm wide.

The margins are trimmed to produce an even end. The resulting structure is shaped like a two-sided comb with a width of 40 to 70 cm. Properly used and cared for, kakabans will last 1 to 2 years.

Kakabans are placed in a spawning pond with a bottom free of silt and mud but not hard enough to bruise the breeders. If the bottom tends toward muddiness, the pond may be dried for some days before use. The bottom may also be cemented or covered with sand.

To prevent eggs being deposited elsewhere than on the kakabans the margins of the spawning pond should be free of aquatic and terrestrial plants. Kakabans are laid transversely on a long bamboo pole held in place between two pairs of shorter poles driven into the bottom at either end of the pond.

They are spaced so that the fibers of adjacent kakabans ouch. The bamboo pole floats, thus thc whole structure moves freely with changes in water level, but the weight of the kakabans keeps it slightly submerged. The number of kakabans required is calculated on the basis of 5 to 8 kg of female spawners.

While spawning is taking place a gentle flow of water is maintained. As in other methods spawning occurs mostly at night. When the lower surface of a kakaban is covered with eggs it is turned over; if both sides are full, it is replaced with a fresh one. When spawning is completed, the kakabans with eggs attached are placed in hatching ponds.

The spawning methods thus far described, all similar to natural spawning, are quite satisfactory in tropical and subtropical countries where carp are perennial spawners.

In warm climates carp of both sexes may become ripe again within three months after spawning or, under exceptionally good conditions, within two months. There are records of individual carp in India which have spawned five times in one year.

Thus a commercial carp breeder in the tropics can count on three spawnings a year by merely placing ripe males and females together in warm water and providing an egg-collecting device.

Temperate Waters-Induced Breeding

In the temperate zones, carp are annual spawners. The carp culturist in a temperate climate is at a disadvantage in comparison to his tropical counterpart, not only because his fish spawn less often but because their spawning is less predictable. Unforeseen changes in the weather, an occasional problem in the tropics, are almost usual in temperate climates.

For example, a cold snap during the spawning period may interrupt or delay spawning at a considerable loss in efficiency and total production. Total control of the carp's environment would undoubtedly prove effective in solving this problem, but costs are prohibitive. Instead the carp culturist may regulate the time of reproduction through inducing spawning by pituitary injection.

This technique is being experimented with as a means of increasing frequency of carp spawning in temperate climates, but at present its chief advantages are in permitting the fish culturist to schedule his work quite rigidly and in allowing strict genetic control. Ripe female common carp are injected intraperitoneally at the axil of the pelvic fin with fresh or fresh frozen pituitary extract from another common carp of either sex and equal weight or with 2 to 3 mg per kg body weight of acetone-dried carp pituitary in 1 cm^3 distilled water.

The importance of using common carp pituitaries should be stressed, for although most fish which have been tested with pituitary extracts respond to materials from unrelated species, even animals belonging to different classes, the common carp has thus far been found to respond only to pituitary extracts of its own species.

For best results fish to be injected should be conditioned and spawned in well-oxygenated water at about 20°C. The simplest spawning procedure is to place injected females in small ponds with an equal number of males and a device to collect the eggs and let spawning occur as in the methods already described.

The males may also be injected, but if they are very ripe it is not necessary. More efficient fertilization and a high degree of genetic control can be achieved by hand stripping the fish. This method is best for very large breeders which would normally require excessive space to spawn.

After injection, females are kept in holding tanks separated from males. Within 12 to 20 hours they are usually ready to strip. Male breeders are injected in exactly the same way as the females. This has the effect of increasing the amount of seminal plasma, thus providing more milt.

Eggs are stripped first, then milt from a male is stripped directly onto the eggs. The eggs and milt should be mixed thoroughly with a nylon bristle paint brush in a plastic container, to which the eggs will not stick as they do to glass or enamel. Care should be taken to prevent any water from coming into contact with the eggs or milt during stripping.

In this connection it is helpful to wipe the fish dry with cheesecloth and work in dry gloves. Shortly after the eggs and milt are mixed, small amounts of water are dripped onto them; fertilization will occur only in the presence of water. Once fertilized, the eggs will begin to clump and adhere to each other.

Before clumping progresses very far the eggs are lifted with the brush and shaken into a holding vessel containing 10 to 15 cm water and a mat of Spanish moss or some other egg collector, or the eggs can be poured onto the egg collector from the plastic container.

In either case the water in the holding vessel should be vigorously agitated during transfer of the eggs in order to disperse the eggs in a manner similar to that attained by carp in nature. Dispersion is important to prevent fungus, which will inevitably form on any dead eggs, from smothering adjoining live eggs.

The egg collectors with eggs attached are tranferred from the holding vessel to ponds or hatchery troughs for hatching. It is worth noting in connection with induced spawning of common carp by pituitary injection that while common carp are unusual among fish in responding only to pituitary extracts from their own species, common carp pituitary is by far the most widely used in inducing spawning of other fish species.

It is relatively large and easy to remove, retains its potency when dried for up to 2 years or, in some instances, as long as 10 years, and common carp are readily available and easily kept nearly everywhere that fish culture is carried out. Thus many state, commercial, and experimental fish culture stations maintain small populations of common carp, often culls from stocks raised for food, as a source of pituitary glands.

Sexing and Selection of Spawners

Two common needs in all types of intensive carp culture are sexing and selection of spawners. Often it is not easy to determine the sex of common carp. When ripe, the female usually exhibits a fuller profile than the male.

Old males usually develop a few nuptial tubercles on the sides of the head and on the pectoral and ventral fins. The only sure way to sex young breeders is by extrusion of the genital product. To avert the need for examination of each fish, carp culturists in India and elsewhere have developed the practice of spawning each female with two or more presumptive males of such a size that the total weight of the "males" approximately equals that of the female.

Thus though a few immature males or females may be included among the brood stock, there is a very low probability of any female's eggs not being fertilized. Male and female carp to be used as spawners are usually kept separately from each other and from other stock.

It is often recommended that ponds used for this purpose be in a sheltered location, for it is believed that exposure to a cold wind with resultant chilling of the water may retard spawning. In Indonesia spawners are fed a special diet of rice bran, porridge, and corn for 3 days prior to spawning.

Immediately after introduction to the spawning pond they may receive a special ration of porridge about 1/20 the total weight of breeders. In general, though, breeders will reach optimum spawning condition under the same dietary regime which produces healthy commercial stock.

However, breeders should not be overfed or encouraged to grow too rapidly, for excess fat hampers gonad development. Rice bran may be fed to spent breeders during the period of recovery. Over the centuries culturists have developed and maintained a number of strains of carp considered to be especially desirable breeders.

Fecundity is of course the primary consideration. But fecundity cannot be empirically determined without considerable expenditure of time and effort and the sacrifice of a number of fish. Thus external indicators of fecundity have been sought.

Presumed characteristics of good breeders have been summarized as follows:

1. Body moderately soft.
2. Lower side of the belly broad and flattened so that the fish will stand on its belly.
3. Relatively great body depth.
4. Caudal peduncle relatively broad but supple.
5. Small head and pointed snout.
6. Rather large and regularly inserted scales.
7. Genital opening nearer to the caudal peduncle than in the average carp.

According to Hora and Pillay (1962), "Some farmers believe that the best mark of a good spawner relates to the insertion of the last scale beforē the genital opening; if a line is drawn from the head along the body to the center of the genital opening it should cross this scale and divide it into two equal parts."

There is also at least one behavioral indicator used in selecting spawners. Females which release large numbers of eggs at one time, so that they are bunched on the collector, are considered poor brood stock.

Discriminatory use of spawners displaying the preceding characteristics of course amounts to selective breeding, a subject which will be covered in detail later.

Age and size of spawners is also a factor to be taken into consideration. Age at maturity varies greatly with climate, as does growth. As a general rule in temperate countries males mature by their second or third year and no later than the fourth; females in their third or fourth year.

In very cold climates, some individuals may not mature until the fifth or sixth year. In the tropics both sexes usually reach maturity within one year, sometimes in as little as six months.

Carp follow the general rule for fish in that the largest females produce the most eggs. Fecundity of course varies with genetic and environmental factors but Table elsewhere in this chapter illustrates the general relationship between size and number of eggs.

It should be pointed out that the spawn of very old fish may be low

Table 8.2: Fecundity of female common carp.

Size (cm.)	*Number of eggs*
15-20	13,512
20-25	29,923
25-30	54,180
30-35	128,434
35-40	141,000
40-45	249,000
45-50	310,000
50-55	488,000
55-60	405,000
60-65	1,507,000
Over 65	2,945,000

in viability. It might seem more efficient to spawn the largest and most productive females, but under the conditions of close confinement characteristic of most of the classical carp spawning methods it may be difficult or impossible to breed very large females. Small males are preferred for the same reason and because they are more ardent courters.

Most Asian culturists select females weighing I to 2 kg and males of the same size slightly smaller. If induced spawning by pituitary injection and stripping of eggs and milt is employed, however, it does make sense to take advantage of the high fecundity of large spawners.

Hatching

The time required for carp eggs to hatch in nature varies widely with temperature. Hatching times from 46 to 144 hours have been reported. Prehatching mortality is nearly always high, and may be as great as 80%. The chief causes of mortality are predators, including the parent fish, low rates of fertilization, low temperatures, and fungus brought on by the presence of dead or unfertilized eggs.

The newly hatched larvae also suffer heavy mortality due to predation and, in relatively sterile environments, to poor food supply. Of these causes of mortality, only poor fertilization need be of little concern to the fish culturist.

Even if stripping of eggs and milt and artificial fertilization are not practiced, cultured carp are usually spawned in close enough confinement that each egg is almost certain to be reached by a sperm. Predation by the parent fish is controlled by removing the eggs from the spawners or vice versa.

If a hatching pond separate from the spawning area is used, the commonest predators, among them fish, crayfish, copepods, and aquatic insects, may be eliminated by leaving the pond dry until just before use. If it is not practical to dry the hatching pond it may be treated with Lexone at 2.5 ppm for 2 or 3 days before stocking.

This will kill most predators and some parasites but will not affect the fertility of the eggs. Other poisons, including quicklime, Camellia seed cake, powdered croton seed, derris root, or commercially available rotenone, may also be used in conjunction with partial draining. Quicklime is especially effective against bottom organisms.

Proper dosages are 60 kg/ha applied to a nearly dry pond or 100 kg/ha of quicklime and 150 kg/ha of tea seed cake if there is considerable water. Camellia seed cake or powdered croton seed are applied at from 50 to 200 kg/ha depending on the amount of water in the pond.

Raw derris root must be soaked in water for a few hours before use. It is then crushed and the juice containing the rotenone wrung out into a bucket of water and diluted for use. One kilogram of derris root will provide enough rotenone to treat one hectare of pond surface.

Rotenone powder should be used at about 5% of this concentration. Predation may also be averted by keeping the eggs indoors in hatching troughs with flowing water until they are eyed. They are then transferred to hatching ponds, however, for it is difficult to provide an adequate amount of zooplankton to feed the newly hatched fry in an indoor environment, although recent experiments in West Germany indicate the potential feasibility of rearing carp fry on a diet of brine shrimp (*Artemia*) in flowing water aquaria.

The temperature for hatching should be the same as that at which the eggs were spawned. The optimum temperature is about 20°C in temperate climates and 25°C in the tropics. Carp are quite temperature tolerant, but eggs and larvae should not be chilled. For this reason, it is best that hatching ponds be sheltered from the wind.

During abnormally cold seasons, Indonesian carp culturists hatch eggs in wooden tubs about 12 cm deep which are placed in the sunshine during the day and kept in a warm building at night.

Fungus as a source of mortality is perhaps more prevalent in culture than in nature. The fungus *Saprolegnia* gains a foothold on eggs which are unfertilized or have been killed by physical shock. The white, fuzzy, foul-smelling masses of mycelia which form on such eggs may spread and smother adjacent eggs, killing them as well.

In this manner *Saprolegnia* can spread throughout a batch of eggs with disastrous results. Carp eggs are large and remarkably resistant to physical abuse as fish eggs go; nevertheless, they should be transferred from spawning to hatching enclosures with the utmost care.

The incidence of fungus can be further reduced by seeing to it that eggs are not allowed to bunch together too closely. If, despite all precautions, numerous dead eggs are seen, growth of fungus may be inhibited when there is a current over the eggs by flushing with malachite green at about 2 ppm.

In primitive methods of carp culture, such as the Dubisch method, the eggs are allowed to hatch in the spawning pond. In more advanced methods the egg collectors with eggs attached are transferred to separate hatching enclosures. Indonesian carp culturists support loaded kakabans in the same manner as for spawning.

Before transfer to the hatching pond they are gently washed to insure that none of the eggs are coated with mud. In the hatching pond the fiber margins of the kakabans are not allowed to touch but are separated by 2 to 8 cm. Bamboo poles are placed across the ends of the kakabans parallel to the center pole and held in place by a board at each end of the pond parallel to the kakabans.

The weight of this device is adjusted so that it will compensate for changes in water level in keeping the kakabans about 8 cm below the surface. Hatching ponds are stocked at rates of approximately 1 ka kaban per 30 to 50 m^2 of water surface.

Masses of plants and other egg collectors may be placed directly into hatching ponds or kept in smaller enclosures within ponds. In Indonesia, carp are sometimes hatched in a sump in the center of the

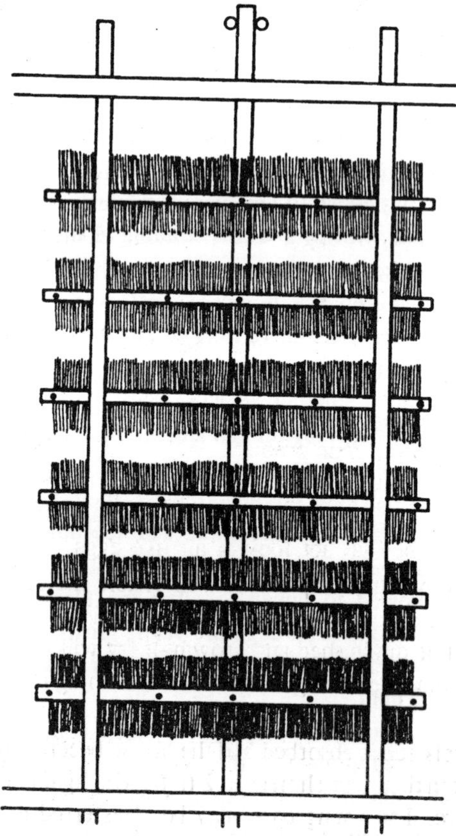

Figure 8.2: Arrangement of Kakabans in an Indonesian carp hatching pond.

pond; thus the pond proper may be kept dry until the eggs hatch. This is especially advantageous where predators are plentiful or water is scarce. In India cloth hapas similar to those sometimes used in spawning are used as hatching enclosures.

Hatching hapas are usually 2 m × 1 m × 1 m and made of cloth fine enough to prevent the fry from escaping but coarse enough to permit zooplankton to enter. In parts of Indonesia the spawning enclosure is a compartment in a larger pond, separated from the pond proper by a temporary earthen dam.

When spawning is completed the dam is opened and the spawners allowed to escape. Then the dam is sealed. After a week the dam is opened again and the larvae are allowed access to the pond. Whether the eggs are hatched in a pond or an enclosure within a pond, it is important that the pond receive ample sunshine to insure the growth of phytoplankton to feed zooplankton which will in turn nourish the young carp.

For the same reason the pond should be no more than 80 cm deep at its deepest point and naturally fertile or artificially enriched. A soft bottom is best; moderate turbidity will do no harm. It is convenient to have the pond so arranged that it can be easily drained. A catching device may be set up at the lower end to trap the fry during draining for transfer to rearing ponds.

FRY REARING AND GROWING FOR MARKET

As previously mentioned, the time to hatching varies, but visual detection of larvae is no problem. When first hatched, the larvae do not swim about but attach themselves to plants or the walls of their container by means of a cement gland. Even so, with their elongate shape and beating tails they do not look at all like eggs.

A little practical experience will enable the culturist to gauge the hatching rate of his fish under normal conditions. Complications in this regard will be diminished and growth of fry will be more uniform if all the eggs from a spawning are placed in hatching enclosures within one day.

The yolk sac is absorbed and the larvae become free swimming and capable of taking nourishment in 2 to 6 days, again depending on water temperature. The young carp may be transferred to nursery ponds as early as 3 days after spawning or they may remain in the hatching pond for up to 3 weeks.

At the time of transfer they may be counted volumetrically. Survival to this point varies greatly; rates as high as 86% of egg production and as low as 20% have been reported, depending on weather, availability of zooplankton, and the success or failure of precautions against fungus and predators.

Once the fry have been transferred to nursery ponds, the culturist's main concern is to raise them to marketable size or for use as breeding stock. In temperate climates, where the carp is an annual spawner, it is often necessary to hold fry at a convenient size so as to have a supply of fish on hand for stocking thoughout the year.

Carp may be kept at a relatively small size for 2 years or more by judicious crowding and feeding just enough for maintenance but not enough for growth. This amount has been calculated as 30 mg of protein per 100 mg of carp per day at 22 to 24°C, or a daily intake of about 1/1000 of the total protein content of a carp.

In general, however, the culturist's aim is to maximize production and profits by growing fish as rapidly as possible consistent with economic considerations.

Maximum production is attained by fertilization of the water to increase production of natural carp foods, supplementary feeding, regulation of population density in the rearing areas, periodic culling of inferior fish, selection of breeding stock, and control of various environmental parameters.

Pond Fertilization

Pond fertilization may be thought of as an indirect method of feeding. Its purpose is to provide nutrients for phytoplankton, the lowest link in the food chain. An increase in phytoplankton will eventually be refleeted in an increase in production at all levels of the food chain on up to the top, in this case the carp.

Although it is possible to raise carp wit] no actual feeding whatsoever if the water used is sufficiently fertile, most successful carp culturists do make some use of direct feeding. But most carp culturists also find it advantageous to let their fish take part of their nourishment from natural foods.

There is no economically feasible diet fed to carp which cannot be improved by the presence of naturally occurring bottom-dwelling invertebrates. In most cases the water used for carp culture will not naturally be so rich in nutrients that the numbers of these animals cannot be substantially increased by proper application of organic or inorganic fertilizers.

While this may require some investment, the amount of money will usually be less than would be spent in adding the same amount of nutrient directly in the form of food. In certain cases, carp may be raised in waters which are exceptionally rich in organic nutrients or, to put it another way, heavily polluted.

The carp perform an additional service by retarding further organic enrichment of the environment. For example, in Java carp are confined in bamboo cages in rapidly flowing polluted streams. They graze on the carpet of small worms and insect larvae in the highly enriched water and yields of 50 to 75 kg of fish flesh per square meter of surface per year are not rare.

Yields of pond fish are usually expressed per hectare or per acre; straight multiplication of the production figures just given would result in a weight of over 500,000 kg/ha. Even with allowances made for the fact that a large portion of a running hectare of such a stream might not be suitable for the placement of cages, this practice clearly represents an extremely efficient and ecologically sound use of sewage.

It is, however, possible only in fairly rapidly running warm water and is not consistent with public health considerations. A more sanitary method of utilizing carp as sewage converters is to grow them in conjunction with conventional sewage treatment operations.

In Munich, Germany, the settled and/or partially treated sewage of the city is diluted and led through a 7-km series of 4- to 5-ha ponds, each containing about 5000 2-year-old carp which are fattened over the summer on the abundant invertebrate fauna.

The annual increment in fish flesh is about 500 kg/ha without additional feeding. The net income of this now amortized installation owned by the Bavarian Hydropower Company is 50,000 DM (about $12,500). Similar installations in Berlin, Germany, and Kielce, Poland, have produced yields of 800 to 900 kg/ha, and 1300 kg/ha, respectively.

Certain industrial and agricultural wastes may be similarly used. In Czechoslovakia effluents from dairies, sugar mills, slaughterhouses, and starch mills have all been utilized in carp culture. When treated with 5 tons/ha of lime, such wastes have produced yields of carp averaging 500 to 600 kg/ha. /ha.

In several European and Asian countries ducks are reared in the same ponds as carp and natural fertilization of the ponds by duck manure results in fish yields of up to 500 kg/ha. These exceptions notwithstanding, most carp culturists will find it highly advantageous to artificially enrich the water.

But it should not be assumed that no harm can be done by fertilizers. Whatever combination of decaying plants, human or animal manure, or chemical fertilizers is used, an overdose may actually reduce production or even have a lethal effect on the fish.

The correct types and amounts of fertilizer to be used vary from locality to locality and even from pond to pond in the same area. For specific advice it is best to determine the chemical and biological characteristics of the body of water to be used or of the soil on which it is to be constructed and to seek advice from local aquaculturists or from agricultural or fishery personnel.

SUPPLEMENTARY FEEDING

Carp culture usually is economic only when the population density of fish in rearing areas exceeds that which could be supported by the natural or augmented fertility of the water. For this reason, supplementary artificial feeding is necessary except for newly hatched fry.

In most culture methods food for very young fry is produced within the pond by fertilization rather than being introduced by the culturist. Notable exceptions occur in Japan, where water fleas (*Daphnia*) are cultured in ponds prior to the introduction of newly hatched fry, and in India, where young fry are commonly fed on various types of oil cakes mixed with rice bran.

Recent research in India tested the effectiveness of 19 carp fry foods fed singly and in combinations of 2, 3, and 4 components. The various food combinations were compared in terms of percentage survival of fry and average growth in millimeters over a 15-day period. Of all combinations tested, a mixture of backswimmers (aquatic insects), freshwater prawns, and cowpeas in a 5:3:2 ratio was judged best.

It produced significantly greater growth than any of the other experimental foods, and while a number of other blends, notably a 1:1:1 mixture of prawns, cowpeas and wheat bran, produced higher survival, this was offset by the difference in growth rate.

Research on fry foods is in its early stages, but some sort of food for newly hatched fry may eventually be adopted by carp culturists throughout the world. Sometime within the first three weeks of life carp fry are transferred to nursery or rearing enclosures.

From then on supplementary artificial feeding is carried out in all types of intensive culture. The sheer variety of feeds used is bewildering, but selection of a feed or feeds will be less confusing if the culturist bears two principles in mind:

1. Artificial feeding is a supplement to naturally available food and food organisms produced by fertilization of the water. Thus food items selected should not duplicate the contributions of natural food but should compensate for nutrients which are in short supply.
2. The goal of feeding is to achieve maximum growth consistent with economic considerations. Total costs to the culturist will, of course, be higher with feeding than without, but cost per ton may be lower with feeding, thus enabling the culturist to realize a greater profit.

A third consideration which is beginning to be taken more seriously, at least in countries where the rationale for carp culture is not to compensate for inadequate protein supplies, is the effect of a particular feed on the quality of carp flesh produced.

A general index of the efficiency of conversion of a feed into fish flesh is a ratio variously called the growth coefficient, food quotient, or nutritive ratio:

$$\text{food quotient} = \frac{\text{weight of food}}{\text{increase in weight of fish}}$$

Table elsewhere in this chapter lists the approximate food quotients of 23 types of carp feed.

Merely to feed the food with the highest growth coefficient does not guarantee that production of carp flesh will be maximized. Carp, like most other animals, do best on a balanced diet. The proportions of protein, fat, and carbohydrate in an ideal diet vary according to the age of the carp and availability of nutrients in the form of natural foods.

In general, artificial feeding should concentrate on foods which are high in carbohydrates. The natural food of carp is very high in protein, reaching 60% of dry weight in Chironomid larvae, one of the most abundant food organisms in most carp ponds.

In nature, part of this protein is converted into energy. Feeds rich in carbohydrates provide more efficient source of energy and free all of the protein to provide for growth. It may be necessary to step up the protein intake in growing large cart; since the need for protein increases with size.

Care should be taken no to feed too much protein, however, for excess amounts will be wasted. Ten to fifteen percent by weight of protein in the diet should be adequate for large carp. Protein intake of

Table 8.3: Food quotients of certain feeds in culture of common carp.

Feed Item	*Food Quotient*
Fresh silkworm pupae	5.0 - 5.5
Dried silkworm pupae	1.3 - 2.1
Silkworm pupae, pressed dry	1.4
Mysis dry	2.0
Chironomids	2.3 - 4.4
Clam meat	1.3
Meat powder	2.0
Dehydrated blood	1.5 - 1.7
Fish meal	1.5 - 3.0
Soybean cake	2.22
Barley	2.60
Oats 2.60	
Wheat flour 7.2	
Peas	2.7 - 2.8
Potato	20.0 -33.9
Rice bran	5.08
Wheat bran	4.22
Peanut cake	2.13 - 2.7
Lupin seeds	3.0 - 5.0
Soybeans	3.0 - 5.0
Maize	4.0 - 6.0
Cottonseed	2.3
Cottonseed cake	3.0

carp may be increased by using feeds rich in protein or by fertilizing the water to increase availability of natural foods. The latter method is ofen economically preferable, particularly in countries such as India where all sorts of protein-rich materials command prohibitive prices.

Whichever method of adding protein is chosen, it is worth remembering the general nutritional principle that a diet is likely to be better balanced in amino acids if it contains a variety of protein sources.

Table elsewhere in this chapter lists the percent composition and nutritive value of 37 commonly used carp feeds. Other foods sometimes fed to carp, but for which no data are available, include cottonseed,

cottonseed cake, sunflower seed meal, soybeans, sorghum, duckweed, fish roe, fish entrails, fish meal, clam meat, meat powder, and brine shrimp (*Artemia*). Maximum food consumption by carp is prodigious; at 25 to 27°C a carp is capable of consuming more than its weight in food daily.

This does not result in great growth, for gorging leads to poor digestion and inefficient conversion of food. The optimum rate of feeding is difficult to determine, for it depends on a number of variables, among them the type of feed used, the amount of natural food available, and especially the water temperature.

At summer temperatures carp may require 30 times as much food as during the winter. Indeed, during the coldest months, long periods of quiescence may occur during which no food whatever is taken.

Thus in temperate climates feeding is intensified in summer and may be reduced in winter to occasional very light feeding on warm days. In the tropics the variation in feeding rate is less, but feeding schedules should still take into account water temperature.

Tables elsewhere in this chapter are examples of feeding schedules for the temperate climate of Japan and the somewhat warmer climate of South China's Kwangtung Delta. Feeding schedules are usually made out on a per day basis, but greater efficiency can be achieved through several light daily feedings than by one massive application of feed.

On the other hand, frequent feeding has the disadvantage of increasing labor costs. This problem may eventually be circumvented by use of automatic feeders which can be programmed to broadcast specified amounts of feed at set intervals.

An improvement on this device is•a feeder being tested at Wielenbach, Bavaria, Germany, which permits carp to learn to release food at any time by pressing against an underwater plate. Using this device, carp soon adjust to taking only as much food as they need.

The central questions in determining what, how much, and how often to feed are, of course, questions of economics. Is it more economic to feed or not to feed?

What feeding regime is most conducive to profitable operation? It has already been mentioned that, except in rare cases o. extremely fertile water, it is economic to feed carp. The relative merits o feeding versus not feeding can be compared or an economic appraisal d various methods of feeding can be made if the cost of feed and feedin labor and the production of carp per hectare is known.

Table elsewhere in this chapter gives ,e sample comparison of

Table 8.4: Composition and nutritive valie of principal common carp feeds (% dry weight).

		Crude		*Carbo-*	
Name of feed	*Protein*	*Fat*	*hydrate*	*Fiber*	*Ash*
Vegetable products					
Groundnuts	27	45	18	3	2
Groundnuts cake	36	10	32	—	19
Coconut oil cake	17-21	7-16	43-44	8-11	5-6
Mustard oil cake	31	10	29	—	30
Lupin, sweet, yellow	42	6	25	10	2
Cowpea	22	4	71	—	4
Soybean cake	44-50	8-11	33	6	6
Bean meal	51	9	31	5	5
Barley	12-27	2	77	7	3
Rice (hulled)	8	2	77	7	3
Rice, broken, white	8	1	80	<1	1
Rice bran	13-16	4-18	43-47	6-9	13-15
Wheat	15	2	75	4	4
Wheat flour, white	12	1	87	<1	<1
Wheat bran	15	5	62	12	6
Oats	14	3	74	6	—
Maize (corn)	7-12	5-6	81	2	2
Maize (fresh)	10	5	70	2	1
Rye	12	2	70	2	2
Italian millet	12	7	75	—	6
Potato	8	<1	83	3	—
Sweet potato	6	2	85	4	—
Ragi	9	9	68	—	14
Animal products					
Silkworm pupae	49	26	7	—	3
Defatted silkworm pupae	83	2	9	—	6
Sardine	71	22	—	—	—
Crustacean (Mysis)	74	15	—	—	—
Crustacean (Daphnia)	42	7	31	—	—
Small shrimps	66	7	5	—	—

Snail (Vivipara)	83	2	—	—	—
Worm (Limoudrilus)	48	24	—	—	—
Worm (Tubifex)	65	15	14	—	6
Insect (Notonecta)	56	4	24	—	16
Insect (Chironomus)	60	26	—	—	—
Mixed zooplankton	46	6	23	—	25

Table 8.5: Feeding schedule for common carp in Japan.

Month	*Monthly feeding rate in percentage of total annual Quantity*	*Essential Foods*	*Daily Feeding Frequency*	*Time required to finish food at each feeding*
January	0			
February	0			
March	0			
April	1	Wheat, snail pupae, soya sauce waste, earthworms, rice bran	1	Within 1 hour
May	4	Mixed foods	1-3	30 min
June	15	Pupae as staple food, also mixed food	3-6	15-30 min
July	20	Silkworm pupae	3-7	15-30 min
August	30	Silkworm pupae	5-9	15-30 min
September	20	Silkworm pupae	5-7	15-30 min
October	9	Pupae, wheat, bean meal, vegetable and fish meal	2-5	15-30 min
November	1		Once to once every 2 days	30 min
December	0		Once, or every other day	

Table 8.6: Feeding scehedule for common carp and grass carp in the kwangbtung delta, china.

Month	Approximate temperature (°C)	Estimated weight of fish in pond: Increment per month (Kg)	Estimated weight of fish in pond: Total (Kg)	Quantity of food required per month (Kg): Grass	Silkworm Waste	Fresh silkworm pupae	Rice bran
February	15	—	70.00	—	—	—	—
March	16	127.80	197.80	1,534	1,022	639	639
April	20	149.10	346.90	1,739	1,193	745	745
May	24	191.70	538.60	2,301	1,534	959	959
June	28	255.60	794.20	3,067	2,054	1,278	1,278
July	30	319.50	1,113.70	3,834	2,556	1,598	1,598
Quantity harvested at the end of July			800.00		—		
New stocking material added			200.00		—		
Stock			513.70		—		
August	31	426.00	937.70	5,112	3,408	2,130	2,130
September	28	319.50	1,259.20	3,834	2,556	1,597	1,597
October	27	149.10	1,408.30	1,789	1,193	745	745
November	23	106.50	1,514.80	1,278	852	533	533
December	16	85.20	1,600.00	1,022	682	426	426

costs and production of fed and unfed carp it, Israel. This type of analysis may be applied to the comparison of any two feeding schedules simply by plugging in the appropriate data.

Table 8.7: Costs per hectare and per ton of common carp culture in Israel with and without feeding.

	Yield with feeding		*Yield without feeding*	
	Per HA	*Per Ton*	*Per HA*	*Per ton*
	2,100 Kg	—	1,000 Kg	—
COSTS	—	0.47 HA	—	1.0 HA
Charges for capital invested in ponds and fishing gear	$ 360	$169	$360	$360
Water	210	99	210	210
Fertilizers	87	41	87	87
Maintenance	106	50	106	106
Feed	370	174	—	—
Labor	286	116	150	150
Marketing costs	32	15	12	12
Interest on working capital	5	2	2	2
General and overhead expenses	10	5	8	8
Total	**$ 1,466**	**$ 671**	**$ 935**	**$ 935**

One other subject that should be considered in a discussion of carp nutrition is food additives. The use of vitamins and other additives in carp culture rests on the same assumption as their use in human nutrition: optimum amounts of these substances are not present in normal diets.

Among the classes of additives which have been given to carp are vitamins, antibiotics, minerals, and tissue preparations. Their use is largely in the experimental stage, but results are encouraging.

Addition to carp diets of hydrolyzed yeast, rich in vitamins of the B and D groups, has resulted in experimental yield increases of 16 to 56%, depending on the other components of the diet, while reducing feed expenditure per unit gain in weight by as much as 15%.

The antibiotic terramycin, applied at a dosage of 5000 to 10,000 units/ kg of feed, has been shown to increase growth by 5 to 25%, with a 10.5% saving in feed costs and a higher survival rate of stock. Terramycin is particularly effective when the feed has a high vegetable content. However, fish culturists may eventually experience a problem encountered by farmers of cattle and poultry who use antibiotics prophylactically.

The eventual evolution of strains of disease microbes resistant to antibiotics has in some cases made disease treatment very difficult and may lead to a net decrease in growth and survival. In all likelihood, those fish culturists who refrain from using antibiotics, except perhaps as a therapeutic measure against specific diseases, will do best in the long run.

Cobalt, a component of vitamin B_{12}, when added to carp diets at a rate of 0.08 mg of cobalt chloride/kg of fish/24 hours, or 3.0 g/ton of feed, resulted in an increase of vitamin B_{12} in the liver with an accompanying rise in growth rate of 30% in fingerlings and 15 to 207, in 2-year-old carp. Cost of feed per unit gain of weight decreased by 20%. Cobalt chloride may also be added to ponds as a fertilizer with similar effects.

Commercial tissue preparations, made from the viscera of slaughtered animals and used as a growth stimulant in warm-blooded animals, may also be added to carp feed. Seven kilograms of tissue preparation per ton of feed when added to the rations of 2-year-old carp increased growth by 12.0 to 13.3%.

Stocking Rates

The amount of space allotted to carp in ponds varies with the characteristics of the pond, the type and amount of supplementary food given, and the size of the carp. Warm, shallow, naturally fertile ponds are best for all sizes and ages of carp, but fertilizers may be added.

Once fertilizer dosages and feed rations have been worked out, the carp culturist's chief concern becomes the regulation of population density. Growth will be greatest at low densities, but space and labor considerations limit the extent to which this principle can be applied.

A suitable population density for newly hatched fry would of course amount to gross overcrowding in adult fish. So it is customary to maintain a series of ponds for raising fish of different ages.

Segregation by size not only aids in regulating population density; it equalizes competition for food and assures that the somewhat different food requirements of carp at different ages can be met. Ponds may roughly be divided into three categories: nursery ponds, rearing ponds, and productnr ponds.

Nursery ponds are the first stop for the young carp after they lea the hatching pond and are usually the smallest of the three types of ponti Small ponds facilitate ecological control and recapture of the fry. Dept; is usually less than 1.5 m, with some ponds as shallow as 0.5 m, to tak, full advantage of the warming effect of the sun.

Rearing ponds all slightly larger in all dimensions but still less than 2 m deep. Production, ponds may be of almost any size consistent with efficient feeding and harvest of fish. In southeast Asia and the Mediterranean area, rice fields are used as rearing or production ponds.

This practice is becoming less prevalent as the use of heavy machinery necessitates periodic draining of the fields and as herbicides and insecticides are increasingly used in doses lethal to fish. A further limiting factor in temperate climates is that the maximum size of carp which can be produced in so shallow an enclosure as a rice field is about 500 g.

In most European and some Asian countries this is well below the accepted minimum marketable size. The size, age, and population density of carp stocked in ponds varies greatly. Table 8 gives samples of still water pond or rice field stocking rates for seven countries. Prospective carp culturists are best advised to follow local custom, at least at first.

The factor limiting the number of carp which can be stocked in a pond is not the amount of space available to each fish, but the volume of water per fish. In still water ponds, which account for the majority of carp culture facilities, available space and water volume are virtually identical, but if water is circulated through an enclosure containing fish, the volume of water per fish is effectively increased with no change in the space allotment.

If conditions are such that a flow of water through a pond can be maintained, stocking rates may be far in excess of those employed in still water. For example, in the Philippines running water ponds are stocked with fry at rates of 280,000 to 850,000/ha as compared to 50,000/ha in still water, with comparable yields.

Often conditions do not permit construction of a flowing water pond. A more frequently applicable method of increasing circulation of water in carp culture involves the use of floating cages as rearing or growing enclosures. Small cages submerged in streams have long been successfully used in growing carp in Java and Cambodia.

More recently, Japanese and Russian fish culturists have investigated the feasibility of rearing and growing carp in floating cages in lakes.

In Japan, carp fingerlings are stocked in rectangular bamboo framed nets, 2 ill deep and van) in', ill area from 7 to 81 m^2. These nets are floated by means of erupt) oil drums and anchored to wooden ,takes tlrisen into the lake bottom, usually rn about 3 to of neater. When stocked With fingerlings at rates of 10 to 80/nr= and heavily fed-carp production may reach 4000 kg/ ha.

Russian experiments in growing adult carp at high densities (50 to 250/m^2) in floats have not been as successful, with growth generally less than that obtained at lower densities in still water ponds. Nevertheless, experiments in the use of floating cages in all phases of carp culture are continuing.

Recirculating Water Systems

A more sophisticated approach to the problem of water circulation in carp culture involves the construction of closed or semiclosed recirculating systems. This approach to fish culture has the advantages of minimizing the amounts of both space and water needed and of allowing nearly complete control over the fish's environment.

On the debit side, elaborate filtration and aeration systems are required to compensate for the heavy oxygen demand and the large amounts of waste products generated by the extremely dense populations of carp. Moreover, although the small size of such systems cuts down on the total amount of labor required, a certain amount of specialized technical aid is necessary.

The first recirculating water system used in commercial carp culture was put into operation in 1951 by I. Motokawa of Maebashi City, Japan. In collaboration with Dr. A. Saeki of the Fisheries Faculty, Tokyo University, a pioneer researcher in the use of recirculating systems in fish culture, Ire converted a concrete fish pond into a 1-ton tank with a closed recirculating system.

Dimensions and working capacity are given in Table anywhere else in this chapter. Water is pumped from the fish tank to an adjoining concrete tank for settling out of sediment, then through pipes to one of a pair of filtration tanks.

It is filtered through 60 cm of 1.5-cm diameter gravel spread on perforated plastic plate placed 20 cm above the bottom of the filtration tank. The filtration tanks are used alternately; the one not in use is washed periodically by compressed air passed through the pipes.

Motokawa later built a 5-ton tank along the same lines as the original. Specifications and results of both systems are given in Table elsewhere in this chapter. When stocked with fingerlings at 30 to 70%

Table 8.8: Stocking rates used in culture of common carp in seven countries.

Country	*Type of pond*	*Age or size of carp Stocked*	*Stocking rate*	*Growth*	*Mortality*
India	Nursery; (stagnant; heavily fertilized	2 days old million/ha	1.25 to 2.5 in 15 days and fed)	to 25 mm	—
Indonesia	Nursery (or rice field)	3 weeks old in 3 weeks	60,000/ha	to 30-50 mm	40-60%
Nigeria	Rearing 30-50 mm	6 weeks old, in 3 weeks	25,000-30,000/ha	to 50-80 mm	20%
Philippines	Nursery	8- 10 mm	50,000/ha	to 50-60 mm in 1 month; may be grown up to 180 mm in nursery ponds	10-15%
	Rearing	60-180 mm	50,000/ha	to 20-50 g	—
	Rearing (running water)	Fry	280,000-850,000/ha	—	10-20%
	Production (stagnant)	20- 50 g	5,000/ha	—	—
Japan	Rice field	Fry	3,000-15,000/ha	—	—

(Table 8.8 Contd.)

(Table 8.8 Contd.)

Country	*Type of pond*	*Age or size of carp Stocked*	*Stocking rate*	*Growth*	*Mortality*
	Rearing 1	1 month old	300-1,500/m^2	—	—
	Rearing 2	2 months old	30-100/m^2	—	—
	Rearing 3	3 months old	10-30/m^2	—	—
	Rearing 4	4 months old	1-3/m^2	—	—
	Production	2 years old	0.8/M^2	—	—
U.S.S.R.	Rice field	Fingerling	10-80/m^2	—	—
(Ukraine)	(nursery)	—	—		
U.S.S.R.	Production	40 g	500,000	—	—
	(floating cage)		2½ million/ha	—	
U.S.A.	Nursery	3-4 weeks	250,000/ha	—	—
(Alabama)	(experimental)				

of total fish holding capacity, production of carp per unit of water utilized reached 400 kg/m^2 the highest level ever achieved in Japan by any method.

Table 8.9: Dimensions and capacity of a one-ton closed recirculation water system used in culture of common crap.

Dimensions	
Fish tank	76.5 m2, 1.3 m deep
Filtration tank	24.8 m^2, 1.9 m deep
Volume of filter	9.2 m3 (gravel of diameter 1.5 cm)
Head of the two tanks	1.7 m
Total volume of water	205 m3
Working capacity	
Working area of filtration	15 m2
Filtration velocity	102 in/day
Pumps	one 2-KW centrifugal and one 2-KW vertical; one 5-HP gasoline engine (for emergency)
Circulation of water	75 m^2/hour
Working oxygen intake	220 liters/day
Filtration	830 g/day as N
Carp reared	up to 1 ton
Carp kept	up to 6 tons

Even more spectacular production of carp with water circulation has been achieved experimentally at the Max Planck Institute in Hamburg, West Germany. There carp have been reared and grown in aquaria at truly incredible population densities. As many as 10 carp have been grown in a 40-liter aquarium.

With rapid water circulation, filtration by activated mud supplemented by a constant inflow of freshwater, temperature control and a daily food ration of 3.5% of the fish's weight, growth rates in aquaria were 500 to 600 times higher than for camparable fish kept in ponds. No ill effects due to crowding were observed.

Comparable results were achieved in the Soviet Union by use of heated water in a similar recirculating system. It is believed that if it had been financially feasible to build a larger filtration complex, the German system could have been operated as a closed system with similar results.

Figure elsewhere in this chapter is a diagram of a closed system of the same sort as the semiclosed system used at the Max Planck Institute.

SELECTIVE BREEDING AND HYBRIDIZATION

We have thus far covered the techniques of spawning, hatching, and rearing carp used by fish culturists in maximizing growth, production, and, ultimately, profit. Another factor which has bearing on carp production is selection of stock. Historically this function has also been the province of the culturist.

Table 8.10: Details of common carp culture in one-ton and five-ton water recirculating systems.

	One Ton	*Five Ton*
Total volume of water (m^3)	205	286.3
Volume of water circulation (m^3/hour)	75	135
Oxygen intake (liters/hour)	2.4	3.5
Fish tank		
Surface area (m^2)	76.5	125.1
Depth (m)	1.3	1.5
Filtration tank		
Surface area (m^2)	24.8	47.6
Volume of filter (m^3)	9.2	28.6
Fish harvested (tons)	0.85	4.12
Fish harvested in unit area (kg/m^2)	11.1	30.3
Period (days)	55	57
Temperature of water (°C)	16.3–27.0	17–27.0
Number of fingerlings stocked	1,216	4,370
Weight of fingerlings stocked (kg)	543	2,250
Food given (kg)	625	1,890
Number of fish harvested	1,182	4,308
Weight of fish harvested (kg)	852.2	4,121
Number of fish died	34	62
Weight increase (%)	57	83
Food conversion	2.02	1.01
Average increase of weight (g)	273	442
Same per day (g)	5.35	7.75

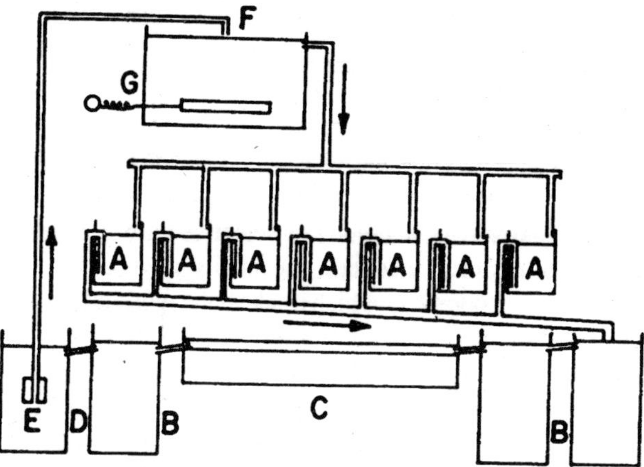

Figure 8.3: Closed recirculating system used in culturing common carp at the Max Planck Institute, Hamburg, Germany.

However, the professional carp culturist rarely has the time or the facilities to carry out large-scale experiments on selective breeding. Such work is most appropriately done by government agencies or other large operators.

Further, it is questionable whether any but the largest producers of carp for the market should spawn their own fish, experimentally or for production. It has been shown that mating of sibs, half sibs, or even cousins produces a marked inbreeding depression of growth rate and viability.

Given the small amount of brood stock carried by most culturists, inbreeding is virtually unavoidable. Since 1964 this rationale has been put into practice in Israel by the Carp Breeder's Union, who carry out research aimed at developing improved strains of carp and supply fry of such strains to production farms, thus allowing the commercial culturist to devote his total effort to the quantitative aspects of production.

By virtue of the ease with which common carp are spawned, their hardiness, and their great fecundity the possibility of selective improvement of the species was recognized very early in the history of fish culture. Selective breeding of carp has gone on for centuries. resulting in the diversity of strains available today. Nevertheless, great differences may still be observed between the progeny of different sets of parents of the same strain, so that selective breeding on this basis is still relevant.

Further improvements may be made by crossing established strains to combine desirable traits and to take advantage of heterosis (hybrid vigor). Offspring of such crosses may in turn be bred selectively.

Whatever the means and ends of selective carp breeding, extreme care should be taken to maintain the purity of selected stocks. The very reproductive potential which makes the possibility of selective breeding so inviting enables one unwanted fish to destroy the results of years of careful breeding.

Hybridization among strains and subspecies has long played a part in genetic improvement of carp. With the development of artificial methods of spawning, interspecies hybridization is beginning to enter the picture. Most interspecific hybrids of the common carp are sterile, but this is not so disadvantageous as it might at first appear.

If adult carp are grown in a pond for a number of years, natural spawning may take place. Spawning retards growth and may result in the introduction of further generations of fish to compete for food with the original stock. Stocking with sterile fish of course eliminates this problem.

It should not be surprising to learn that the qualities most frequently selected for are those directly advantageous to the culturist, among them high fecundity, high viability, good food assimilation, and, in particular, rapid growth.

Mass selection for rapid growth has gone on for so many centuries that there is probably little potential for further improvement and such improvement as might occur could only be expressed under optimum conditions.

The tendency to rapid growth is linked with the strain known as mirror carp, which has only a few large, scattered scales. In Europe and Israel this is the most commonly cultured strain. It is relatively difficult to spawn, however. Recently young of a strain of blue carp (*Cyprinus carpio*, var. *cerulea*) developed in Poland have also shown more rapid growth than is normal for cultured carp.

One might expect heterosis to be expressed in higher growth rates of hybrids, and this is usually the case when geographically remote varieties and subspecies are crossed. Such hybrids are also commonly hardier and more viable than are pure strains.

Some interspecific hybrids, among them mud carp (*Cirrhinus molitorella*) *X Cyprinus carpio* may grow more rapidly than either parent. Carp X goldfish (*Carassius auratus*) is the only common carp hybrid which regularly occurs in nature, and is an exception to the general rule of sterility in hybrids. Backcrosses of carp X goldfish with either parent show somewhat better growth than the parent fish.

The hybrid of male common carp with female Prussian carp, *Carassius auratus gibelio* is known as the "Savinsk silver crucian" and is reported not only to grow faster than either parent but to mature one year earlier and to be highly disease resistant.

This hybrid has the added advantage of feeding almost exclusively on plankton. Hybrid carp are in general more disease resistant than are pure strains. Hybridization and selective breeding have also been used to increase hardiness relative to environmental factors.

Mention has already been made of Israeli efforts to develop a more salinity-tolerant carp. In the Soviet Union, cold resistance is of equal importance. Crossing European cultured carp (*Cypriuus carpio carpio*) with the wild Amur carp (*Cypriuuscarpio haematopterus*) of East Asia produced a cold-resistant variety known as the Kursk carp, which has made possible the extension of carp culture in the Soviet Union as far north as latitude 60°N.

Breeding for quality from the consumer's standpoint has lagged behind selection for characteristics advantageous to the producer. The heightlength ratio has long been accepted as an index of quality applicable by both consumer and producer.

Carp with a high height-length ratio supposedly grow faster and have better quality flesh. This belief has sparked the production of such breeds as the German *Aischgrund,* which exhibits height-length ratios as high as 1:2, compared to the 1:3 to 1:4 ratios typical of wild carp.

Recently, however, it has been shown that body conformation has nothing to do with growth rate and little if any connection with quality. Thus the only justification for continued selection on the basis of body conformation is on economic grounds: If a particular shape is more salable than others it is worth breeding for.

The efficacy of even this sort of breeding for shape is questionable, since environmental conditions exert such a profound influence on body conformation. Recent experiments carried out at the Max Planck Institute with the aim of selectively breeding carp without intermuscular bones (the small, often forked bones which make many fish, carp included, so annoying to eat) might indeed do the consumer a service as well as increasing the market value and salability of carp. The mirror carp has already been mentioned.

Two other varieties with reduced numbers of scales have been developed: the line carp, which has one row of scales along the lateral line, and the leather carp, which is almost devoid of scales. Selection for few scales has been rationalized on the basis that nearly scaleless carp are easier to prepare for the table, but this advantage is doubtful in a fish which has such large scales in any event.

Be that as it may, in Europe the "scaleless" varieties of carp are considered superior as food. All three varieties bring better prices than scaled carp, but most culturists concentrate on the mirror carp, which grows faster and is more viable than line or leather carp and, unlike them, breeds true.

Scaleless carp were not introduced to Asia until this century. Although they have not done well at low altitudes in the tropics, they have proven superior to the scaled varieties at high altitudes. The Asian consumer, however, is as prejudiced against mirror carp as his European counterpart is against scaled carp.

Before leaving the subject of selective breeding mention should be made of the fancy and colored varieties of carp which have been developed in China and Japan. Among the colors which have been produced are gold, lemon yellow, orange, rose pink, blue, dark green, and gray.

Colored carp are used mainly for decorative purposes, but in recent years some of these colors have been used as genetic markers in experimental carp breeding. Selection and hybridization for resistance to cold are not the only methods available for increasing carp production in temperate climates.

In the Soviet Union carp are reared in floating cages placed in cooling reservoirs of power stations. These reservoirs receive effluents 10 to 15°C warmer than neighboring natural waters. When mixed with river water, the resulting temperatures are often within the optimum range for growth of carp.

Even in midwinter the temperature of these reservoirs may be above 20°C. Before this practice was adopted, carp culture in floating cages was limited to the extreme south of the Soviet Union. Now it is practiced wherever thermal waters are available in central Russia. Yields compare favorably with, and in cold summers surpass, those achieved in ponds.

POLYCULTURE

Dramatic increases in yield of carp ponds frequently can be obtained through polyculture (rearing of several species together) to make more efficient use of the total pond environment. Chinese fish culturists, who use common carp as one of a complex of species, have developed this method to an art. (For details see Chapter anywhere else in this book on Chinese carp culture.)

Even when monoculture of common carp is intended, the culturist may find it advantageous to stock one of the Chinese species, the grass carp (*Ctenopharyngodon idellus*), if dense growth of weeds, which has been shown to adversely affect growth of common carp, becomes a problem.

Polyculture of carp is not as well developed in other parts of the world, but encouraging results have been obtained in the Soviet Union from raising common carp with *Cyprinus carpio X* crucian carp (*Carassius carassius*) hybrids, goldfish, bream (*Abramis brama*), and sterlet (*Acipenser ruthenus*).

In Yugoslavia carp are reared together with tench (*Tinca tinca*). Tench compete for food with carp, grow more slowly, and reach a much smaller size, thus although they bring a high price, the economic feasibility of culturing carp and tench together is doubtful.

Carp are commonly reared with roach (*Rutilus rutilus*) in France and experimental polyculture of carp with mullet and *Tilapia* is going on in Israel.

An aspect of polyculture that has developed chiefly in Europe is the use of predatory fish in conjunction with carp raised in ponds which support populations of trash fish or where "wild" spawning of carp takes place. The predators control the population of potential carp competitors and are eventually harvested with the carp.

The traditional fish for this purpose is the pike (*Esox lucius*). The rainbow trout (*Salmo gairdneri*), imported from America, has two advantages over the pike. Unlike the pike it inhabits the open waters of ponds as well as shorelines and weed beds, and it brings a better price than pike.

Use of rainbow trout in carp ponds is limited by oxygen supply; they require at least 5.6 ppm of dissolved O_2. Russian fish culturists report 25% increases in carp yield through use of another American predator, the largemouth bass (*Micropterus salmoides*), which like the pike is a shoreline dweller.

Among the native European fish that have been more or less

successfully used as predators in carp ponds are common whitefish (*Coregonus lavaretus*), peled (*Coregonus peled*), brown trout (*Salmo trutta*), English perch (*Perca fluviatilis*), and pike-perch (*Lucioperca lucioperca*).

YIELDS OF COMMON CARP CULTURE

Most of the techniques thus far discussed have been developed for the purpose of realizing the carp culturist's primary goal, a high yield of carp per unit area of water. Just what constitutes a high yield varies with locality and type of culture. Table elsewhere in this chapter lists actual yields achieved by various culture methods in various countries.

HARVESTING

Carp are harvested by draining the growing pond or by use of a seine or cast net. Cast nets are preferred for harvesting small quantities of fish, since they can be operated by one man. Seining requires additional labor and, if the pond to be seined is large, the use of a small boat. Size at harvest varies according to local custom.

In Indonesia, carp as small as 0.08 to 0.15 kg are not only accepted but preferred for table use. On the other hand, in most European countries 1.2 kg is considered near the minimum marketable size.

In general, Asian consumers will accept smaller fish than Europeans, but the carp culturist should ascertain local preference before scheduling for harvest.

It is good practice to periodically harvest the largest, fastest growing fish in production ponds. This not only gives the culturist a constant source of income but serves to thin out the stock, thus improving the conditions of growth for stock remaining in the pond. Seines are preferred to cast nets for this purpose, since it is easier to sort fish in a seine.

TRANSPORT AND MARKETING

In Asia carp usually are sold live and may pass directly from producer to consumer. Iced or dried carp also are sold, but live fish bring a higher price, particularly in tropical areas, where preservation is a problem. Marketing may consist simply of displaying the fish in cages placed in the growing pond or in small, shallow ponds nearby.

Where it is necessary to transport the fish to market tanks mounted on vehicles are used. Although carp are not as resistant to crowding

Table 8.11: Yields of common carp culture in various countries.

Country or area	*Culture method*	*Yield (Kg/Ha)*
Czechoslovakia	Growth in ponds with ducks	500
Europe	Natural growth in ponds	25-400
	Growth in ponds with feeding	100-400
	Intensive culture in ponds	1,500
West Germany	Growth in sewage treatment ponds, without feeding	500-900
Guatemala	Intensive culture in ponds	4,000
Haiti	Government hatcheries	2,300+
	Farm ponds (subsistence culture), usually without feeding	550
India	Natural growth in ponds	400
	Growth in ponds with management	1,500
Indonesia	Intensive culture in ponds	1,500
	Growth in cages in polluted streams without feeding	500,000-750,000
Israel	Intensive pond culture of mirror	1,500 carp
Japan	Growth in irrigation ponds (low fertility)	76
	Growth in irrigation ponds (medium fertility)	180
	Growth in irrigation ponds (high fertility)	490
	Growth in irrigation ponds with very heavy feeding	5,000
	Intensive culture in ponds	5,000
	Growth in running water ponds or streams	400,000-2,000,000 (depends on velocity of water)
	Growth in rice fields	700-1,200
	Rearing in floating cages	4,000
	Rearing in closed recirculating systems	4,000,000

(Table 8.11 Contd.)

(Table 8.11 Contd.)

Country or area	***Culture method***	***Yield (Kg/Ha)***
Nigeria	Commercial culture with fertilization and feeding	371-1,834
Philippines	Intensive culture in stagnant	5,500 ponds
	Intensive culture in running water ponds, with heavy feeding	80,000
Poland	Growth in sewage treatment without feeding	1,300 ponds,
U.A.R.	Experimental culture in ponds, feeding	2,500 with
United States (Alabama)	Intensive pond culture with inorganic fertilization, without feeding	314
	Intensive pond culture with inorganic fertilization and feeding (not economically feasible)	784-1,930
U.S.S.R.	Growth in rice fields (Ukraine)	150-200
U.S.S.R.	Experimental culture in ponds in peat hags (unfertilized)	50
	Experimental culture in ponds in peat hags (fertilized)	250-300
	Pond culture on collective farms	200-500
Yugoslavia	Culture in ponds, without fertilization	780
	Culture in ponds, with manure added	1,500-2,000

as certain Asian fish which have accessory breathing organs, they are hardier than most fish and may be transported in closed containers under semicrowded conditions.

In Israel it is recommended that adult carp be shipped in tank trucks in a 1:1 ratio of carp to water. Up to four times as much water may be required at high temperatures. If crowding in transport is necessary, aeration by means of a pump or oxygen cylinder is advisable. In regions which have extensive inland waterway systems, oxygen problems are solved by transporting carp in streamline shaped cages suspended over the side of boats, thus providing a constant exchange of water as long as the boat is in motion.

At the market, carp are usually kept in cement cisterns about I m deep, which may be supplied with a crude running water system. A 3-m X 2-m cistern with running water is satisfactory for up to 300 kg of carp.

If the fish are to remain in the cistern for more than one day, they should be fed. Thus maintained in clear water and fed regularly, they soon lose any "muddy" taste acquired in pond life. Some carp are sold live wherever carp are caught or cultured for human consumption, but in Europe there is a greater market for processed carp.

The oldest method of preservation is to salt the fish and dry them in air. Dried fish is often sold as a snack, to be eaten without cooking. Carp is also sold as fresh or frozen whole fish or fillets or in cans. In the case of canned fish, the producer usually sells to a processor rather than to a retailer or consumer.

Carp destined for canning may be cut up and processed as is, in which case it requires cooking before eating, or it may be fried or smoked prior to canning. A common canned fish product is gefilte fish, favored by Jewish people throughout the world.

The preferred fish for this dish is whitefish (*Coregonus spp.*), but as stocks of whitefish have become depleted in many countries, carp has increasingly been used for this purpose.

PROBLEMS OF COMMON CARP CULTURE

Diseases and Parasites

We would be remiss in our discussion of culture of the common carp if we did not mention some of the problems the culturist may encounter. Some problems have already been discussed, including methods of compensating for a sterile environment and means of controlling or eliminating predators, competitors, excess plants, and *Saprolegnia* on eggs.

The carp culturist should also be prepared to cope with a number of diseases and parasites of carp. Among the disease and parasites afflicting carp are *Argulus*, ascites disease, bothriocephalosis, caryophyllosis, chilodonellosis, coccidiosis and coccidiosal enteritis, dactylogyrosis, *Ichthyophthirius* (sometimes known as "Ich"), infectious air bladder disease, infectious dropsy or red spot disease, infectious gill necrosis, philoin etrosis. *Prymnesium,* and sanguinicolosis. Some of these are curable and most are susceptible to treatment to prevent their spread.

The carp culturist wishing to provide an ounce of prevention will do well to use disease-resistant strains of fish if they are available, drain ponds which are not in use, maintain good water circulation, handle all carp carefully so as to avoid injury, avoid unnecessary mixing of stock or introduction of wild stock, feed an adequate diet, and to do whatever else is conducive to keeping the stock in good condition. In some instances eradication of specific disease hosts may also be undertaken as a preventive measure.

Socioeconomic Problems

The feasibility of carp culture in some regions, particularly the United States and Canada, is reduced by the presence of a complex of attitudes only partially attributable to the carp. Carp were introduced to the United States in 1877 attended by a great brouhaha of publicity anent their value as food fish.

About that time, high-ranking fishery officials went so far as to suggest that the carp was so desirable that it might be advisable to eradicate some "undesirable" native species, for example, the largemouth bass and the northern pike.

The apostles of the carp seem not to have considered the differences between American and European conditions. In North America human population density was low compared to Europe, land was plentiful, and farming of mammalian and avian stock, together with freshwater and saltwater fisheries, provided for a supply of protein far more abundant than that of any European country.

There was simply no incentive for the intensive culture of carp. The enthusiasm accorded the first introductions soon waned, and in 1896 the U.S. Fish Commission ceased to import, distribute, and stock carp.

But the carp had gained a foothold. Escapees from private ponds populated those waters where carp had not been deliberately introduced. Today *Cyprinus carpio* inhabits 46 of the 50 states of the United States as well as the more southerly portions of Canada.

Left to fend for themselves, they quickly reverted to the wild strain without a thought for the labors of the European fish culturists who had painstakingly developed the breed. Carp caught in North America are usually scaly, extremely bony, coarse-textured fish with a poor height-length ratio. Sport fishermen, who comprise a much larger segment of the population in the United States and Canada than in Europe, found these fish a far less attractive quarry than the native game fish.

Neither did they appreciate the table qualities of the wild carp. As the human population grew, attendant pollution, siltation, and overfishing decimated game fish stocks while the carp thrived.

Anglers had noted the carp's habit of raising small clouds of mud while industriously rooting in the botton and in short order the nuisance became a villain, accused of increasing turbidity, destroying aquatic vegetation, and preying on the spawn of game fish.

With the designation of the carp as the scapegoat for the sins of man in the decline of sport fisheries its rejection was complete. Price and prejudice went hand in hand, so that today in North America carp bring only a third the price of such comparable "rough" fish as buffalo fish.

Some carp are marketed by commercial fishermen, but sales are virtually limited to the poorest members of society. With the continued eutrophication of American waters and the predicted narrowing of the gap between protein supply and demand, sport and commercial fishermen, fish culturists, and housewives may all have to reconsider the carp. For the present, however, carp are scarcely considered edible in North America and their culture is not economically feasible.

PREREQUISITES FOR SUCCESSFUL CULTURE OF COMMON CARP

The common carp remains the easiest of all fish to culture intensively. For this and other reasons it is also one of the best fishes for culture in many countries. Commercial culture of carp is likely to be feasible if the following conditions are met:

1. There must be a market for carp. This may be a mass market, as in countries where carp are traditionally eaten, or a specialty market, as in Guatemala where a small European population sustains a successful carp culture enterprise.
2. There must be an economical means of getting live or iced carp to market or a suitable means of preservation for shipping.
3. The carp culturist must begin with stock which is both adapted to culturists all over the world, particularly in the Soviet Union, Poland, $ungary, West Germany, Yugoslavia, Israel,

Japan, mainland China, and southeast Asia, strive to improve their techniques. For the foreseeable future the common carp will continue to he one of the chief suppliers of fish protein to man and an increasing proportion of that protein will come from intensively cultured carp local conditions and suited to regional tastes in such matters as size and scaliness.

4. There must be adequate space for ponds. While it is possible raise some carp in a single pond, the competitive advantage goes culturists who use a number of ponds, each designed for a particid purpose.

   Ideally there should be a separate pond or ponds for spawnin;, hatching, nursing, rearing, growing, and holding male and female brood stock.

5. There must be an adequate supply of reasonably warm water. If water is scarce, a recirculating system may solve the problem, but such systems require a very large initial investment of money.
6. Ponds used in carp culture either must be naturally fertile or then: must be an economical means of fertilizing them.
7. Unless the waters to be used are extremely fertile, carp feed mus; be available at a reasonable price.
8. There must be an adequate supply of labor available at moderate cost. If induced spawning or a recirculating system is to be used, cut ployees must have some technical training. Otherwise unskilled labor will do.
9. Sufficient capital must be available to meet the initial expenses for stock, feed, equipment, and so on.

COMMON CARP IN SUBSISTENCE AQUACULTURE

Most of the foregoing conditions assume that the carp are to be sold. Carp also play a role in subsistence aquaculture, for which all that is absolutely necessary is a source of stock and a fertile body of water where they may be held and harvested.

Today subsistence aquaculture is being promoted chiefly in Africa and Latin America. *Tilapia* spp. are the fish most frequently advocated, but in Haiti carp is used. Government hatcheries do the actual culturing, attaining yields of 2300 kg/ha and more.

Young carp are distributed to small farmers who stock them in ponds, usually less than 100 m^2 and 50 cm to 1 m deep, then simply wait until they reach harvestable size. Without feeding, this takes 7 to 9 months. It would appear that a considerable local enhancement of protein supply is achieved in this manner.

9

CULTURE OF THE INDIAN CARPS

It has become a cliche that the people of India need protein. Even the most socially unaware persons have some grasp of the magnitude of India's problem. One can cite statistics *ad infinitum* to demonstrate that India is in a steadily worsening state of nutritional crisis, but however one defines the problem, it is clear that the solution, if there is ever to be one, will not come as any single panacea, but from effective population control coupled with increased and more efficient protein production by many means, including fish culture.

Fish culture shows promise in India, for there is a considerable demand for fish (total landings of fish in 1965 amounted to 1331 thousand metric tons), a number of native fish well suited to culture, a tradition of fish culture, and a great abundance of cultivable waters (an estimated 7,307,642 ha of fresh and brackish water).

The potential for fish culture in India has not gone unnoticed, and according to R. V. Pantulu, formerly of the Indian Fresh Water Fisheries Research Institute at Barrackpore, fish culture operations in India have increased sevenfold to eightfold during the last decade.

Yet large areas of potentially rich waters still lie fallow and, technologically, Indian fish culture lags behind much of the world. Though brackish water culture is practiced in some areas, notably the states of West Bengal and Kerala, freshwater culture is better developed and will probably remain more important.

Freshwater fish culture is favored not only by the availability of suitable waters and fish, but by the strong preference for fresh fish in most parts of the country, which permits locally raised freshwater fish to compete favorably with saltwater fish in inland areas.

As elsewhere in Asia, the most commonly cultured fish in India and Pakistan are members of the carp family (Cyprinidae). Indian cyprinids used in fish culture are popularly separated into two groups: the most desirable species are referred to as major carps; the smaller, less desirable species are called minor carps.

The minor carps persist in Indian fish culture largely because as fry they are extremely difficult to distinguish from the major carps, and are thus unintentionally stocked. Minor carps may also be deliberately stocked when stocks of major carps are scarce.

In the south of India, in the states of Madras and Mysore, a third group, the Cauvery carps, largely supplant the major carps. Indian carps have not yet become as popular for introduction and culture outside their native habitat as the common carp (*Cyprinus carpio*) or the Chinese carps, but the catla (*Catla catla*) has been introduced to Ceylon, experimentally cultured in Israel and the United States, and commercially raised in Malaysia. All the Indian major carps have been recommended for use in the Philippines.

ECOLOGICAL NICHES OF THE INDIAN CARPS

The Major Carps

The major carps comprise the catla, the rohu (*Labeo rohita*), and the mrigal (*Cirrhinus mrigala*). Some authorities also include the calbasu (*Labeo calbasu*). These three or four species are often grown in polyculture, though their ecological niches are by no means as distinct and well defined as those of the Chinese carps, nor is Indian polyculture nearly as sophisticated as the ancient Chinese practice.

In general, the catla feeds on plankton and decayed macrovegetation on the surface and throughout the water column, the rohu is a column feeder on decayed vegetation with a taste for higher plants, the mrigal a bottom-feeding herbivore, and the calbasu a benthic omnivore.

Certain of the Chinese carps have been experimentally included in Indian carp polyculture systems and in the future further combinations of Indian carps, Chinese carps, and other fish may be expected in both experimental and practical culture.

The Cauvery Carps

The niches of the Cauvery carps overlap; thus polyculture of these three species could probably be enhanced by introduction of other species. The species association for fish culture in southern India has already been diversified by the introduction of catla.

The catla joins the fringelipped carp (*Labeo fimbriatus*), which consumes mostly filamentous algae and some zooplankton; the white carp (*Cirrhinus cirrhosa*), a plankton feeder with a preference for zooplankton, and the Cauvery carp (*Labeo kontius*), which competes with the fringe-lipped carp for filamentous algae, but also eats pieces of plants and detritus.

The Minor Carps

Minor carps present in fish ponds vary from region to region. Among those commonly found in one or another part of India are the reba (*Cirrhinus reba*), which feeds largely on phytoplankton and decayed plants; the nagendram fish (*Osteochilus thomassi*), a benthic and marginal feeder on filamentous algae and diatoms; and the sandkhol carp (*Thynnichthys sandkhol*), which consumes mostly phytoplankton plus some zooplankton; also the bata (*Labeo bata*), the carnatic carp (*Barb us carnaticus*), *Barb us chola, Labeo boga, Labeo dyoechilus, Labeo gonius, Labeo nandina,* and *Barb us sarana*.

One more Indian cyprinid should be mentioned: the omnivorous copper mahseer (*Barbus hexagonolepis*). Not exactly a "minor" carp, the copper mahseer attains a maximum length of 90 cm. It is cultured in some parts of India but is not included in the traditional Indian poly cultural scheme.

SPAWNING THE INDIAN CARPS

For many years a major obstacle to the development of culture of the Indian carps has been the inability of culturists to consistently breed them in captivity. All species spawn naturally in rivers and will not reproduce in standing water, although the major carps may be spawned in specially constructed reservoirs, or bunds, where there is enough current to approximate river conditions.

The copper mahseer will also spawn in running water ponds provided the temperature is about 20°C, or ripe fish may be hand stripped and the eggs fertilized artificially. Little or no effort has been expended on hand stripping or reservoir spawning of the Cauvery carps or minor carps.

Bund Spawning

The technique of bund spawning can be applied only where the drainage from an extensive catchment area can be accumulated in a natural depression. The low end of such a depression is blocked off by a strong embankment, so that during the rainy season intermittent streams will inundate the depression.

Or a dam may be built in the uplands to concentrate runoff in one place, from which it is channeled into the bund. During the dry season a minimum of 1.5 m of water is maintained in a pool perhaps 3000 m^2 in area, which is stocked with catla, rohu, mrigal, and calbasu in a 4:2:1:1 ratio at a sex ratio of 2 males per female; males may be distinguished by the rough dorsal surface of the pectoral fin.

The exact number of fish stocked depends on the extent of the spawning area; about 1 fish per 15 m2 is appropriate. The pool is usually fished just before the start of the monsoon, and the numbers of each species and sex estimated, so that losses can be rectified by stocking.

The spawning area is a flat piece of land on which grass is grown during the dry season so that the water will not be easily muddied when it is flooded. It may comprise the entire bund other than the permanent pool, or it may be just one corner of the bund.

When the rains come and flood the spawning ground an outlet channel in the embankment is opened up so that water circulates through the bund. The breeders then move out of the pool and begin chasing in the shallow areas. Spawning usually occurs at night during the full moon or new moon.

When spawning is completed, the eggs are collected by dragging seines, about 4 m long × 1.5 m deep, made of mosquito netting, over the spawning ground. Unfortunately a large percentage of the eggs is often destroyed by being trampled by the fishermen.

The eggs are placed in spawning pits dug as near as possible to the bund and supplied with bund water. These pits may be 1 to 1.3 m long, 0.6 m wide, and 0.3 m deep and accommodate from 100,000 to 300,000 eggs. When the inlet to the pit is closed, the water temperature rises rapidly, accelerating hatching time to 12 to 18 hours, instead of the 36 hours that might be required at lower temperatures.

The rate of hatching in these pits is low due to bacterial decay and lack of aeration in the stagnant water. Some improvement may be effected by suspending a hatching net or "hapa" in a hatching pit. The hapa is rectangular in shape and constructed as a net within a net.

The eggs are placed in the inner net, which is made of material just fine enough to hold them. The newly hatched larvae pass through into the outer net of fine cloth and are nursed there until they are 4 to 5 days old, by which time they have become fry.

Artificially Induced Spawning

As mentioned, the technique of bund spawning may be used only in areas where the topography permits. Induced spawning with the aid of pituitary injections is more generally applicable. The first attempts to apply this technique to the Indian carps were made in 1956, but it is only in the last five or six years that consistent success has been achieved.

Today all four major carps and a number of other Indian cyprinids are bred in this manner. Success has been found to hinge on the quality of pituitary glands used and the correct dosage. Pituitaries used in induction should be taken from fully mature, ripe, or freshly spawned fish of the same species as the fish being spawned, or a very closely related species.

Dosage is variable, depending on the stage of maturity of the breeders. Since best results are obtained only with fully mature fish, only dosages for such fish will be described.

Breeders are usually selected from 1.5- to 5.0-kg, 2- to 4-year-old fish stocked in spawning ponds a few months prior to the breeding season, which usually coincides with the southwest monsoon, then segregated at maturity.

Maturity of males is easily determined; fully mature specimens ooze milt when the abdomen is gently pressed. Selection of females is more difficult, but fish with soft, rounded, bulging abdomens and swollen, reddish vents are preferred. A catheter may also be used to assess ripeness.

Intramuscular injections are made on the caudal peduncle or near the shoulder region. Females are injected two or three times, while males receive only one injection. The first injection, of females only, consists of 2 to 3 mg of pituitary extract/kg of body weight, after which the sexes remain separated for 6 more hours.

Then males are given a dose equal to the first injection administered to females, while the females receive a second dose of 5 to 8 mg/kg. Following this injection, the fish are placed together in groups of three (two males and one female) in covered breeding hapas, 1.6 to 6.5 m^2 in surface area and 0.9 m deep, fixed on bamboo poles in the marginal waters of ponds.

Spawning ordinarily takes place within 3 to 6 hours, but if after 10 to 12 hours no spawning occurs, females only are given a third, slightly higher dosage of pituitary extract. If the water temperature is near optimum (about 27°C for most species), 60 to 100%, success may be expected by this method.

Once the eggs have hardened, 8 to 10 hours after spawning, they are transferred, in batches of 75,000 to 1,000,000, to 1.6-m², 0.9-m deep hatching hapas set in marginal waters of ponds, where they hatch in 15 to 18 hours at 27 to 31°C. Spawners may be sacrificed to obtain their pituitary glands.

As induced spawning of cyprinids becomes more prevalent in India, selective breeding and hybridization of Indian carps can assume greater importance. Experimental hybridization of Indian carps with each other and with Chinese carps has already been done, but the resulting offspring have for the most part been unpromising if not incapable of survival.

One exception is the hybrid catla × rohu, which combines the wide body of the catla with the small head of the rohu. These traits would give it an advantage at the market wherever consumers do not eat tip head of the fish, while at the same time effectively giving the consume; more nourishment for his money. The catla × rohu hybrid is fertile and has produced a healthy F_2 generation.

Despite recent improvements in induced spawning methods, the main source of stock for culture in India and Pakistan continues to be collections of eggs, larvae, fry, and fingerlings taken from rivers.

COLLECTION OF EGGS, LARVAE, FRY, AND FINGERLINGS

Collection and Hatching of Eggs

Eggs are collected only from the Halda River in the Chittagong area of Bangladesh. Drifting fertilized eggs are captured 12 to 14 hours after spawning, which generally takes place within 3 weeks before or after each full moon from April through July. The precise time of peak spawning is determined by test collections at the start of the season.

The number of eggs caught in these collections enables the collectors to forecast the peak of spawning so that they can fish about that time or shortly after, when the maximum number of eggs is available.

The net used in egg collecting is simple, consisting of no more than a rectangular piece of mosquito netting 11 to 12 m long and 2.7 m wide with a bamboo pole attached at each end. Such nets are usually operated by two men in a boat stationed at right angles to the current, but they may also be moored in the river or used by men wading.

Captured eggs may be placed in a compartment of the collecting boat for some time, even up to hatching, but this results in high mortality due to congestion and inadequate aeration.

Better methods of holding and hatching eggs involve nets suspended from a bamboo framework. bamboo baskets lined with fine cloth and suspended in the river, or hatching pits dug in the river bank and supplied with water through a system of pipes.

Suspended nets are more often used as a temporary device to accommodate the eggs immediately upon collection, after which the eggs are transferred to pits or baskets, which are believed to produce healthier larvae.

A typical hatching pit was 448 cm long × 244 cm wide × 46 cm deep and could accommodate 120 to 300 kg of eggs (900,000 to 2,200,000 eggs). The hatching rate in all these traditional devices is usually 25 to *50%*. Somewhat better results may be obtained using hatching pits in conjunction with the double net device already described in connection with bund spawning.

Collection and Transport of Larvae and Fry

The most commonly collected life stages of the Indian carps are the larvae and fry, which are taken at various times of year, depending on the locality. Favored locations for fry collection are along gently sloping banks of rivers where the current is not too strong and at the mouths of small creeks.

In such locations special fry-collecting nets are fixed in 1 to 3 m deep water. These nets are funnel shaped, tapering from 2.5 to 3.5 m wide at the mouth to 20 to 25 cm at the cod end, which is kept open by means of a ring. Two lateral wings may be attached at the mouth so as to cover a wide area.

A detachable tail piece, or "gamcha," shaped like a monk's hood, is attached at the cod end. The gamcha may be 1 to 2 m long and 40 to 100 cm wide at the rear end. These and other dimensions of fry nets vary widely according to local need.

Equally variable is the mesh of the net, which may be of mosquito netting or nearly any available cloth. Experiments conducted by the Allahabad Substation of the Central Inland Fisheries Research Institute have shown that 0.3 cm. netting is much more effective than the materials in general use.

Finer netting may be called for where there is a fast current and low turbidity. Fry nets are anchored in the stream bottom by bamboo poles, two each at the mouth and middle of the net, and one at the tail.

Usually a battery of 15 to 25 nets, owned and operated by a group of 7 to 12 fishermen, is placed at each collection site.

While the nets are in use two fishermen in a boat move from net to net emptying the gamchas every ½ to 1 hour or as often as is necessary to prevent crowding of the catch. Captured fry and larvae are passed through a wire or bamboo sieve to separate them from debris, then transported in large earthen basins to rectangular cloth live wells about 2 m long × 1.25 m wide × 0.7 m deep anchored in the river so that the top is just above the water level.

The average daily catch from one fry net may be from 300,000 to 750,000 fry and larvae. The next step is transportation of the fry to market at one of the larger cities where they are sold to owners of nurseries for raising to fingerling size.

The classical container for transport is an open earthen vessel of variable size, called a "hundi." The density of fry in a hundi varies according to the time to be spent in transit.

However many fry are to be transported, it is advisable that the water in the hundies be kept constantly agitated. Manual agitation is sometimes necessary, as when fry are shipped by rail and the train is stopped in a station. Oxygen depletion is further prevented by the addition of 50 to 100 g of colloidal earth to each hundi.

It has been suggested that the colloidal earth serves as a buffer to maintain proper pH, but its principal function is to attract and concentrate in the bottom sludge dead fry and other potential sources of organic pollutants.

In recent years a variety of more sophisticated transport containers

Table 9.1: Numbers of Indian carp fry recommended for transport in earthen hundies of 27.3 liter capacity.

Length of fry (mm)	*No. per Hundi*	*Maximum Duration of Transport (Hours)*	*Percentage of mortality*
12-19	1,500	24	2-5
	1,200	36	2-5
19-25	1,000	20	2-5
	800	30	2-5
25-51	500-800	24	10.0
51-77	200	8	10.0

made of metal or plastic and equipped with circulating pumps, aerating devices, or a supply of oxygen have started to supplant the earthen hundi, but many fry are still shipped with no means of oxygenation other than agitation of the water by hand or by the motion of the transport conveyance.

Table 9.2: Numbers of Indian carp fry recommended for transport in closed 22.7-liter metal containers with and without oxygenation.

initial dissolved oxygen content (PPM)	*size of fry to be transported (MM)*	*no. of fry to be put in each container*	*Approximate safe period during which transport can be effected (Min)*
4	6—7	50,000	19
4	6—7	30,000	31
4	6—7	20,000	47
4	15—20	1,000	40
4	15—20	500	80
4	30	300	120
4	30	150	240
5	6—7	50,000	25
5	6—7	30,000	42
5	6—7	20,000	62
5	15—20	1,000	60
5	15—20	500	120
5	30	300	165
5	30	150	330
6	6—7	50,000	31
6	6—7	30,000	51
6	6—7	20,000	77
6	15—20	1,000	75
6	15—20	500	150
6	30	300	207
6	30	150	414
oxygenated	12—20	1,000—1,25	12 hours
oxygenated	39—51	500	24 hours
oxygenated	25—32	400	16 hours

Even without supplementary oxygenation, metal containers are sometimes preferred to hundis since there is no danger of breakage. The number of fry which can be transported in closed metal containers with and without oxygen is shown in Table anywhere else in this chapter.

As a more general rule of thumb in transporting Indian carp fry, the minimum volume of water per fish has been estimated for different sizes of fry. On arrival at the market the fry are transferred to 70- to 90-liter earthen pots, or "galmas," each containing 150 to 200 g of colloidal earth. After 10 to 15 min, the colloidal earth is removed and with it the dead larvae and fry.

Young fry sold at market are usually a mixture of major and minor carps, for no method of fry sorting comparable to that used for Chinese carps has been developed for Indian carps, although numerous attempts have been made.

Catla can be separated from other species with fair success by 'placing the mixed fry in a tall, narrow container and allowing the oxygen supply to become severely depleted, at which point the catla come to the surface and most of them can be skimmed off, but the other species do not sort themselves out as the Chinese carps do.

About all that can be done otherwise is to separate and discard young predatory fish, most of which are slightly larger than the carp fry, by sieving. Visual identification of advanced fry is possible but excessively tedious.

Collection and Conditiong of Fingerlings

Fingerlings as well as fry of catla, carnatic carp, and Cauvery carps are collected in Madras and certain parts of East Bengal, Delhi, and Uttar Pradesh. Fingerlings are collected from back waters of rivers, paddy fields, irrigation channels, tanks, and so on, which they enter

Table 9.3: Minimum volume of water required during transport by Indian carp fry of different size groups.

Length of Fry (cm)	*Minimum Water Av. Wt. of Fry (g)*	*volume required per Fry (cc)*
4—7	1.91	25
3—5	0.92	15
2—4	0.35	8
2—4	0.25	7
1—2	0.076	2

from large rivers. In such confined waters they may be captured with seines, dip nets, cast nets, or, in Madras, with special rectangular basket traps made of palmyra roots, called "mavulu."

These traps, 1.2 m long, 30.5 cm wide, and 0.9 to 1.2 m high, are placed in gaps in dams constructed across channels for the express purpose of obstructing the movements of young fish. A number of holes about 15 cm in diameter are located along the side of the mavulu near the bottom.

Fish enter the holes and swim into the trap but find it very difficult to leave due to inwardly narrowing funnel-shaped structures connected to each hole. In parts of Andhra Pradesh state, similar traps are used to collect fingerlings of catla, mrigal, and fringe-lipped carp from irrigated paddy fields.

Fry of these species enter paddy fields naturally in June and July and are allowed to grow there until September or October, when they are trapped. In the Cauvery River delta Indian carp fingerlings are captured by regulating the flow of water through irrigation sluices. Fingerlings congregate below the sluices and are stranded when the sluice gates are closed.

This operation is carried out at intervals of about 4 hours and the stranded fingerlings easily captured by seining. Since by the fingerling stage Indian carps have acquired adult specific characters, they are easily sorted visually. If the fingerlings are to be stocked nearby, they may be transported in jars and stocked immediately, but if the rearing ponds are distant, it is considered advisable to "condition" them so as to eliminate all food and excreta in the gut.

If fingerlings are transported in crowded containers without conditioning, feces and vomited remnants of food may severely pollute the water. Conditioning basically involves nothing more than starvation for 48 to 72 hours, although it may also help accustom the fish to crowded conditions.

Rapid elimination of food and feces may be achieved by placing the fingerlings in a net basket fixed in a pond, they splashing water on them from all sides, which frightens them so that the% pass excreta and vomit immediately. No analysis has been made of the stress factor induced by this practice.

It has been suggested that some feeding with animalcules such as cladocerans may be preferable to total starvation in both conditioning and transport.

Practically any container with mesh or perforated sides which can be placed in a pond or stream may be used for conditioning. Conditioning containers should be kept in a shaded area to protect the fingerlings from sudden changes in temperature; an optimum temperature for conditioning is considered to be between 26 and 29°C.

Conditioning containers should not be placed where the water will be muddied by the activities of fishermen.

NURSERY PONDS

Preparation and Stocking

Captured and conditioned fingerlings may be placed directly into growing ponds to fatten them for consumption or stocked in rearing ponds for further intensive care. Fry, however, must be nursed for 12 to 15 days to insure their health and satisfactory growth.

Both seasonal and perennial ponds, ranging from 7 m^2 to 0.5 ha in area and 0.9 to 3.6 m deep, are used as nurseries. Sample stocking rates for nursing ponds are shown in Table elsewhere in this chapter. Perennial ponds have the serious disadvantage of harboring a host of predators, parasites, and competitors of carp fry, which seldom can be entirely eliminated.

For this reason, in stocking perennial ponds it is best to scatter the fish, rather than dumping them all in at once. Stocking at night is also advisable, since most fry predators feed visually and the fry are especially vulnerable to predation during the period of acclimatization to a new environment. Temporary ponds are somewhat better, but the ideal is a pond which can be drained at the discretion of the culturist.

In the relatively few modernized nursery units in India, the ponds are drained and sun-dried before use, the bottom is plowed, and a short-season crop of leguminous plants is grown as a source of nitrogen for the soil. After harvesting the legume crop, the plants are plowed under and the bottom is levelled.

Further fertilization may be carried out using various kinds of manure or refuse, mixed with oil cake, applied at 200 to 325 kg/ha before the pond is filled. Vegetable manures are usually applied in heaps, weighted down with stones rather than scattered about the pond, so as to reduce the danger of widespread deoxygenation.

Animal manure is placed in bags or baskets for the same reason. Dilute sewage is used as a fertilizer in some areas, notably in the Bidyadhuri Spill in Calcutta. In using sew age, care should be taken that the dissolved oxygen concentration in the pond does not drop below 3 ppm. Inorganic fertilizers, though too expensive for use by many culturists, have been used on an experimental basis.

Table 9.4: Sample stocking rates of Indian carps in Nursery ponds.

Type and/or area of pond	*Approximate stage and/ or size*	*number per ha or water surface*	*Duration of rearing (Days)*
Shallow, seasonal nurseries, 91-152 cm deep, 1,524 cm × 1,524 cm or 1,828.8 cm × 914 cm in with a depth of over 30 cm	Fry up to 8.5 mm	741,300-1,235,500, depending on density of plankton available as food area, and paddy fields	15-30
Seasonal nurseries 1,524-1,828 cm × 914-1,219 cm × 91-122 cm	Fry up to 8.5 mm	1,235,500-1,976,800	15
Seasonal, shallow nurseries 1,524 cm × 1,524 cm in size and 91-122 cm depth	Fry few hours to 3 days old	222,390 without feeding, 1,235,500 with artificial feeding	15
0.62 ha in size	—	—	30
Seasonal nurseries, 0.9 1.5 In deep, 2.4 × 3 In in size, or perennial ponds 1.8-3.6 m deep and 0.5 ha in area	Fry	7,812,500	12-15
Cement cisterns	Fry up to 19-25 mm	8,401,400 without artificial feeding (must be thinned after 10 days)	—

They would appear to be especially promising for use in arid areas, where organic manures are relatively scarce and more appropriately used as a source of humus for the soil. Unfortunately, most of the research on inorganic pond fertilization in India has involved use of the N-P-K mixtures, with little testing of the individual elements.

Use of N-P-K mixtures may be wasteful, as limnological data from many parts of India show an abundance of potassium. The nitrogen-fixing bluegreen algae so prevalent in Indian fish ponds, along with the occasional practice of growing legumes in dry ponds, may make the addition of nitrogen superfluous as well.

There is some experimental evidence that phosphates alone are as effective as or better than N-P-K mixtures in many situations, but the lack of adequate controls in this research leaves room for doubt. In parts of Bangladesh a 3:1 mixture of cow dung and superphosphate is applied to ponds at 555 kg/(ha)(year).

Clearly, pond fertilization practices in India and Pakistan can be improved, through research and by greater appreciation of the fact that the waters of the region vary widely in chemical characteristics, so that each body should be treated individually rather than according to some custom or general formula.

If the soil is acid, it may also be necessary before filling to treat the pond with lime until a pH of 8 or 9 is reached. Large perennial ponds are generally acid, but 300 to 500 kg/ha of lime is usually sufficient to correct this situation.

In ponds which cannot be drained and dried, pest control is a major preoccupation of the culturist. Predators include fish such as the snakeheads (*Ophicephalus spp.*), frogs, several varieties of insect, and aquatic birds. Competitors of the carp fry include many species of small, commercially undesirable fish as well as tadpoles.

Fishing is usually inadequate to control predator and competitor fish, and poisoning must often be relied on. A number of pesticides of plant origin are used, but the most common is derris root powder. Applied at 4 to 6 ppm, it eliminates virtually all fish as well as killing some aquatic insects and tadpoles.

Larger doses may be more effective, but the prescribed dosage is preferred since it initially only stuns the fish, and edible predators can be salvaged by quickly transferring them to clear water. Further control of insects can be achieved by applying an emulsion of 56 kg of mustard or coconut oil and 18 kg of washing soap per hectare.

These poisons lose their effectiveness within 2 to 12 days of application, at which time manuring or stocking may be initiated. Ducks and geese must be fenced out of nursery ponds.

Weeds may also cause a problem by competing for nutrients with plankton and by providing hiding places for predators. Manual or mechanical removal is preferable to chemical control, but the possibility of ecological control, using shading or herbivorous fishes, should be considered. A lengthier treatment of weed control methods follows in the discussion of growing ponds.

Fertilization of Nursery Ponds and Supplementary Feeding of Fry

The fry remain in the nursery 12 to 15 days and are not ordinarily fed, since plankton produced by fertilization is adequate for growth. It has been customary to stock nurseries when the water turns bottle green, indicating a heavy growth of phytoplankton. Inorganic fertilizers are particularly effective in producing this condition.

Recent research, however, has shown that early fry of the major carps prefer zooplankton. Application of fresh or partially dried cow dung at about 11,000 to 16,000 kg/ha will, after about 10 days, produce a vigorous growth of zooplankton lasting 7 to 10 days. Heavier doses are actually less effective in producing zooplankton.

This sort of manuring should be carried out before stocking. If the initial dose does not produce an adequate amount of zooplankton, treatment may have to be repeated at 2500 kg/ha or less every 4 to 5 days until production is satisfactory.

Fertilizers applied after the pond is filled should be handled in much the same manner as fertilizers placed in dry ponds: they should be placed in a heap at one corner of the pond. Or a separate culture of zooplankton may be grown in a small, heavily manured pond.

The presence of adequate quantities of zooplankton can be tested for very simply. If 50 liters of pond water are filtered through a plankton net into a test tube and a few drops of formalin or a pinch of common salt is added to kill the plankton, a layer of sediment about I cm deep should develop.

The color of the sediment, brown or green, indicates the relative proportions of zooplankton and phytoplankton, respectively. If a pond simply does not produce enough food organisms, or if other problems such as deoxygenation or reinvasion of predators develop, the fry may be transferred to another pond. This is not necessarily an emergency measure, as a change of environment may accelerate growth in any case.

Table 9.5: Feeding schedule for Indian carp fry.

	Artificial food totalling:
first five days after stocking	One to two times the weight of the fry at stocking daily
Second five days after stocking	Two to three times the weight of the fry at stocking daily
Third five days after stocking	Three to four times the weight of the fry at stocking daily

If a heavy bloom of phytoplankton develops, it may be controlled by dissolving cow dung or dye in the surface water to block the penetration of light into deeper water. An abundance of duckweed or other small floating plants serves the same purpose.

Some Indian carp culturists make use of artificial fry feeding. Various types of dried and powdered oil cakes mixed with rice bran are the customary food, although water fleas (*Daphnia*) have also been recommended. The normal feeding schedule for oil cakes and rice bran is given in Table elsewhere in this chapter.

There has been speculation that oil cakes and rice bran placed in ponds function more as fertilizer than as food. Extensive feeding experiments carried out at the Central Inland Fisheries Research Substation, Cuttack, India, compared the effects on common carp and rohu fry of 19 food items, fed singly or in combinations of two, three, and four items, with the effects of the oil cake-rice bran diet.

In laboratory tests many of the diets studied produced better growth and/or survival than did the normal diet. The best of the diets tested, a mixture of notonectids (aquatic insects), prawns, and cowpeas, was then field tested on nursery fry of catla, rohu, and silver carp.

Although fry of these species are plankton feeders in nature, all showed better growth and survival on the mixture than on conventional diets. Mrigal fry also grew well on the mixture but were not compared to mrigal fry fed oil cakes and rice bran.

The Biometry Research Institute of the Indian Statistical Institute has been the site of other research on diets for Indian carp fry, in this case involving micronutrients. Addition of yeast, vitamin B complex, and ruminant stomach extract with cobalt nitrate to ponds containing 3- to 26-day-old, *Daphnia-fed* fry of catla and rohu resulted in higher survival and, especially in the case of yeast, better growth.

Yeast and B complex also reduced density effects on survival. Yeast, in particular, may find application in commercial culture of the Indian carps. However, while addition of yeast to fry diets enhances growth, it also decreases the total protein per gram dry weight of fry.

REARING PONDS

When the nursing period is over, at which time the fry have reached a length of 20 to 50 cm, they should be left in the nursery pond for about 2 days, during which time they are not fed, then captured in a fine-mesh seine and transferred to rearing ponds. The nursery pond may then be prepared for the next lot of fry.

Rearing ponds are poisoned, fertilized, and if necessary limed in the same manner as nursery ponds. Stocking rates for rearing ponds are shown in Table elsewhere in this chapter.

From this time on, artificial feeding is only rarely practiced in the culture of the Indian carps, the plankton production of a fertilized pond providing adequate food for growth.

PRODUCTION PONDS

Preparation

Production ponds are prepared similarly to nursing and rearing ponds. First all bottom deposits are removed, either manually after draining or, if draining is impossible, by use of nets or long-handled scoops. Lime added not only to adjust the pH of acidic ponds but also as a disinfe, tant.

If a pond has not previously been limed, a heavy dose, perhaps much as 10,000 kg/ha, may be necessary, but in regularly limed pons; 100 to 200 kg/ha is sufficient, except where the soil is very acidic or pug, in carbonates.

Manuring practices vary greatly; one recommended dosage for produe tion ponds is 1000 kg or more of cow dung, 560 to 1200 kg of poultry ma pure, and 5000 kg of green compost/ha. Other fertilizers such as oil cakes or commercial inorganic fertilizers are also used. Water containing sewage may be used in fattening Indian carps for consumption.

This practice might seem questionable from a public health standpoint, but at concentrations of sewage great enough that human pathogens are abundant, dissolved oxygen levels are too low for high survival of fishes.

Stocking

Stocking practices in Indian carp production ponds seem haphazard when compared with polyculture practices in China and elsewhere. This

Table 9.6: Sample stocking rates of Indian carps in rearing ponds.

Type and/or area of pond	*Stage and/or size (mm)*	*number per ha or water surface*	*Duration of rearing (Days)*
Perennial or seasonal rearing ponds, 122-183 cm deep, 0.62-1.24 ha in area, and paddy fields with a depth of 46 cm or more	25-51	49,420-74,130 without feeding; 148, 260-197,680 with regular feeding	30-60
Rearing ponds slightly larger than nursery ponds	25-38	98,840-123,550 without feeding, 148, 260-197,680 with artificial feeding	60
Perennial or seasonal rearing ponds retaining water for a long period, but not deeper than 183 cm, long and narrow in shape for easy, inexpensive fishing operations, and paddy fields 45-61 cm deep	19-25	24,710 without feeding; 197,680 with artificial feeding	60-90
Rearing ponds	25-51	4,000-5,000	60
Rearing ponds	35	250,000-500,000	

Table 9.7: Sample stocking rates of Indian carps in production ponds.

Size Stocked	*Fish/ha*	*Species Ratio*
50-100 mm	4,000	catla:rohu:mrigal, 6:3:1
75-130 mm	ca. 11,000	catla:rohu:mrigal, 2:3:4
juveniles	—	catla:rohu:mrigal, 3:3:4
80-130 mm	6,250	catla:rohu:mrigal, 3:6:1 or catla:rohu:mrigal:calbasu, 3:5:1:1
—	—	catla:rohu:mrigal, 3:3:4 or catla:rohu:mrigal:calbasu, 3:3:3:1

is partly due to the extreme difficulty of distinguishing the various species as fry, but also because the whole question of suitable polycultural techniques for India has not been adequately explored.

Not only are the numbers and proportions of the different species of fish stocked not standardized, neither is the size at introduction to the growing pond. All sizes from fry to juveniles 300 mm long are used. Table elsewhere in this chapter includes a sample of various stocking policies which have proven at least partially satisfactory.

Since the characteristics of the bodies of water in which these stocking practices are employed are unknown, it is not possible here to make recommendations for pond stocking. In general, the numbers of the major carps stocked should be determined by the relative availability of preferred foods for each.

Calbasu are usually added to the basic three species when there are mollusks available in the growing pond, since these are not utilized by the other major carps.

GROWTH AND YIELDS OF INDIAN CARPS

In stocking production ponds, allowance is usually made for an annual mortality of 30% or more. Very large fish bring poor prices, so Indian carps are seldom left in growing ponds longer than 3 years. Most fish are sold after the first year, at which time catla, rohu, mrigal, and calbasu may have attained weights of 900 to 4100, 675 to 900, 675 to 1800, and 450 g, respectively.

The Cauvery carps are smaller fish, attaining firstyear weights of up to 450 g for the fringe-lipped carp, 330 g for the white carp, and 300 g for the Cauvery carp. In very fertile waters, comparable weights may be reached in as little as 6 to 8 months. Few data are available on yields of Indian carp culture, but they vary widely.

In semiwild waters, where the fish are merely stocked and forgotten until harvest, yields seldom exceed 110 kg/ha. With cultivation this expectation may be increased to 300 to 900 kg/ha. With artificial feeding yields as high as 2802 kg/ha have been achieved.

In recent experiments at the Central Indian Fisheries Research Station at Cuttack, the unprecedented yield of 3564 kg/ha was obtained by stocking catla, rohu, mrigal, silver carp (*Hypophthalmichthys molitrix*), grass carp (*Ctenopharyngodon idellus*), common carp, and calbasu in the ratio of 5:10:5:10:4:5:1 at 5000/ha, with fertilization and supplementary feeding.

MARKETING

Indian carps usually are sold fresh, in accordance with the regional preference. Most fish are not sold directly to the consumer, but through various middlemen; sometimes as many as five are involved in handling one lot of fish.

Obviously, this greatly increases the price to the consumer and reduces the amount of protein food available to those who most need it. In some states of India, notably Ahmedabad and Maharashtra, cooperatives market a substantial proportion of fishery products at considerable saving to the consumer, a practice which may be extended to aquacultural products.

PROBLEMS OF INDIAN CARP CULTURE

Among the routine problems facing Indian fish culturists is the presen$_0$ of unwanted plants in growing ponds. Depending on the plant species be dealt with, a diversity of methods, including poisoning, is used in weed control. Many of the most effective poisons are chlorinated hydrocarbon, such as 2,4-D, which are scarcely to be recommended for introduction into ecosystems or human food supplies.

Other poisons, such as copper sulfate, sodium arsenite, and anhydrous ammonia gas, lack the longterm cumulative effects and the dangers to man presented by the chlorinated hydrocarbons, but they may be toxic to fish.

In all but the most desperate cases therefore, it is safer (and usually cheaper) to use mechanical or ecological methods of plant control. For floating weeds, outright manual removal is the best treatment. Emergent plants may be controlled by cutting of leaves at weekly intervals for about 6 to 8 weeks before fruiting.

Marginal weeds may be controlled by many methods, including plowing under, grazing by livestock, burning during the dry season, or deepening the margin of the pond. Rooted submerged weeds may be removed, albeit with considerable labor, by netting with strong nets, by dragging chains, or with the aid of various types of fork and rake.

The commonest agents of ecological weed control are herbivorous fish. The most commonly used species for this purpose is the grass carp, which in addition to destroying or reducing most submerged and emergent plants and adding to pond fish production, contributes to the nourishment of other fish by dropping partially digested plant remains in its feces.

All four of the major carps and a number of the minor carps, although unable to utilize fresh macrophytes as food, consume the partially decayed plant material in grass carp feces. However, grass carp are not a panacea for weed problems, since there are some plants, such as *Eichornia and Salvinia,* which they eat only with reluctance if at all.

There is also the possibility that if grass carp find their way into natural waterways, they may be destructive of the native flora. Another herbivore, already introduced to Ceylon for use in weed control, is the tawes (*Barb us gonionotus*). A number of species of tilapia, including *Tilapia melanopleura, Tilapia mossambica, Tilapia nilotica,* and *Tilapia zillii,* may effectively control certain types of weed. However, *T. mossambica* has on at least one occasion been found to depress total yield in polyculture involving catla.

Another ecological method of weed control is shading. Trees around the border of a pond may provide sufficient shade to discourage marginal weeds, but to control offshore weeds in most ponds the culturist must rely either on floating plants such as duckweed (*Lemna*), individuals of which are small enough not to interfere with netting and routine management operations, or on creation of an algal bloom.

A heavy bloom can be induced by repeated application of N-P-K fertilizers, but this may be prohibitively expensive. An unusual combination of effects results from application of superphosphate or urea at 50 ppm or more.

These substances at that concentration are toxic to most submerged plants, but they act as fertilizers and produce an algal bloom as well. The desirability of an algal bloom must of course be evaluated in terms of the characteristics of the individual pond and the feeding habits of the fish present.

Other pond management practices used in India and Pakistan include the treatment of foul water by doses of 1.5 ppm or less of potassium permanganate, raking the pond bottom to release accumulated gases, and addition of minute amounts of alum to settle suspended or colloidal matter and reduce turbidity.

Among the diseases reported in Indian carps are gill rot, *Saprolegnia* infection, dye disease, fin rot, Ichthyophthiriasis, costiasis, argulosis, ligulosis, gyrodactylosis, and dropsy. For a detailed discussion of some of these diseases and methods of treatment, the reader is referred to Davis.

PROSPECTUS AND RECOMMENDATIONS

The prospectus for culture of the Indian carps is one of growth, as it must be if India's protein crisis is to be abated or merely kept from worsening. Significant growth can be achieved if a greater proportion of India's available waters are brought into fish production.

But to even approach the type of production increase that is needed, great scientific, technological, and social strides must be made. Among the steps which must be taken are the following:

1. The ecological niches of the various Indian carps must be better understood, so that pond stocking and management can be carried out on a more rational basis. If research discloses that not all available niches are being filled, additional species, for example some of the Chinese carps, could be introduced to Indian polyculture.

   More precise knowledge of the ecological role played by the species cultured would also eliminate such unfortunate practices as encouraging a phytoplankton bloom in a pond full of zooplankton feeders.
2. More effective means of spawning Indian carps must be developed. This almost certainly means perfecting existing techniques of induced spawning by hormone injection. Only when Indian fish culturists can consistently and selectively spawn their stock will Indian fish cultic approach its full potential.
3. When successful breeding is assured, it will be possible and deli able to proceed with experiments in selective breeding and perhal, hybridization.

4. Far better methods of hatching eggs must be adopted. A hatching rate of 25 to 50% is simply not satisfactory for a major fish culture enterprise.
5. Mortality in transportation of fry must be reduced and transpon made more efficient. Again the technology exists, but economic considerations restrict its usage. Some progress is being made in this area, however.
6. As long as river-caught fry sustain a major portion of the market, there will be a need for a workable method of sorting fry to species. The present inability of culturists to determine what species they are stocking renders current knowledge of suitable stocking ratios useless and results in inadvertent stocking of inefficient protein producers, that is, the minor carps.
7. More and more efficient hatcheries and culture stations must be built, using artificial ponds that can be drained and otherwise ecologically controlled. Losses to predators and other natural hazards which could be controlled undoubtedly significantly reduce the total yield of Indian fish culture.
8. Much more research needs to be done on pond fertilization. In conjunction with this research, surveys should be made of the chemical characteristics of Indian soil and waters so that the culturist may know precisely what the effect of a certain dosage of a substance in a given pond will be.

   This would eliminate loss of fish due to fouled water, unutilized phytoplankton blooms, and so on. For the present at least, emphasis should continue to be placed on organic fertilizers, for ecological as well as economic reasons, but inorganic fertilizers should not be ignored.
9. Ecological means of weed control, particularly those involving herbivorous fish, should be encouraged and use of chlorinated hydrocarbon herbicides discouraged.
10. Artificial feeding of all ages of Indian carps should be studied, and if useful and economically feasible foods are found, such feeding should be encouraged.
11. Indian fishery and fish culture research should be directed toward potential application of its findings. The Indian scientific literature should not be further burdened with masses of needlessly precise data detailing, for example, the lengths of

carp fry in hundredth of a millimeter.

12. Cooperatives and other schemes to eliminate middlemen and supply protein food efficiently and cheaply to those who need it should be encouraged and aided.

Though research undoubtedly holds the key to many of the problems of Indian fish culture, given the urgency of the situation, development must be given preference. Implementation of presently known feasible techniques for increasing protein production in India is of utmost importance and must succeed if India is to feed her people.

10

CULTURE OF FROG

The status of commercial frog culture is nebulous. On the one hand, United States government publications repeatedly advise prospective frog farmers that intensive commercial culture of frogs as food animals has yet to he achieved. On the other hand, one continually encounters individuals who claim to be operating profitable "frog farms."

Such establishments generally turn out to be slightly modified shallow ponds or swamps, where frogs are harvested in much the same manner as wild frogs. In some cases, husbandry is limited to erecting a fence to retain the frogs and exclude predators, and the chief market is other would-be frog farmers.

Other such farms, however, are more sophisticated and sell to restaurants and other food outlets. Intensive indoor culture methods have also been developed for several species, but at present they are applied only to the production of laboratory frogs, and opinions differ as to whether modifications of these methods could economically be applied to the culture of frogs for human consumption.

SOURCE OF STOCK

Most attempts at frog culture have been made in the United States, where frogs are among the most expensive luxury foods. Numerous species are harvested from the wild and are generally not discriminated among by buyers or consumers except on the basis of size. The largest and the most widely used in attempts at culture is the bullfrog (*Rants catesbiana*).

Bullfrogs lay their eggs in shallow standing water during April in the South and May or June in the North. Hatching requires 4 days to

3 weeks, depending on temperature. The aquatic larvae, generally known as tadpoles, feed chiefly on benthic algae.

In 5 months to 2 years they metamorphose into the semiaquatic and exclusively carnivorous adults, which may reach lengths of up to 20 cm. Prospective frog farmers may obtain bullfrog stock from commercial sources, or eggs or tadpoles may be taken from the wild.

Bullfrog eggs and those of a few other large frogs) may be distinguished from those of small, undesirable species by the size of the floating egg mass, whit' covers about 0.5m^2. Size is also the distinguishing characteristic of bull frog tadpoles, which are much larger than most other tadpoles of the same age.

Stocking

Whichever life form is taken, they should be distributed around the perimeter of the body of water to be stocked. Although this method may be suitable for new operations, the culturist should endeavor to breed his own stock as soon as possible.

In addition to the taxonomic uncertainty in collecting wild stock, wild tadpoles often harbor pathogenic organisms and suffer high mortalities in the late stages of metamorphosis. All known attempts at frog farming in the United States have failed to incorporate any form of control over breeding but have allowed the frogs to spawn as they would in the wild.

The resulting tadpoles have sometimes been reared separately from adult frogs, and adults have been segregated by size in the belief that extensive cannibalism would otherwise result. However, some researchers have found cannibalism rare or nonexistent among well-fed bullfrogs of all ages.

Feeding

Feeding is the key not only to averting cannibalism, but to health and satisfactory growth of frogs. Frogs and tadpoles maintained outdoors will obtain some food naturally, but at commercially feasible population densities, the natural food supply must be supplemented. Tadpoles, while primarily herbivorous in nature, will accept any soft animal or vegetable matter.

Among the feeds which have been employed are boiled potatoes, meat scraps, and chicken viscera. An especially attractive idea is the use of the viscera and other scraps from butchered frogs as tadpole feed. Once metamorphosis to the frog stage is complete, feeding becomes much more difficult. Adult frogs feed exclusively on moving animals.

Japanese researchers have reportedly been able to induce frogs to ingest stationary silkworm pupae by mixing them with live nightcrawlers, then removing the nightcrawlers when the frogs have become accustomed to the pupae.

Another Japanese method of eliminating dependence on live food involves the use of wooden trays containing about 12 mm of water. Dead silkworms or other food items are placed in the trays, which are anchored in shallow water near shore. A small motor keeps the trays oscillating slowly, so that the silkworms roll back and forth.

So far as is known, these Japanese techniques have not been tried with bullfrogs in the United States. Most American frog culturists have relied on stocking or attracting live food animals. One farmer, located near the ocean in Florida, stocked his ponds with marine fiddler crabs (*Uca spp.*), which are abundant on Florida beaches.

Smaller species of frogs and their tadpoles may be eaten by bullfrogs and are sometimes stocked as food. Aquatic plants may be encouraged as shelter and food for tadpoles, crayfish, and other potential food animals.

Terrestrial flowering plants serve a similar function by attracting flying insects, which are hunted by frogs on shore. More insects may be attracted by illuminating the shore of the pond at night with 100- to 200-W clear lamps. No combination of these methods has yet proven entirely satisfactory, and the difficulty of supplying adequate amounts of food remains the principal obstacle to successful bullfrog farming.

Design of Ponds

Another problem faced, and largely overcome, by early experimental frog culturists is territoriality. A large bullfrog may require about 7.5 m of shoreline as a feeding territory, a trait which severely limits the number of bullfrogs in most natural environments.

Natural bodies of water, however, usually include large expanses of deep, open water which are of little use to bullfrogs during the growing season. Culturists are therefore able to maintain frogs at population densities much higher than those usually observed in nature by reducing the amount of open water in their ponds, while increasing the length and irregularity of the shoreline through construction of islands and peninsulas extending into the centers of the ponds.

If natural ponds suitable for such modification are not available, the shoreline of artificial ponds may be maximized by constructing them as a series of narrow trenches. Such trenches should run north and south insofar as possible, so that vegetation on the banks will serve as shade for the frogs.

Whatever form of pond is used, a small portion of it should be deep enough to protect frogs and tadpoles from extreme heat or cold. In the South, 30 to 45 cm is adequate, but in the North, deeper water may be necessary to insure the survival of hibernating frogs.

In any location, a large portion of the pond should be only 5 to 15 cm deep to facilitate the feeding behavior of frogs and tadpoles. Predators of frogs and tadpoles are numerous, and some tadpole predators, such as large aquatic insect larvae, are virtually impossible to exclude from frog ponds.

Some terrestrial predators may be kept out by enclosing ponds with a small-mesh wire fence about 1 m high, sloping outward at an angle of 35°. Birds are more difficult to exclude, but a wire net stretched above the shallows may be partially effective. No predator control method developed to date is 100% effective, and the culturist should allow for some loss.

Harvesting

Harvesting of bullfrogs from ponds as just described is extremely inefficient. The methods employed are the same used in hunting wild frogs -fishing with hook and line, spearing, and hand capture. Live bait is occasionally used in fishing for frogs, but a more common practice is to dangle a crude lure, made of red cloth or yarn, in front of the frog to simulate a hovering insect.

Spearing and hand capture are done at night with the aid of a bright spotlight, which dazes and immobilizes the frogs. Clearly, these methods must be supplanted by mass harvesting techniques if successful commercial pond culture of frogs is to become a reality.

Data on the commercial status of frog culture in the United States are few and sometimes contradictory. Most of the reports of success have come from Florida and Louisiana, where the growing season is very long, if not year-round, but commercial suppliers of frogs are located as far north as Vermont and Wisconsin.

INDOOR CULTURE OF FROGS

Species Cultured

A newer approach to frog farming, and one which largely eliminates climatic considerations, is indoor culture. Practical methods of indoor propagation and rearing of frogs for use as laboratory animals were first worked out by T. Kawamura of the University of Hiroshima, Japan. Kawamura's methods were subsequently adapted for use with

American species by George W. Nace of the Department of Zoology, University of Michigan.

Nace's methods have been the model for several other institutions which have undertaken to produce their own experimental animals, but to date no one has attempted indoor commercial culture of frogs as food animals.

However, the species routinely cultured at Michigan include the green frog (*Rana clamitans*), the pickerel frog (*Rana palustris*), and the leopard frog (*Rana pipiens*), all commonly marketed as food, and there is no reason to believe that any of the larger American frogs could not be similarly cultured. Thus the possibility of indoor commercial production of frogs for human consumption cannot be ignored.

Water Supply

As might be expected in an indoor culture system, pains had to be taken to provide a suitable water supply for the University of Michigan Amphibian Facility. Based on the experience of Nace and his associates, there are four requirements for maintenance of a self-perpetuating frog colony:

1. The water supply must be abundant at all times; the Michigan facility uses up to 90 liters/min.
2. Line pressure should be adequate to permit individual fine control of flow through each container.
3. The pH should be slightly acid.
4. The water temperature must be constant at 20 to 22°C.

The source of water at Michigan is the city of Ann Arbor municipal system, which is unsatisfactory on the last three counts. Booster pump· pressure regulating valves, and carefully designed plumbing have beer installed to compensate for irregular main pressure, pH is maintained a6 to 7 by the monitored introduction of acetic acid, and the temperature is regulated with the aid of heaters and industrial capacity mixing valve.

A commercial culturist would of course seek to locate so as to avoid these expenditures if possible. Ann Arbor city water is chlorinated, which would seem to present yet another problem, as it does for tadpoles. It has proved necessary to instal; an industrial activated charcoal dechlorinator to provide safe water for tadpoles.

However, while chlorine is toxic to tadpoles at concentrations well below the 0.6 ppm found in Ann Arbor city water, adult frogs can stand chlorination up to 4 ppm. In fact, mild chlorination serves as a prophylactic measure against bacterial diseases. Adults art thus kept in water provided by lines which bypass the dechlorinator.

Tadpole Bottles

Differences in water quality requirements, along with other aspects o the life history of frogs, dictate that separate housing facilities be provided for each life stage. Fertilized eggs and very young tadpoles an' held at low density in shallow enamel pans.

Dead embryos are remove,' regularly, and the water is changed at least every third day. When vigorous swimming commences, the tadpoles are transferred to special tadpole bottles.

A tadpole bottle is constructed by removing the bottom of a conventional 1-gal glass or plastic bottle, stoppering and inverting it. Water is supplied from below through a 10-mm glass tube and removed through a 15-mm plastic siphon tube extending to the stopper.

In this manner constant flow is maintained, and the oldest, "stale" water is removed Flow through each bottle is adjusted so that the water is exchange·' about three times daily, yet dangerous currents are not created.

A circular stainless steel screen inserted over the inflow and siphon tubes prevents tadpoles from becoming trapped in the neck of the bottle. Tadpole bottles, each containing 25 to 75 tadpoles, depending on size and species, are held in racks provided with waste troughs to dispose of the water which is siphoned out.

In nature, certain individuals of each batch of tadpoles grow most rapidly at first. These large individuals release a growth-inhibiting substance which acts upon the smaller tadpoles. The result is that tadpole; metamorphose and emerge as frogs in waves, rather than all at once.

While in nature this helps avert mass mortality due to predation or unfavorable conditions in the terrestrial environment, commercial culturist would not be likely to find this arrangement advantageous. Fortunately, the use of continuously flowing water, as described here, prevents the a: cumulation of the growth-inhibiting substance and results in relatively uniform growth and more or less simultaneous metamorphosis.

Cages for Metamorphosed and Adult Frogs

Metamorphosis is considered to have occurred when the forelimbs erupt, at which time the young frogs are transferred to rectangular plastic containers lined with rubber mats and containing a few pieces of broken clay flower pots to serve as cover. These cages are placed on racks at an incline, so that one end contains water while the other is dry. The containers are cleaned and the water is changed every third day.

Transformation into the frog form need not be complete for the young to be treated as adults. Rather they are transferred to adult containers as soon as their vigor is assured. Housing for adult frogs should have the following characteristics:

1. Both aquatic and terrestrial areas.
2. Flowing water and facilities to permit flushing.
3. Construction design which permits ready access and allows cleaning with minimal handling of the frogs.
4. Closures which are strong enough to prevent the escape of frogs, fine enough to retain insects presented as food, and open enough to provide adequate ventilation.

These conditions are met by the rather elaborate two-story plastic cages used at Michigan. The opaque bottom section of each cage contains not only water but ledges so that the frogs may remain dry but secluded. Nested into the bottom sector is a dry, transparent cage with a rubber mat and clay shelters like those used in containers for newly metamorphosed frogs.

A hole in the bottom of the upper section permits the frogs to move from level to level. Water is supplied through a tube in the rear of the bottom compartment and leaves via a 25-mm-high overflow tube. Tops are made of stainless steel wire cloth and incorporate an access port.

Adult cages, which are either 48.3 cm × 26.7 cm × 16.5 cm deep or 50.8 cm × 40.6 cm × 21.6 cm deep, are mounted on racks so that each cage can be individually withdrawn for inspection, cleaning, and so on. The overflow tubes are connected to a telescoping drain so that circulation need not be interrupted during such operations.

A simpler device for holding adults, which may be more readily adaptable to commercial culture, is a 5-m-long trough, equipped similarly to the cages just described, but not incorporating the two-story structure. Such troughs may be divided into compartments, without losing the desirable feature of easy flushing, by simply leaving a 6-mm open space under each divider.

Separate housing facilities are maintained as a quarantine for newly received frogs. Such animals are first held 10 min in water containing enough calcium hypochlorite to produce a chlorine concentration of 6 ppm. Following this treatment, they are placed in isolated containers and provided with an excess of food until their health is assured.

Feeding

Feeding is critical to the success of all forms of frog culture, and Nace's system is no exception. Tadpoles may be fed a variety of greens, but boiled romaine or escarole lettuce has been found best. Spinach is avoided, as it may cause formation of kidney stones.

A good deal of judgment is required in feeding, for, although tadpoles consume great amounts of food and must be fed twice daily, they may be killed by overfeeding. The basic lettuce diet is supplemented two or three times weekly with cubes of raw or boiled liver.

It should be noted that a number of other forms of food may be equally suitable from the tadpole's point of view, but that the nature of the tadpole bottles dictates a number of the properties of the food.

Specifically, it must not float to the surface, produce a scum which inhibits gas exchange, or be fine enough to settle through the screen into the neck of the bottle or be flushed out. As in outdoor culture methods, feeding presents more of a challenge once metamorphosis is reached.

So far, optimal growth and rapid attainment of sexual maturity have been attained only when the frogs are fed on live insects. Nace has settled on three species, the meat fly (*Sarcophaga bullata*), the greenbottle fly (*Phoenicia sericata*), and the field cricket (*Acheta domestica*).

Crickets are obtained commercially and maintained on a diet of chick mash and water, but the flies are raised in the laboratory. Adult flies are maintained on water, sugar, and a sugar solution and allowed to deposit their eggs on a moistened mixture of sawdust and dog food, topped with several thin slices of raw liver, placed in a plastic tray.

After 24 hours in a breeding cage, each such tray is placed in a 31.0 cm × 28.5 cm × 8.1 cm deep stainless steel pan, lined with paper toweling. Escape of maggots is prevented by means of a nonlethal "electric fence" created by running a 10-V current through a copper strip mounted on insulation affixed around the lip of the pan.

Upon reaching full growth, the maggots migrate from the food tray into the pan, where they pupate Pupae may be stored at 4°C for as long as 3 to 4 months, then warmed to 30°C for hatching. After hatching, the flies may again be chilled or anesthetized with CO_2 and fed to the frogs while in a torpid state.

The entire fly culture operation, which produces 25,000 flies daily is confined to a 2.4-m × 3.0-m room. The species raised both require eh vated temperatures for reproduction, thus escapees cannot become a nuisance in the Michigan climate.

Potential frog culturists in tropical an,' subtropical climates, where meat flies and greenbottle flies might become established, might consider the possibility of relying entirely on cricket or some other species of insect.

The diet of flies and crickets has proved satisfactory for green frog and leopard frogs, but pickerel frogs and some smaller species apparently develop a vitamin deficiency and do not survive well.

Ultraviolet lighting has been found to help, but it is more efficient and equally effective to dust the food animals with powdered Pervinal, a commercial preparation containing ten vitamins, as well as calcium, magnesium, an and various trace elements.

Breeding and Selection

Laboratory breeding procedures for frogs have been standardized and are well described in a number of embryology texts, thus need not be repeated here. Commercial adaptations have yet to be worked out.

Frogs have been selectively bred for some time, a process which has been greatly enhanced by the discovery that the skin markings of each frog are unique and may be used like human fingerprints as a means of individual identification.

All frogs in the Michigan colony are routⁱnely identified at metamorphosis and a complete breeding record kept for each individual, a procedure which could easily be applied by commercial culturists to selected breeder frogs.

Possibility of Indoor Commercial Culture

Obviously, the methods just described will have to be simplified somewhat if frogs are to be commercially cultivated indoors. The first to attempt to adapt Nace's and Kawamura's techniques to commercial culture, and also the first to culture bullfrogs indoors, is Dudley D. Culley, Jr., of the Department of Forestry and Wildlife Management, Louisiana State University.

The principal difference between Culley's procedure and that used at Michigan is the source of food. Tadpoles are fed on Commercially available rabbit pellets or trout chow. Adult bullfrogs have been found to prefer fish to other food organisms, thus experimental animals at Louisiana State are maintained on a diet of mosquito fish (*Gambusia affinis*) and sailfin mollies (*Mollienisia latipinna*), both of which are easily bred and maintained in captivity.

Bullfrogs are also fond of tadpoles, and experiments are being conducted with excess tadpoles as food. The principal obstacle to total biological success in indoor bullfrog culture is the difficulty of breeding them, but Culley is optimistic that this problem will eventually be solved.

DISEASES

Diseases present a relatively small problem in frog culture. The most commonly reported "disease" is "red-leg," usually attributed to over crowding. Actually there are two conditions which may give rise to a reddish discoloration of the legs. Red-leg in recently transported frogs most often indicates simple irritation of the skin caused by prolonged contact with a dry surface.

Such irritation may, if not treated, afford access to infectious microbes, but it is not a disease symptom in itself. Infection by certain bacteria, most frequently *Aeromonas,* produces a similar response. The best preventive measure is adequate nutrition.

Cures may be effected by isolating the infected individuals and treating them with such antibiotics as chloramphenicol and sulfadiazine. In severe cases, it is also advisable to keep the frogs in a salt solution approximating 25 to 30% frog Ringer's solution.

GROWTH AND DEVELOPMENT

Growth and development of well-fed frogs in both outdoor and indoor culture systems compares favorably with that observed in nature. The chief determining factors are food supply and length of the growing season. On the average, two years are required from metamorphosis to maturity in the South and four years in the North.

Similar variations exist in the growth rates of tadpoles. Of perhaps more interest to the culturist is the time required from metamorphosis to marketable size. The only reliable data of this sort come from Culley's experiments.

Taking a length of 20 cm (including the outstretched legs) and a weight of 130 g as minimal for marketing in Louisiana, almost all of Culley's bullfrogs reached commercial size within 12 months of metamorphosis. The fastest growing individuals reached this size in 8 months. Through selective breeding, Culley hopes to reduce the average time required to less than 8 months.

UTILIZATION

A serious obstacle to the development of commercial frog culture in the United States is the American attitude that only the hind legs are useful as food. There is in fact an ample portion of meat on the back and front legs of any large frog, but its utilization would increase the cost of processing.

Even if the back and front legs are eaten, there is still a large amount of waste. In certain Oriental cultures frogs are prepared so that the bones become soft and digestible, or even cooked with the entrails and skins intact, but it is doubtful that such practices would find favor in the United States at this time.

Culinary practices aside, if markets or uses could be found for presently wasted parts of the frog, frog culture in the United States would be closer to the threshold of economic feasibility. Mention has already been made of the practice of feeding frog entrails to tadpoles.

It is also possible that frog wastes could be processed into a product similar to the marine protein concentrate (MPC) made from fish, and used as an animal feed or nutritional supplement. Efforts have also been Made, with some success to tan frog skin and use it iii the manufactuere of leather items.

In addition to the economic and gastronomic incentive, frog culture should be encouraged as a conservation measure. Wherever there are large populations of hogs in the United States, they are sought by hunters not only as a source of food but for sale to schools and research laboratories.

Intensive hunting, along with drainage of wetlands, continue r, reduce already depleted populations and sonic authorities foresee the disappearance of the wild frog industry within 10 years. Already .Aerie educators and scientists must import large quantities of frogs.

Disappearance or drastic depletion of frogs would mean the loss n(, only of an industry but of an important component of the ecosystem Adult frogs are among the most effective insect predators, and both adults and tadpoles are important in the diets of many fish, birds, reptile and mammals.

Tadpoles occupy a unique position in the food chain by virtue of their benthic feeding habits, which result in their recycling nutrients that might otherwise be trapped in the substrates of ponds. It is thus to be hoped that aquaculturists in the United States will make increased efforts to propagate and rear frogs for both laboratory and table use.

Table 10.1: Stocking rates and yields of Fish-Frog culture in India.

Frog species stocked	*Stocking Rate/Ha*	*Stocking rate of Major Carps Per Hectare*	*Yield of Frog (Rg/Ha)*	*Yield of Fish (Kg/Ha)*	*Total Yield (Kg/Ha)*
R. hexadactyla	2,000	none	259.0	0.0	259.0
R. tigrina	2,000	none	235.6	0.0	235.6
None	—	3,705	0.0	886.1	886.1
R. hexadaclvvla	2,000	3,705	234.8	1,611.0	1,845.8
R. tigrina	2,000	3,705	218.3	1,093.1	1,311.4

EXPERIMENTAL FROG CULTURE IN INDIA

Frogs support industries of some value in many of the Latin American and Asian countries, but only India maintains an extensive frog cairns program, although small-scale experimental culture is reportedly heirs. carried out in China and Cuba.

The main center of experimental frog culture in India is the Pond Culture Substation of the Central Inland Fisheries Research Institute, Barrackpore, Cuttack, but preliminary work is also being done at the Freshwater Biological Station, Bhavanis agar, 'Madras.

In both cases the species cultured are *Rana hexadactyle* and *Rana tigrina,* both of which are in high demand for export as h·O, legs. Officials at Cuttack are not generous with information, but it I - known that some of the studies conducted concern induced spawning food and habitat requirements. and polyculture with fish.

Spawning

Both species of frog, which spawn naturally during the northeast monsoon (September to November), can be induced to spawn throughout the year by the administration of frog pituitary hormones with a priming dose of progesterone.

The natural rate of fertilization of *R. tigrina* is poor, so stripping of eggs and artificial fertilization have fertilization have been employed. Nearly 100% fertilization has been obtained using the dry method.

There appears to be no basis for fear that either species will be a serious predator in fish ponds. Preliminary observations indicate that they feed primarily on worms. gastropods, and aquatic insects, with ;mall fish constituting only an incidental item in the diet. It submerged weeds are encouraged by fertilization, a frog pond should produce an ample food supply.

Polyculture with Fish

Indications are that the combination of frogs and fish would be more profitable than frog monoculture. Experimental yields obtained when small frogs were stocked with fingerlings of the Indian major carps catla (*Catla catla*), rohu (*Labco roluta*), and mrigal (*Cirrhina mrigala*) are shown in Table elsewhere in this chapter.

No explanation has been advanced for the higher yields of fish in ponds stocked with frogs, and they may or may not be related to the presence of frogs.

PROSPECTUS

Experimental frog culture has thus far dealt almost exclusively with the production of frogs for laboratory use or as a luxury food. If the commercial status and prospectus of such culture is uncertain, even less can be predicted about the eventual role of frogs in supplying human nutritional needs.

Whatever form of frog culture one considers, an authority can be found to support any prognosis, from glowing optimism to a "can't be done" attitude. Rather than add to the confusion, let us simply acknowledge that attempts at commercial frog culture will continue, and state that its future is in the hands of a few biologists and adventurous entrepreneurs.

11

Culture of *Tilapia*

Members of the genus tilapia (*family Cichlidae*) have been an important source of food for man at least since recorded history began. The fish Saint Peter caught in the Sea of Galilee and those with which Christ fed the multitudes were tilapia.

An Egyptian tomb frieze, dated at 2500 B.C., illustrates the harvest of tilapia and suggests that they may have been cultured. Since that time, and probably before, the various species of tilapia have been of major importance in the fisheries of their native lands, the Near East and Africa.

DISTRIBUTION OF *TILAPIA SPP.*

From the point of view of human nutrition, tilapia was already firmly entrenched as one of the world's most important fish by the start of the twentieth century. But with greatly increased emphasis on fish culture in this century, plus the advent of modern transportation, tilapia became even more valuable to man.

Today no fish, with the probable exception of the common carp (*Cyprinus carpio*), is more widely cultured. As early as the 1920s experiments in tilapia culture were being carried out in Kenya. Tilapia had become an intercontinental traveler by 1939 when naturally propagating stocks of *Tilapia mossambica,* native to the streams of Africa's east coast, were discovered in Java.

No one is quite sure how they got there, but it is likely that aquarists, who have long been intrigued by the bizarre "mouth-brooding" habits of this and most other tilapia species, were implicated. However

T. niossambica arrived, they made themselves at home and spread rapidly throughout the island. So prevalent did they become that, despite the geographic reference in the scientific name, the generally accepted common name for *T. mossambica* is "Java tilapia."

They were originally regarded as a nuisance, but when facilities for the traditional Indonesian practice of milkfish (*Chanos chanos*) culture began to deteriorate under the Japanese occupation, the less demanding nature of tilapia became apparent, and by the end of World War II tilapia were not only too well established in the waters of Java but too deeply entrenched in Indonesian fish culture for anyone to consider control measures against them.

The Japanese, always a nation cognizant of the nutritional possibilities of fish, helped spread tilapia throughout Indonesia, where today it is found in virtually every body of water, including ditches and stagnant pits where few other fish of value can be grown.

The retreating Japanese also introduced tilapia to Malaya, from whence it spread throughout southeast Asia, achieving considerable importance as a food fish in virtually every country.

Today, due to the enthusiasm generated by the research of such men as H. S. Swingle at Auburn University in Alabama and C. F. Hickling at the Tropical Fish Culture Research Institute in Malaysia, plus the missionary efforts of such organizations as FAO and the Peace Corps, the Java tilapia and its congeners are cultured, at least experimentally, not only in southeast Asia, but in Japan, Asiatic Russia the Indian subcontinent, the Near East, virtually all of Africa, parts of Europe, the United States, and many of the Latin American countries.

SELECTION OF SPECIES FOR CULTURE

The Java tilapia was the first member of the genus *Tilapia* to come to the attention of large numbers of fish culturists and has remained the most widely cultured species. However, according to the late A. Yashouv of the Fish Culture Research Station at Dor, Israel, it is "the most difficult to manage" member of the genus.

This is not to say that there is a "best" tilapia for culture. At least 14 species have been cultured and all share the hardiness, ease of breeding, rapid growth, and high quality of flesh which have made the Java tilapia popular.

Any one of them or some as yet untried species or hybrid might be the right fish for culture in a given situation. Too often problems in tilapia culture have resulted from hasty or uninformed selection of a species.

In choosing a species the culturist should take into account the factors listed in Table 1 and discussed further here.

Availability

The Java tilapia is practically universally available, but some species are still available only within their home range or have been introduced elsewhere on a limited scale. This will probably become a less important consideration as time goes by and the more desirable species are distributed among fish culturists.

Food Habits

All tilapia are more or less herbivorous, but some prefer higher plants, whereas others are adapted to feed on plankton. If the food habits of a species are not known, they may be predicted by examination of the gill rakers. Numerous long, thin, closely spaced gill rakers indicate a plankton feeder; the opposite shows that the fish consumes larger particles of food.

Some tilapia are relatively omnivorous and will benefit from artificial feeding with vegetable materials and in some cases even accept animal food if nothing else is available: others are obligate herbivores. Some macrophyte feeders are sufficiently voracious to function well as biological weed controls, whereas others are useless in this capacity.

Salinity Tolerance

Most tilapia are tolerant of brackish water, but some are better adapted to it than others and may thrive and even breed in sea water.

Temperament

Tilapia are less aggressive than most carnivorous cichlids, but they may attack and nip the fins of other species, an undesirable habit if a fish is to be used in polyculture. This behavior is not necessarily species-specific; there are conflicting accounts in the literature for several species. Such factors as sex, temperature, and population density are known to affect aggression and may be involved in the reaction of tilapia to other fish.

Temperature Tolerance

Tilapia are essentially tropical lowland fish, but some species and some stocks withstand cool temperatures much better than others. Where no data are available, valid inferences may often be drawn from consideration of the climate of a species' native habitat.

One more word should be said in behalf of the Java tilapia and Nile tilapia. Both of these species may be and are cultured where great amounts of organic enrichment make it scarcely possible for other edible fish to survive.

SPAWNING AND GROWTH OF THE YOUNG

In many forms of fish culture, obtaining spawn is one of the most difficult tasks. Tilapia present no such problem; indeed it is difficult to prevent them from spawning. The fact that it takes no skill whatever to spawn tilapia in ponds is one of the reasons they have been widely promoted as a fish for subsistence culture, and certainly these prolific fish have enabled many an African or Asian farmer to produce his own fish without acquiring extensive skills or technological know-how.

To spawn tilapia little more is needed than a pond, preferably one with a loose, sandy bottom, and some breeding stock. The spawning pond should be stocked with 25 to 30 females/1000 m^2 and about half again as many males.

If the water is warm enough (see Table anywhere else in this chapter for suggested breeding temperatures for some species), the males will begin digging holes, perhaps 35 cm in diameter × 6 cm deep, in the pond bottom. A female deposits 75 to 250 eggs in such a nest then picks them up in her mouth. Next the male discharges sperm into the depression and this too is picked up by the female.

Fertilization thus takes place inside the female's mouth, where hatching occurs within 3 to 5 days. The larvae are retained in the mouth until the yolk sac is absorbed, after which they may venture forth, but for 10 to 15 days they still return to the female's mouth when threatened. During this time the female eats seldom if at all.

If the young are separated from the mother during brooding, they may be raised quite satisfactorily by themselves. Apparently the chief function of mouth-brooding is protection from predators. The young tilapia mature at an age of 2 to 3 months, at which time they are 6 to 10 cm long.

From then on they breed every 3 to 6 weeks as long as the water is warm. Whenever the water temperature approaches the lower limits of tolerance for a particular species, breeding activity is suspended. Thus the nonreproductive period ranges from about 2 months in subtropical climates to none whatever near the equator.

As for other environmental factors impinging on spawning, it can be stated that tilapia will reproduce in almost any sort of water they can survive in. Java tilapia have been successfully spawned in water with a salinity of 35%.

This description of spawning applies specifically to Java tilapia, but it generally fits all the cultured species except *T. heudeloti*, in which the male incubates the eggs, *T. galilea*, in which both sexes share in mouth-brooding, and *T. sparmanni* and *T. zillii*, which spawn in typical cichlid fashion, on a clean stone or other smooth object, and do not mouth-brood, although the parents do guard the eggs and young.

T. sparmanni and *T. zillii* compensate for the lack of the protective mouth-brooding trait by producing more eggs-up to 5000 in large *T. zillii*. In nature the survivors from a few thousand eggs in the open would probably approximate the survivors of a few hundred mouthincubated eggs and young, but in the protected environment provided by the fish culturist, more eggs are likely to mean more young.

Thus *T. sparmanni* and *T. zillii* are even more prone to overpopulate a pond and produce a stunted population than are other tilapia.

THE PROBLEM OF OVERPOPULATION AND METHODS OF CONTROL

Mouth-brooders or not, overpopulation is the greatest problem encountered in raising any species of tilapia. Stunting is bad enough in countries such as the Philippines where tilapia as small as 75 mm may be marketed, but in places like East Africa, where large fish are preferred for the table, it can spell the difference between success and failure.

The seriousness of the problem may be emphasized by describing the situation in Kivu Province of the Congo. There yields to tilapia culture of 4325 kg/ha were considered normal, which sounds quite good until it is pointed out that 707, of such yields consisted of fish less than 15 cm long.

Classical methods of preventing overpopulation and stunting include separating parents and young immediately upon hatching, monosex culture, and stocking predators along with the tilapia. Selective breeding for large fish has been attempted, but with no success. Apparently environmental override genetic factors in determining size.

Separation of Parents and Young

Separation of adults and young could theoretically be accomplished by netting out the adults after spawning. When the brooders are sufficiently disturbed by nets and the like they will usually spit out the fry. The captured adults could then be placed in another pond and the spawning pond used for a rearing pond.

This technique is not practicable, however, since the breeding cycles of individual adults are far from synchronous, so that in a sizable population spawning occurs more or less continuously. It is possible to remove the young.

A method practiced in Indonesia makes use of a drainable spawning pond at a higher elevation than the fry pond. When the eggs hatch, the adults are disturbed so that the larvae are released and drained into the fry pond. Different sizes of fry may then be periodically cropped from the fry pond for further use in culture.

Monosex Culture

Monosex culture is much more commonly employed. Stocks of a single sex may be obtained by sexing and sorting the stock individually. The structure of the genital papillae is indicative of sex. In males there is a single urogenital opening on the tip of the papilla; in females the genital opening is separate and located on the frontal wall of the papilla, close to the apex.

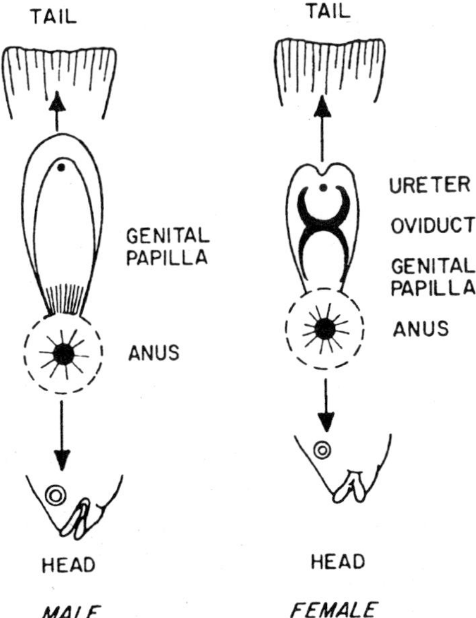

Figure 11.1: Distinguishing characteristics of male and female Tilapia mossambica.

This method has the disadvantage of being laborious. Moreover, even experienced workers can usually achieve only 80 to 90% accuracy. Since all it takes is one female inadvertently introduced into a pond of males being fattened for consumption to undo all the labor involved in sexing, easier and more effective methods for obtaining monosex stocks have been sought.

The best results have been achieved by hybridization. Of the many interspecific and intraspecific tilapia crosses which have been attempted, at least three have produced 100% male offspring.

Attempts to produce monosex stocks of tilapia have generally concentrated on obtaining males since, unlike females, males continue to grow during breeding periods. However, males have one disadvantage, Whether or not there are females present, they optimistically construe spawning nests.

The favored location for nest building is at the base of the pond bank, and the nest-building activities of a great number of males may eventually undermine the bank. For this reason there has been some speculation as to the feasibility of stocking growing ponds with females.

No crosses which consistently produce high percentages of females have been reported, but at the Tropical Fish Culture Research Institute in Malacca, Malaysia, one male Java tilapia of Malaysian origin turned up which, when bred to two females of the same stock, produced 88 and 97% female offspring. Unfortunately this male was lost.

As one might gather from this discussion, the possibilities of hybridization in monosex culture have by no means been fully explored. Only a few of the possible interspecific hybrids have been produced, to say nothing of crosses between different strains of the same species, which vary in sex composition of the F_1 generation as widely as interspecific crosses.

Further, the F_1 generation of many tilapia crosses are fertile and might be used in further breeding experiments. Add to this the fact that the taxonomy of tilapia is by no means cut and dried, and it can be seen that the possibilities are almost unlimited, but that duplication of a desirable hybrid may be quite difficult.

Monosex culture requires a certain amount of technical supervision to be successful. The small farmer often lacks the time, expertise, or inclination to sex fish or keep spawning records. Thus monosex culture is best suited to large commercial operations, or wherever there can be considerable governmental supervision. (A minority of authorities, notably S. Tal, Israel's Director of the Inland Fisheries, are skeptical of its practicability in any situation.) Thus while monosex culture of tilapia has been somewhat successful in Uganda, where the government has largely taken over fish culture, in the neighboring Congo, where fish culture is the responsibility of the individual farmer, it has failed.

Control by Predators

Where tilapia are to be raised on small, technologically unspecialized farms, a more suitable method of population control is the stocking of predaceous fish to crop the young tilapia.

The use of predatory fish is most common in Africa, where stunted fish are often simply unacceptable as food. The most commonly used predators there and in southeast Asia are catfishes of the enus *Clarias,* but eels (*Anguilla japonica*), largemouth bass (*Micropterus salmoides*), and carnivorous cichlids such as *Serranochromis robust us* and *Hemichromis spp.* have also been used.

Cage Culture

Experiments at Auburn University suggested a completely different approach to population control: culture in floating cages. Nile tilapia stocked at 7000 to 15,000/ha in such cages exhibited growth and survival comparable to that obtained through pond culture but were apparently unable to reproduce.

It was supposed that the eggs and sperm passed through the bottom of the net. More recently, however, Java tilapia have been found to have successfully reproduced in floating cages in Lake Atitlan, Guatemala.

STOCKING SYSTEMS

Monoculture

Inclusion of a predator is one form of polyculture, a practice which is becoming nearly universal in raising tilapia. Indeed, except for very primitive subsistence culture, or in waters that will not support other edible fish, monoculture of tilapia for human consumption seems scarcely defensible.

Monoculture is practiced, on a small scale, in rice fields in southeast Asia. Stocking rates for this practice are 120 to 180 fingerlings/ha. Care must be taken to use plankton- and algae-feeding species, since macrophages might destroy the rice crop.

Polyculture

Since the ecological niches of the various *Tilapia spp.* are imperfectly known, and since the history of tilapia culture is so short compared to that of some other polycultural systems, species combinations and stocking practices are by no means codified. Table elsewhere in this chapter outlines some of the stocking systems which have been commercially or experimentally applied, along with their results, when known.

It bodes well for the future of tilapia in fish culture that in almost every case where tilapia have been added to an existing pond culture community, total production has risen with no reduction in the nontilapia components of the harvest.

One exception was found in India where tilapia of an unknown species depressed total production of a pond and apparently virtually eradicated milkfish and catla. Where tilapia are accused of exterminating other fishes, one must wonder whether some hyperaggressive species with a more typical cichlid temperament may not have been stocked.

Tilapia have not been accused of eradicating other fish in the Philippines, but milkfish farmers there are ambivalent if not hostile toward the presence of Java tilapia. Part of their dislike of tilapia stems not from any direct effect of tilapia on fish production but because tilapia, in addition to consuming phytoplankton and naturally occurring algae, eagerly devour the elaborately cultured "lab-lab" meant for thtmilkfish.

In other countries, though, there are numerous examples of tilapia being deliberately stocked with milkfish, usually with good results. Surprisingly little work has been done on the combined use of two or more *Tilapia* species. Although an all-tilapia counterpart of Chinese carp culture may never be developed, certainly the variety of food habits among tilapia-plankton feeders, filamentous algae feeders, macrophages, and omnivores-points in this direction.

The association in Africa of the plankton-feeding *T. macrochir* and the macrophage *T. melanopleura* also usually involves an assortment of ages and sizes, not to gain any particular polycultural advantage but because, given the prolific nature of tilapia, it is simpler. Initial stocking of growing ponds is carried out with a mixture of fry, large breeders, and various in-between ages.

At harvest time all but a few of the large breeders are taken for consumption. Excess fry are also harvested for consumption or, more often, for use in stocking other ponds. Restocking may not be necessary, but if artificial feeding is employed, 10 to 20% of the estimated production by weight may be stocked after harvest.

Granted the relative simplicity of mixed-age culture, a harvest consisting of many sizes of fish may be economically disadvantageous. Stocking fish of approximately the same size will not produce a harvest of even-size fish, even if monosex culture is employed, but may more closely approach it. M. Huet of the University of Louvain, Belgium, has devised a formula for restocking single-size artificially fed tilapia ponds:

$$\text{number of tilapia to be stocked} = \frac{\text{total production}}{\text{individual growth}} + (\text{waste})\left(\frac{\text{total production}}{\text{individual growth}}\right)$$

Individual growth of fish may be fixed within certain limits by referring to the normal growth of the species cultured, or it may be determined more precisely by weighing a sample of the stock at stocking and again at harvest.

Waste percentage is largely a matter of estimation or perhaps intuition. Values normally used in the application of Huet's formula are 10, 15, and 20%.

Total production equals natural production plus production due to feeding. Natural production must be known from previous culture, without feeding, in the pond to be stocked or a similar pond. Production from feeding may be obtained by dividing the weight of food used by its nutritional quotient.

Huet does not give a method for determining production due to fertilization, but many of the commonly used organic fertilizers double as feeds and may perhaps be treated on that basis. As an example of Huet's formula in application, let us suppose a 0.5-ha growing pond which is cropped twice a year.

Its natural production is estimated at 400 kg/(ha)(yr). Now 3000 kg of cottonseed oil cakes, which have a nutritive quotient of 5, are available as feed, and waste is reckoned at 15%. Total production for 6 months thus equals

$$\frac{400\text{kg/(ha)(yr)} \times 0.5\text{ha}}{2} + \frac{3000 \text{ kg good}}{5} = 700 \text{ kg}$$

Individual growth of fish is estimated at 0.1 kg and waste at 15_0. So, plugging in the data, we get

$$\text{no. of fry to be stocked} = \frac{700}{0.1} + (0.15)\left(\frac{700}{0.1}\right) = 8050 \text{ fry}$$

The formula is of course applicable only if the pond is to be restocked with the same size fish at the same species ratio as originally stocked. The only other noteworthy example of multiple-species tilapia stocking is H. W. Swingle's work at Auburn University in Alabama.

In addition to two or three species of *Tilapia,* one of which, *T. nilotica,* has unknown feeding habits, Swingle used a presumptive predator, the largemouth bass (*Micropterus salmoides*).

The bass may have gotten some nutrition from young tilapia, but when fathead minnows (*Pimephales promelas*) were added to the pond, they were eradicated by the bass over the course of 7 months, resulting in a fivefold increase in bass production but only a slight increase in tilapia production.

It has long been part of fishermen's lore, though not well substantiated, that many predators, including the largemouth bass, are reluctant to take spiny finned prey. If so, then perhaps the role of some predators in tilapia culture should be reevaluated.

Swingle has also stocked Java tilapia and Nile tilapia separately with channel catfish (*Ictalurus punctatus*), which, though not as piscivorous as the largemouth bass, might conceivably act as a predator on tilapia fry.

Significant consumption of tilapia fry by the catfish was not noted, but the tilapia apparently utilized not only plankton, but wastes and excess feeds intended for the catfish, and production of catfish was' substantially increased.

Stocking Rates

Most of the reported stocking densities for tilapia are lower than necessary, at least where monosex culture is employed. The problem of excess small fish in tilapia ponds is more closely allied to excess reproduction than to initial overstocking.

Experiments at Auburn University in which 1-year-old, 100-g *T. nilotica* were stocked in 2.02-ha ponds at various rates demonstrated increased production at each density increment up to 5039/ha, the highest tested.

Research in Uganda on the hybrid *T. mossambica* (Zanzibar stock) *X y T. nilotica* (Lake Albert stock) showed that, up to a weight of 50 g, fry did not suffer retarded growth at densities as high as 8000/ha. Above that size it was found necessary to transfer them to rearing ponds at 1000 to 1500/ha if normal growth was to continue.

Much higher stocking densities were successfully employed in further experiments at Auburn University involving tilapia fingerlings. Nile tilapia fingerlings stocked at 20,000/ha and fed gave a production of

2822 kg/ha in 196 days, but those stocked at 40,000/ha produced 3699 kg/ha. Of these fish, 98.5% and 91.9%, respectively, were considered to be of usable size.

Similar results were obtained with Java tilapia at densities up to 50,000/ha, but the percentage of usable fish, 99.7 at 10,000 fish/ha, declined to 67.7 at 50,000/ha, due presumably to the very prolific nature of Java tilapia. Of course it should not be assumed that more is better than less in tilapia stocking.

Many factors other than density enter the picture, not the least being the question of available food supplies and its corollary, the economics of feeding.

MANAGEMENT OF TILAPIA PONDS

Segregation of Age Groups

The practice of segregating different ages of fish in nursing, rearing, and growing ponds, so prevalent in culture of species where spawning is strictly controlled, is rare in tilapia culture. However, in parts of Africa, fry may be nursed from 6 weeks to 2 months, or until they begin to breed, in 0.01- to 0.1-ha ponds. This technique may become more widespread, particularly for use in monosex culture.

Pond Fertilization

Pond fertilization is of vital importance in culture of tilapia, particularly the plankton-feeding species, but has yet to be treated systematically. This is largely due to the short history of tilapia culture, as well as to the frequent use of tilapia in "crash" programs designed not to provide data for more sophisticated efforts but to alleviate existing critical protein shortages.

In southeast Asia, tilapia may be cultured in ponds which are already heavily enriched by agricultural runoff and/or domestic pollution. Some of these waters carry such heavy loads of organic nutrients as to be uninhabitable by other desirable fishes. Fertilization would thus be superfluous, and fertilizers are set aside for use in culture of carps, milkfish, mullet, and so on.

But even in southeast Asia, such ponds are the exception rather than the rule. It may be expected that as tilapia culture matures, especially if tilapia becomes a commercial product sought by all economic classes, fertilization will be studied in some detail.

A certain amount of research on fertilization of tilapia ponds has beer. carried out, most of it involving Java tilapia and all of it involving the use of phosphates, which are the most effective group of fertilizers for enhancing phytoplankton production.

The importance of phosphorus in production of Java tilapia was demonstrated by a series of experiments at Auburn University in which ponds received 8-8-2 (N-P-K) fertilization, 0-8-2 (N-P-K) fertilization, or no fertilization at all. Both fertilizers significantly increased tilapia production at population densities of 4942, 9884, 14,826, and 19,768/ ha.

Except at the highest density, the 0-8-2 (N-P-K) mixture was actually more effective than the mixture containing nitrogen compounds. Although it can be predicted that use of phosphates will enhance phytoplankton production, the digestibility of various phytoplankton differs widely.

Java tilapia digest *Anabaenopsis* and *Oedogonium* well, *Botryococcus* partially, *Microcystis and Spirogyra* poorly, and perhaps cannot digest *Oscillatioria* or *Anabaena* at all. Unfortunately it is not yet practical to produce cultures of a particular phytoplankton species on a large scale.

Experiments in South Africa yielded the none too surprising xesult that 185 kg/ha of 19% superphosphate in conjunction with lime increased yields of Java tilapia by a factor of greater than 4. Basic slag, which is often used in practical fish culture in Africa, achieved similar results when applied at 225 kg/ha.

More surprising is the similar effect of experimental application of 19% superphosphate at 330 kg/ha to ponds containing the macrophagous *T. melanopleura*. Over a 5-month period an increase in production of 240 kg/ha over natural production was recorded.

Phosphatic fertilization in the form of P,,O, applied at 40 to 120 kg/(ha)(yr) to Malaysian ponds containing Java tilapia and *Barbus gonion.otus* raised the total yield of fish by 261 to 1260 kg/(ha)(yr). It should be pointed out, though, that both of these species are plankton feeders and highly tolerant of turbidity.

The effects of organic fertilizers on tilapia are not well known, but such fertilizers are fairly widely used, for example, in Indonesia, where marigold plant is used as a green manure. It is also likely that where such artificial feeds as oil seed cakes are used in tilapia culture, a large percentage of the intended feed is not consumed by the fish but functions as a fertilizer.

Sewage is used to fertilize tilapia ponds in southeast Asia and has been suggested for use in semiarid regions of Africa where green manures are not abundant and animal manures are better employed in agriculture.

This suggestion has met with little enthusiasm since unlike most Asians, Africans in general are as squeamish with regard to human wastes as are Europeans and Americans.

Pond fertilization in fish culture is of course not merely a matter of knowing the characteristics of the fish to be cultured, but must also take into account the chemistry of the water and soil.

Thus fertilization experiments carried out with Java tilapia in, say, Alabama, are of only limited value to the prospective tilapia culturist in Uganda. As time goes on and more on-site research is carried out, scientists and fish culturists will be in a better position to evaluate the pros and cons of fertilization in culture of tilapia and all fishes.

Supplementary Feeding

Supplementary feeding in tilapia culture is as important and as little understood as fertilization. Most authorities are of the opinion that supplementary feeding is essential for success in large-scale culture of tilapia, but nowhere is it carried out in a systematic manner.

Among the feeds employed in Asia and Africa are rice bran, broken rice, oil cakes, flour, corn meal, kitchen refuse, rotten fruit, coffee pulp, and a variety of aquatic and terrestrial plants.

In South Africa, *T. melanopleura* are provided with fodder by growing rice to a height of 20 to 30 cm, then flooding it and allowing access to the fish.

In countries where little money is available to purchase feeds, use of waste products should be encouraged. For example, in the Congo the simple expedient of throwing mill sweepings into tilapia ponds has resulted in production well above normal for the area.

There is great need for research in tilapia nutrition, not only to determine what feeds are best but also what rates of feeding are most effective.

The only worthwhile study of tilapia feeding rates was carried out on Java tilapia and Nile tilapia at Auburn University, using a mixture of 35% peanut meal, 35% soybean meal, 20% ground beef liver, 15% fish meal, and 15% distiller's dry solubles.

Experimental feeding rates were 1, 2, 3, and 4% of body weight per day. Java tilapia drew best at but nearly as well at 2%. Growth of Nile tilapia improved with each increment of feed. Feed conversion rates were best at 2% and loo, respectively.

The feed used seems unusual for tilapia in its high animal content;

certainly such a feed would not be economically feasible where tilapia are raised to offset protein deficiencies in human diets.

USE OF TILAPIA IN WEED CONTROL

Correlated with the feeding habits of the various *Tilapia* species is their use in weed control. Five species have to date been used or tested in this capacity:

T. heudeloti fed on higher plants in experiments at Auburn University, but they did not exert effective control over any species.

T. melanopleura vies with the grass carp as one of the best agents of biological control of aquatic weeds.

T. mossambica eats filamentous algae, a principal habitat for many species of mosquito larvae, thus is often used, in combination with insectivorous species, as an agent of malaria control. For this purpose, 2500 to 5000 fish/ha are recommended.

Its role in relation to higher plants is not clear. Some authorities claim that it does not consume them in appreciable quantities. However, in ponds in Texas it appeared to effectively control some aquatic and emergent plants, though it would not touch *Elodea* or *Riccia*. Consumption of higher plants probably depends in part on the availability of other foods.

T. nilotica experimentally stocked at 2500 to 5000/ha controlled filamentous algae and reduced some higher plants. It may be even more effective in malaria control than *T. mossambica* since it not only eats algae but is reputedly fond of mosquito larvae.

T. zillii in experiments in Malaysia controlled higher plants, including *Funbristylis acuminata,* which grass carp will not touch.

Weed control by tilapia is generally a matter of stocking them in ponds where weeds interfere with fish culture. Thus stocked, they not only perform a service by eating weeds, but add to the total fish production of the pond.

Tilapia have occasionally been suggested for use in control of nuisance plants in natural waterways where they are not native, as in the St. John's River of Florida where water hyacinth interferes with sport fishing g and boating.

Such suggestions are usually y resisted since the total effect of a voracious herbivore in a new environment is, to say the least. difficult to predict.

GROWTH AND PRODUCTION

Growth of tilapia varies greatly with stocking density, frequency of spawning, and food supply. Under very favorable conditions, individual Java tilapia may reach a weight of 850 g in 1 year; in brackish water they may reach 450 g in 8 months.

But in most ponds 85 to 140 g is a more realistic weight to expect after a year if the sexes are raised together. Males grow two to three times faster than females, thus monosex culture of males produces correspondingly better growth.

Monosex culture of females would also improve growth by eliminating periods of no growth associated with spawning, but no data are available on this rarely practiced technique. Heterosis is not unknown in tilapia, but the subject has been insufficiently investigated.

It has been shown that both of the reciprocal crosses of Java tilapia and Nile tilapia exhibit better growth and food conversion than either parent. The same is true of both the intraspecific crosses of Java tilapia of African and Malaysian stocks.

Since the future of tilapia culture appears to be largely bound up with polyculture, it seems superfluous to discuss production at length. The question to be asked is not "How many kilograms of tilapia can be produced in this pond?" but rather "Will tilapia add significantly to this pond's fish production?"

As we have seen, in most cases the answer to the second question is yes. The amount of added production will of course vary, but even in instances such as the experimental culture of Java tilapia with channel catfish, where only 266 kg/ha of tilapia were produced, the effect of adding tilapia must be regarded as significant.

Although if the total production of a fish pond were 266 kg/ha it would be a poor pond indeed, the production of tilapia in this case must be considered as supplementary to the production of the primary crop, channel catfish.

The 266 kg/ha of tilapia produced, *plus* an increase in catfish production of 168 kg/ha over the 1400 kg/ha achieved by monoculture, amounts to an increase of 434 kg/ha of fish, or a total production gain of 30.3%.

Addition of tilapia to carp ponds in Israel has, on occasion, resulted in production gains of more than 165%. Where monoculture of tilapia is practiced, the "normal" figure usually cited for natural production is 500 kg/ha in the tropics and somewhat less in moderate climates.

Witli fertilization and/or supplementary feeding yields of 1000 to 2500 kg/ha can be achieved. Huet suggests that 2500 kg/ha is a minimum desirable production in Africa but, at least in subsistence culture, smaller yields surely accrue some benefit to the culturist Maximum yields of tilapia may be as high as 18,000 kg/ha, but report, of such yields must be taken with a grain of salt since they are likely to contain a preponderance of fish too small to be usable.

HARVENSTING AND MARKETING TILAPIA

Harvesting of tilapia crops is usually done by seining or, where feasible, pond draining. However, experiments indicate that if only a portion of the stock is to be retained electrofishing may be more efficient and result in less injury to the fish.

In most places where tilapia is cultured it is marketed as fresh or iced fish, but it may also be sold frozen. The market price for tilapia varies greatly. In Israel, tilapia now brings a better price than the traditionally cultured common carp. In Africa the commercial value of tilapia is largely dependent on size.

In southeast Asia, size is not an important factor, but the market price varies regionally. In some areas the acceptability of tilapia is lessened by its black skin, and consumption of tilapia is largely limited to people who cannot afford, say, milkfish. In other areas it is marketed as a gourmet food, which is quite appropriate, for the quality of tilapia flesh is usually very high.

Tilapia too small to be marketed for human consumption need not be wasted, as they may be used as fodder for more expensive fish such as trout, as an ingredient in livestock feeds, or as bait in commercial fishing.

Experiments in Alabama indicate that tilapia could be produced in the United States at extremely low cost. Data are not available for other parts of the world, but it would appear that tilapia could compete favorably with other aquacultural and fishery products in most tropical and moderate climates.

Some authorities, however, notably S. Tal and C. F. Hickling, do not view tilapia as a good commercial proposition, at least not on a large scale. Even Tal and Hickling do not dispute tilapia's importance where there is an immediate need to feed large numbers of people or where fish can go directly from pond to pot.

Whatever the commercial feasibility of tilapia culture may prove to be, it must be conceded that, thanks to subsistence culture and small-scale commercial culture, tilapia is currently one of the most important fish crops in much of the world, including most of Africa, Jamaica, southern Taiwan, and parts of Indonesia.

DISEASES AND PARASITES

Diseases and parasites are somewhat less of a problem with tilapia than with many cultured fishes. Among the parasites found on tilapia are *Trichodina, Chilodon,* and *Saprolegnia.*

The only disease mentioned in the literature is bacterial fin rot, but one might expect that, at least in marginal climates, tilapia would be subject to ichthyophthiriasis, the preconditiorn for thick is usually chilling. 'filapia also act as carriers of catarrhal enteritis.

STATUS AND PROSPECTUS OF TILAPIA CULTURE

The prospectus for tilapia culture can best be outlined on a regional basis.

The Near East

The future of tilapia in Israel is debatable, but as long as the present demand is sustained it seems likely that tilapia will hold their own in fish culture as well as in fisheries.

There are perhaps more institutions carrying on fish culture research in Israel than in any other country, so breakthroughs in tilapia culture techniques may well be made and applied in Israel. The growth of fish culture in other Near Eastern countries is hampered by the lack of an aquacultural tradition and, in some cases, a shortage of water.

Present emphasis in the region is on culture of the common carp, but one may expect tilapia to play some role in the development of fish culture.

Africa

There is perhaps more excitement over tilapia in tropical Africa than anywhere else, but results to date vary greatly, as does the prospectus. The problem of stunting, which must be reckoned with wherever tilapia are raised, is crucial in Africa due to the reluctance of most Africans to accept small fish.

The future of African tilapia culture is thus dependent on the improvement and spread of population control techniques. Culture of tilapia will undoubtedly continue to be practiced in virtually all African countries but, as in the past, success may be expected to be greatest in those countries where government supervision and assistance are greatest. Most noteworthy in this respect are Uganda and the Malagasy Republic.

Government supervision is necessary not only for economic reasons but because Africa lacks a tradition of fish culture. Thus a farmer who is perfectly willing to work long and hard on a terrestrial crop is culturally conditioned to think of fish as wild game rather than as livestock to be tended, and he may let a carefully constructed and stocked fish pond deteriorate for lack of attention.

Southeast Asia

lilapia may be expected to continue to play an important role in fish culture, particularly in Taiwan and Indonesia. Whether significant expansion will occur depends on the results of research, on the extent to which eutrophication renders inland and brackish water unsuitable for culture of other fish, and, in some countries, on whether or not regional attitudes toward tilapia change.

United States

The consensus of workers at Auburn University is that tilapia are not presently feasible for culture in the United States, due to the premium placed on large fish, the difficulty in overwintering (even in Alabama, tilapia used in research must be brought indoors during the winter), the doubtfulness of consumer acceptance, the availability of a wide variety of native fishes for culture, and the justifiable concern of conservationists and sport fishermen over the possible ecological effects of the intentional or accidental stocking of tilapia in natural waterways.

Large-scale culture of tilapia is not expected in the United States but, despite the warnings of ecologists, occasional introductions may be made. Java tilapia and/or Nile tilapia have already been stocked locally as food or sport fish or for mosquito control in at least six of the southern states and Hawaii. There is as yet no indication of their impact on fisheries or the ecology in any of these areas.

Temperate Regions of Europe and Asia

Little future is seen for tilapia in these regions, except perhaps in industrial cooling waters. Experiments along these lines are being carried out in England, the Soviet Union, and West Germany. Some success has also been reported from tilapia culture in the south of France, but details are not available.

Latin America

In no other major area of the world is fish culture so poorly developed. Widespread protein deficiency in Latin America has in recent years prompted the various national governments and international aid agencies to investigate the potential of fish culture in the region.

The most frequently suggested group of fishes for culture there are the *Tilapia* spp. The only serious objection which can be raised is that if tilapia find their way into natural waters, their effect on the local ecology could be disastrous.

With this in mind studies have been undertaken in a number of countries, notably Brazil, Guatemala, and Peru, to determine the aquacultural potential of native fish species.

Results to date are not encouraging, so experimental culture of tilapia is proceeding in many Latin American countries, especially Brazil and Costa Rica.

Commercial production of tilapia is already under way in Jamaica and Trinidad. In Jamaica tilapia culture is quite successful in terms of yield but shows little promise of being able to add significantly to the abundant fish supply contributed by marine fisheries.

In Trinidad the situation is much the same as regards pond culture, but Trinidad and some other Caribbean islands have further resources for fish culture in the form of extensive fresh and brackish water swamps.

It has been suggested that tilapia could be cultured and stocked in these swamps to supplement the take of fishermen who regularly exploit them.

CURRENT AND FUTURE RESEARCH IN TILAPIA CULTURE

There is no form of fish culture that cannot benefit from research, but tilapia culture, as a young branch of the art involving 12 or so species grown under widely differing conditions all over the world, is in particular need of information obtained through research.

Growing Tilapia in Thermal Effluent

One aspect of tilapia research-the experimental culture of tilapia in industrial cooling waters-may result in still further geographical expansion of tilapia culture, but most tilapia research is aimed at improving production in the tropical and moderate climates where they are already successfully raised.

Population Control

Easily the most important advance which would be made would be a foolproof method of preventing overcrowding and stunting. This has usually been approached through hybridization. As mentioned earlier, there are at least three tilapia crosses that yield 100% male offspring, but one of these is difficult to produce, one involves the use of stocks from rather limited geographic areas, and one involves *T. hornorum,* which is not available to many culturists outside east Africa and Malaysia.

What is needed is not only an easily obtained and duplicated all-male hybrid, but a series of them, including plankton feeders, macrophages, salinity and temperature tolerant strains. Such hybrids might also exhibit heterosis, as does the existing all-male hybrid *T. nossambica* (Zanzibar stock) × *T. nilotica* (Lake Albert stock).

Taxonomy and Genetics

To achieve the ends of hybridization it will be necessary to better understand tilapia genetics, both at the specific and subspecific levels; to understand, for example, why mating male *T. mossambica* from Zanzibar with female *T. nilotica* from Lake Albert produces 100% male offspring, whereas mating the same sexes of the same species from other parts of the world may not.

The attainment of this understanding will entail careful examination of the taxonomy of the genus *Tilapia,* which is currently quite confused.

Ecological and Ethological Studies

Concurrent with hybridization experiments should be studies to more precisely determine the ecological niche occupied by each of the cultured species. Many attempts at tilapia culture have yielded unsatisfactory results merely because the culturist did not have the necessary information to choose the right species or hybrid for the job.

Once the roles of the various species are known, hybridization can proceed more intelligently and the culturist will have an even wider selection of tilapia types to choose from. One of the best means of approaching the problem of ecological niche would be to study tilapia behavior and food habits under natural or seminatural conditions.

When the roles played by the various species and hybrids are known there will be a real basis for the foundation of tilapia polyculture, with or without nontilapia species, at a level of sophistication comparable to that of Chinese carp culture.

Even now, studies aimed at finding better species combinations and stocking rates for pond communities would not be amiss.

Pond Fertilization and Supplementary Feeding

Among the less glamorous tasks facing researchers on tilapia culture is the assessment of bodies of water for culture. It is all very fine to do research on pond fertilization in Alabama or Israel, but to attempt to extrapolate from there to a pond of unknown physical and chemical characteristics in East Africa is scarcely realistic.

For this and other purposes, regional research stations should be established wherever largescale tilapia culture is contemplated, and surveys should be made of all waters to be cultivated so that the culturist may proceed intelligenth with specific management measures appropriate for his area.

Much more work needs to be done on pond fertilization and feeding in tilapia culture. Both laboratory research on nutritional needs and field work on the effects of different feeds and fertilizers in practical culture are needed.

Not only the yields which may be achieved, but the protein content and marketability of the fish produced should be assessed. With a sound basis in research, further development of tilapia culture can proceed apace.

Development will surely include at least some practical culture in Latin America, gradual replacement of individually operated subsistence cultures with more efficient commercial or communal operations, education of would-be tilapia growers, particularly in Africa, as to the need for population control, proper feeding, and other management measures, and further mechanization wherever tilapia are cultured.

More precise means of economic analysis of culture methods should also be applied. At the present time there seem to be more questions than facts with regard to tilapia culture, but it is a safe bet that, for the foreseeable future at least, the tilapia complex will continue to be an important contributor to the world's protein supply.

12

Culture of the Shrimp

Decapod crustaceans of the suborder Natantia (*shrimps* or *prawns*) are found in fresh and salt waters virtually all over the world and many of the larger species are highly valued as human food. In most countries, shrimp culture is nonexistent or at best in the experimental stages, but some species have been cultivated in southeast Asia for five centuries or more.

The methods in use are crude, often consisting of no more than trapping and confinement of young shrimp in brackish water ponds for several months before harvesting. In most southeast Asian countries production of shrimp has long been incidental to the culture of brackish water fish, but monoculture of shrimp, with concurrent technological advances, is emerging in a number of countries.

Truly intensive shrimp culture, with breeding in captivity, has yet to play a significant role in southeast Asia but has been part of the picture in Japan since 1934, when Motosaku Fujinaga achieved the first success in spawning and partial rearing of the kuruma shrimp (*Pena.eus japon-cus*).

Fujinaga strove to perfect his techniques until 1959 when, with the financial assistance of several fishery companies, he was able to set up a pilot hatchery and farm. By 1967, some 20 operators were using his techniques to produce 4000 tons of shrimp annually from 8500 ha of water. There is presently no successful commercial shrimp culture in the Western hemisphere, but scientists and entrepreneurs in the United States and several Latin American countries have noted the similarity between American commercial shrimps and the kuruma shrimp and have attempted to apply Japanese culture methods, to date with only partial success.

Attempts have also been made in the United States to apply southeast Asian methods, but would-be shrimp culturists have been held back not only by biological and technological problems but by legal difficulties with regard to the ownership and use of estuarine waters.

Shrimp of various species are fished virtually from pole to pole, but commercial shrimp culture is, with the notable exception of Japan, confined to the tropical and subtropical regions. In recent years, however, experimental shrimp culture has been initiated in temperate zone countries.

Nor is freshwater exempt. Experiments in Malaysia and elsewhere have demonstrated the potential for culture of freshwater prawns.

SHRIMP CULTURE IN SOUTEAST ASIA

Despite the long history of shrimp culture in southeast Asia, little is known about the biology of the species cultured there. Up to thirteen species of Penaeid shrimps and seven species of Caridean shrimps, all edible, may be found in ponds used in culture, but none of the Carideans

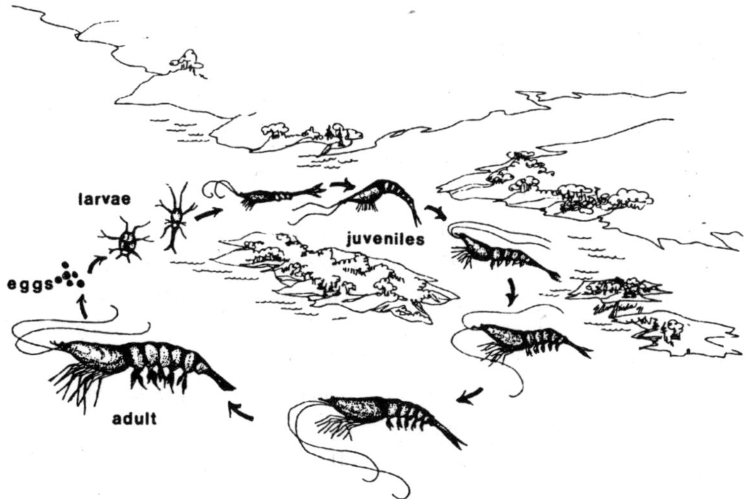

Figure 12.1: Life cycle of Penaeid shrimps.

and only seven of the Penaeids (the banana prawn, *Penaeus merguiensis;* the Indian prawn, *Penacus indices;* the sugpo prawn or giant tiger prawn, *Penaeus monodon;* the green tiger prawn, *Penaeus semisulcatus;* the yellow prawn, *Metapenaeus brevicornis; Metapenaeus ensis* and *Metapenaeus burkenroadi*) are eaten.

In India *Penaeus carinates, Metapenaeus dobsoni,* and the Palaemonid species *Leander styliferus* may be added to the list of cultured shrimps. All the cultured species share the habit of entering shallow coastal waters when very young. There they settle to the bottom, where they grow rapidly for several weeks then return to the sea.

It is a matter for debate whether postlarval shrimp actively seek out brackish water or if only a small fraction of the total population find their way to the estuaries by chance. Whichever is the case, several species occur in estuaries in sufficient abundance to support a fairly significant shrimp culture industry.

Selection for species occurs only at the harvest or marketing stages, except in the Philippines where the sugpo prawn is cultured exclusively.

Malaysia and Singapore

Unlike most parts of southeast Asia, the Malay Peninsula has no tradition of brackish water pond culture. However, there is a large demand for shrimp by the predominantly Chinese population of Singapore.

There is no local shrimp fishery, so shrimp had to be imported until the initiation in 1937 of shrimp culture in modified mangrove swamps in rural Singapore. Singapore thus became the first country to support shrimp culture exclusive of fish.

The demand for shrimp remains high today, but shrimp culture is on the decline due to the rapid usurpation of coastal lands for industrial purposes. Consequently, shrimp culture has spread into neighboring areas of Malaysia.

Before attempting to modify a mangrove swamp for shrimp culture, its suitability for that purpose must be evaluated. The first step in site evaluation is sampling by cast net to determine the relative abundance of various shrimps. If large numbers of Caridean shrimps are captured, the site is likely to be rejected.

There are seven additional factors important in site selection.

1. Tidal range and swamp elevation. Tidal inflow and outflow should ideally be such that the pond can be harvested every day, since premium prices are paid for very fresh shrimp. If the swamp is too high or high tides too low, no sea water will

enter on neap tides, even at high tide, thus reducing the number of fishing (lays. In practice it is not possible to harvest any pond every day; culturists aim at 20 to 22 harvest days per month. Very low swamps and high tides provide more potential harvest days, but expenditures for construction and maintenance of dikes and sluice gates may be prohibitive under these circumstances.

2. Depth. It should be possible to maintain about 0.7 m of water in the pond at all times.
3. Location relative to the coast. If the pond is too near the beach, the dike may be damaged by wave action. Usually a fringe of at least 15 m of mangroves is left undisturbed between the shore and the pond for protection. On the other hand, if the pond is too far from the coast it may be less accessible to shrimp and there may be a danger of flooding with rainwater during the monsoon season.
4. Soil quality. The bottom should be mostly hard clay, perhaps mixed with sand and organic detritus. Soft, porous bottom materials are to be avoided, since the swamp bottom is the source of construction material for the dike. There should be no more than 50 cm of silt on the bottom since, for unknown reasons, heavy silting reduces shrimp catches. Large amounts of organic matter are also to be avoided, since their decay may produce anaerobic conditions leading to mass mortalities of shrimp.
5. Surface area. The smallest ponds require at least two workers daily for maintenance and operation. For this reason ponds of less than 12 ha are not economically feasible.
6. Salinity. Salinity of sea water entering a shrimp pond should be at least 18c/ at all times; 24 to 30%, is considered optimal.
7. Drainage basin. Heavy freshwater run-off can reduce salinity below the preferred level for shrimp. For this reason swamps which receive large freshwater streams are not favored. If a swamp is otherwise suitable, however, it may be feasible to divert such streams.

Once a suitable swamp is located it is converted into a pond by surrounding it with an earthen dike, or bund. The bund must be high enough to prevent the highest tide from flowing over the top, strong enough to withstand water pressure differentials, and wide enough for operating personnel to walk on top. Construction is usually by manual labor. Given the soft soils of mangrove swamps, this is more efficient than dredges, tractors, bulldozers, and so on.

Indeed, where machinery has been used in bund construction it has been necessary to make tl, bund wider and higher merely to support the machinery. Clay for bund construction is taken from the swamp bottom in slat about 30 cm × 15 cm × 10 cm thick.

These slabs are laid side by site around the perimeter of the pond and each layer is sun baked before the next is added. The quality of workmanship at this stage will largely de termine the amount of maintenance necessary in the future.

Even a well constructed bund will sink about 30 cm/year, but poorly constructed bunds may sink as much as 90 cm. Clay slabs are excavated so as to create a pattern of channels radiating from the sluice gates to the farthest corners of the pond. Experience has shown that this practice increases yields.

It may be that the channels serve to distribute young shrimp evenly so that they are less vulnerable to predators and make more efficient use of the food supply. Not onl\ the channels but the entire bottom is cleared of mangrove stumps and leveled, since stumps and other irregularities provide hiding places for predators.

The bottom should slope toward the sluice gates to permit total drainage if desired. Sluice gates must be large and numerous enough to allow tides to enter and leave the pond rapidly, thus avoiding extreme pressures on either side of the bund. Sluice gates should be located so that the incoming tide will not generate eddies and whirlpools, which may trap the incoming shrimp.

The gates themselves should be built with a concrete foundation and sides, and the bund adjacent to the gates should be reinforced by wooden pilings. A simple wooden windlass is used to operate the gates. The channel connecting the pond to the sea should be straight or nearly so and kept clear of plants.

It is believed that plants vibrating in the current frighten young shrimp. Owing to the rapid turnover of water in such ponds, fertilization is not practiced. A few experimental attempts did not appear to produce any significant differences in yields. It is customary, however, to drain the pond completely at least once a year and let it sun bake for 3 to 4 days before refilling.

This is believed to increase the rate of production of plankton and other microorganisms. Next to normal sinking and erosion, the biggest problem in pond maintenance is the mud lobster (*Thalassina anomala*), which burrows in bunds, weakening them and causing leaks. Mud lobsters may be killed by placing a piece of calcium carbide about 25 mm in diameter into the funnel-shaped burrow.

A small amount of quicklime poured into the funnel has the same effect. Daily stocking of shrimp ponds is usually uncontrolled. When the incoming tide in front of the sluice gates reaches a height of 60 cm above the pond level, the gate is simply opened and shrimp and various other organisms are allowed to swim in.

A 60-cm head is necessary to ensure that no shrimp swine out of the pouch. At (lead high tide a 0.13-cm mesh wire screen is placed across the gate to retain the young shrimp. Although there are undoubtedly seasonal spawning peaks for each of the cultured species, there is some reproduction of all species throughout the year, so that this method is practicable year-round.

This sort of stocking permits entry of numerous predators which, if not controlled, will substantially reduce the yield of shrimps. The most serious predators are fish, which may be effectively controlled by poisoning with teaseed cake every 4 months. Ponds so stocked always contain shrimp at all stages of growth.

Large shrimp, up to 4 cm in carapace length, are harvested at dusk or night on ebb tides as they seek to return to the sea. Daytime harvesting is not practiced since few of the shrimp are swimming about during the day.

Shrimp are captured in a conical net about 9 m long with mesh decreasing from 2 cm at the mouth to 1 cm at the cod end. The mouth is constructed so as to fit in place of the sluice gate. The net is affixed directly behind the gate just before the tide ebbs. When the tide begins to ebb the gate is opened and shrimp attempting to leave the pond are captured.

Damage to the net by the rushing current is averted by supporting it in a troughlike wooden raceway on the outer side of the sluice gate. When the water level in the pond is reduced to about 60 cm the sluice gate is closed and the net hauled up. Reliable production figures are not available for this form of shrimp culture primarily because culturists are reluctant to reveal their incomes. Yields of 300 to 800 kg/ha are reported, but it is likely that well-managed operations yield up to 1200 kg/ha of edible Penaeid shrimps annually.

India

Methods similar to that just described are used in India, but the usual sites for culture are 1- to 10-ha rice fields, which are stocked with shrimp only (luring the 6 months when rice is not grown.

Production varies greatly; figures from 300 to 1600 kg/ha for the 6-month growing season are cited in the literature.

Indonesia

Even less intensive methods are used in Indonesia, where Indian prawns, green tiger prawns, yellow prawns, and *Metapenaeus ensis* find their way into tambaks used in brackish water fish culture and are harvested at the rate of 25 to 400 kg/(ha)(year). Various tiny shrimps, notably Mysids, which are not used elsewhere, are also harvested to make trassi, a flavoring product used in Indonesian cookery.

The philippines

The traditional method of shrimp culture is also used in the Philippines, but Philippine shrimp farmers are increasingly adopting more sophisticated methods of growing the largest of the Penaeid shrimps, the sugpo prawn, alone or in combination with milkfish (*Chanos chanos*). Monoculture of the sugpo prawn of course depends on the availability of pure stocks of sugpo fry (postlarval stage).

Eight- to fifteen-millimeter sugpo fry may be captured from rivers by dip-netting from a boat, or by wading fishermen, but more often they are taken by use of lures, called "bonbon." These lures consist of bundles of twigs or grass tied at intervals of 1 to 2 m to a line strung between two poles set in a river near the bank. Sugpo fry entering the river attach themselves to these bundles and are captured by being shaken off into a dip net.

Both methods are practiced day and night on all tides and in all weather. At the peak of fry migration it is possible to collect 1000 fry in an hour. These collection methods result in the capture of a number of species of shrimp, but the sugpo are easily distinguished by the band of dark brown pigment running through their otherwise transparent bodies.

After sorting, they are kept in lots of 100 to 250 in earthenware pots provided with banana leaves for attachment. Later they are placed in plastic bags for sale and delivery to shrimp culturists. Sugpo fry collection is a fairly profitable business, but as in any business where the supply of the commodity cannot be controlled by the operator, prices vary widely with time and place.

As in Malaysia and Singapore, pond site selection is crucial. Philippine culturists concern themselves chiefly with two factors, soil

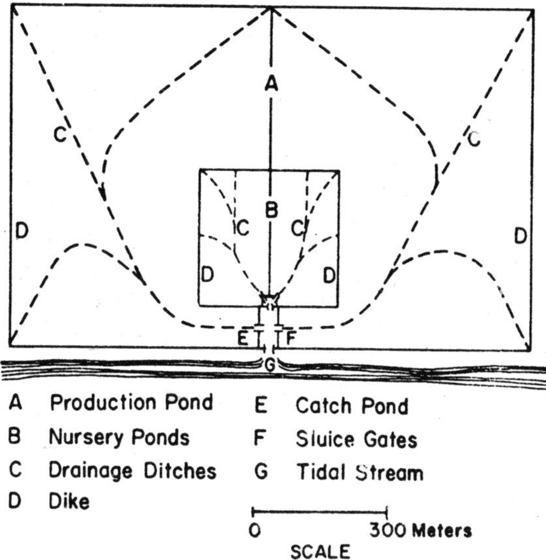

Figure 12.2: Philippine shrimp pond.

type and elevation. Sandy clay is the best type of soil, because it lends itself to dike construction, produces good growth of algal food for the young shrimp, and facilitates the burrowing habits of the sugpo prawn. Clay loam is an acceptable second choice.

Ordinary tides should fill the pond to a depth of at least 0.9 m. Ideally, it should be possible to exchange half the water in the pond as often as is necessary to maintain a temperature of approximately 25°C and a salinity of 20 to 25%.

Owing to the tidal range in the Philippines, which averages only 0.3 m during neap tides, this is not always possible. Fortunately, the sugpo prawn is capable of withstanding temperatures as high as 30°C and salinities as low as 10% or as high as 35% for 1 or 2 days.

Pond construction in advanced Philippine shrimp culture is more elaborate than in the Malayan method. Figure 2 illustrates a rather elaborate but highly effective design for a 10-ha pond. Much larger ponds may be used, in which case they are usually subdivided by dikes into smaller units.

Many ponds currently in use are much less sophisticated in design than the one illustrated. Dikes and sluice gates are constructed as in Malaysia and Singapore. The outer sluice gate opens into a catch pond, which is somewhat deeper than the rest of the pond. The entire pond bottom should slope toward the catch pond and sluice gates.

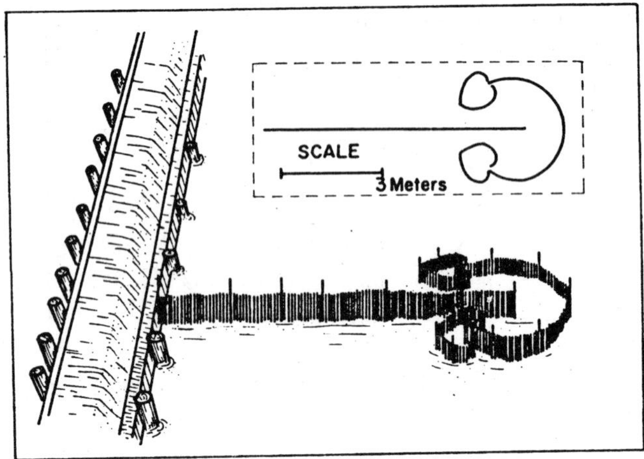

Figure 12.3: Philippine bamboo shrimp trap.

A nylon mesh screen behind the sluice gates filters out predators and other undesired organisms. The drainage ditches in the bottom serve chiefly to facilitate harvest. Vegetation and large obstructions are removed from the bottom, but small branches and twigs are provided as places of attachment for the young shrimp.

After cleaning and leveling the bottom, the pond is dried for 2 to 6 weeks, depending on weather conditions. During this time agricultural lime should be applied at 400 kg/ha or more to absorb excess carbon dioxide and supply the calcium required by the shrimp during their moulting periods.

Then the pond is filled with tidal water to a depth of 3 to 10 cm to induce the growth of the microbenthos complex known as lab-lab, which serves as food for the young shrimp. After about a month the pond will be ready for stocking.

Sugpo fry are stocked at 300,000 to 500,000/ha, in the nursery section if the pond is provided with one. Newly stocked shrimp do not disperse rapidly, so stocking is best done by scattering them around the pond to lessen the danger of mass predation or sèvere competition for food.

When sugpo are raised together with milkfish it is best not to stock until after the milkfish fry are large enough to be immune to predation by the sugpo. This sort of polyculture is becoming less popular since, although total yield in kilograms per hectare is higher than that for monoculture of shrimp, the dollar yield currently is lower.

Growth of floating, green filamentous algae, which might serve as food, is discouraged in nursery ponds since very young shrimp may become entangled in it.

Lab-lab is the primary food but rice bran or dead fish and other animals ground into meal may be given as supplementary food. Such feeds are piled in the corners of the pond and serve as a source of fertilizer as well as food.

Another supplementary food used with good results is small fish, boiled to soften the flesh and placed along the dike in late afternoon and early evening when the sugpo start feeding. After 3 to 8 weeks in the nursery the shrimp are stocked in production ponds at 10,000 to 12,500/ha.

In ponds set up as in Figure elsewhere in this chapter this may be accomplished by opening the nursery dike and driving them out. If separate nursery ponds are maintained, the shrimp are caught in bamboo traps. After trapping there will still be numerous shrimp left in the nursery.

Some of these may be captured by removing the branches and twigs to which they attach. The rest must be picked out of the mud after draining the pond. Production ponds are operated similarly to nursery ponds except that, in addition to lab-lab, growth of filamentous green algae is encouraged. Sugpo prawns are reared for 4 months to 1 year.

Throughout the nursing and rearing periods a continuous exchange of filtered tidal water is maintained in the ponds. Average size at harvest, which is the chief determinant of the price the shrimp will bring, may be increased by lengthening the rearing period.

Supplemental feeding enhances not only growth but survival. Average survival from stocking to harvest for unfed shrimp is only 20%, but as many as 60% may survive when supplemental feeding is employed.

Harvest may be carried out by draining the pond and concentrating the shrimp in the catch basin or, if there is no catch basin, by attaching bag nets such as used in Malaysia and Singapore to the sluice gates.

A more frequently used practice is to place bamboo traps similar to those used in nursery ponds in the pond. Lights are often used to attract shrimp into the traps at night. Whatever method of harvest is used, the burrowing habits of the sugpo prawn occasion some loss, which may be reduced by draining the pond and picking them out of the mud.

It is customary to refer to Philippine shrimp culture as more "advanced" than that practiced in other southeast Asian countries, but production per hectare lags behind the rest of the region; annual yields

Table 12.1: Average rate of growth of cultured sugpo prawns (Penaeus monodon) in the philippines.

Duration of Culture	*Total Length (mm)*	*Body Depth (mm)*	*Weight (g)*
Fry 15.3	1.6	0.025	
1 week	21.5	2.5	0.06
2 weeks	28.2	3.6	0.08
3 weeks	38.8	4.5	0.92
4 weeks	45.3	5.7	0.78
5 weeks	57.1	7.8	1.63
6 weeks	60.3	9.7	3.39
7 weeks	69.5	10.9	4.36
2 months	79.0	9.8	4.34
3 months	94.7	11.1	6.88
4 months	120.0	15.3	14.5
6 months	141.9	18.3	22.3
7 months	152.6	16.4	25.1
9 months	178.0	27.8	57.3
10 months	211.6	30.2	62.8
11 months	223.0	32.0	70.7
1 year	229.8	32.0	95.1

are from 250 to 900 kg/ha. It may be that monoculture of the sugpo prawn leaves open ecological niches which would normally be occupied by other species of shrimp.

Philippine shrimp culture is also severely limited by the undependable supply of sugpo fry and the inefficiency of harvesting. Research on the natural behavior of the sugpo prawn might result in increased yields by providing the key to both artificial spawning and effective harvesting.

Even the most dramatic improvement in breeding and harvesting techniques may not be adequate to counteract the damage done in recent years by industrial pollution of Philippine coastal waters.

Taiwan

Methods of shrimp culture like those practiced in the Philippines are supplanting traditional methods in Taiwan as well. Unlike Philippine culturists, most Taiwanese shrimp producers continue to grow shrimp and milkfish together and seldom practice supplemental feeding. Nevertheless, the average annual yield of shrimp culture in Taiwan is

750 to 1500 kg/ha. This may have something to do with the ecological diversity of Taiwanese shrimp ponds, since Taiwanese culturists do not select a single species of shrimp but culture a combination of species, which may include green tiger prawns, kuruma shrimp, sugpo prawns, *Metapenaeus ensis, Penaeus carinatus,* and *Penaeus teraoi.*

In 1968, fisheries officers at the Tainan Fisheries Experimental Station successfully spawned and reared several of these species in captivity, using the methods developed for kuruma shrimp in Japan (discussed later).

Thus Taiwan may soon become the second country to support truly intensive shrimp culture. Successful introduction of Japanese techniques to the southeast Asian countries would certainly increase production, but the rate of biological and technological advance is not the only factor that will influence the uncertain future of shrimp culture in the region.

Shrimp is presently a luxury food, and it is unlikely that shrimp culture will become so efficient that the price will drop to a level competitive with that of brackish water fish.

Thus, if increased human population or agricultural failure create a need for increased production of inexpensive protein foods in southeast Asia, the present trend toward shrimp culture and. away from brackish water fish culture in such countries as the Philippines may be reversed.

INTENSIVE SHRIMP CULTURE IN JAPAN

The model for improvement of shrimp culture in southeast Asia and throughout the world is the Japanese method of farming the kuruma shrimp. Whereas in traditional methods of culture shrimp are allowed to pass through all the larval stages before human intervention occurs, in modern Japanese culture all life stages, from egg to adult, are passed in captivity.

This not only provides a more dependable supply of shrimp but allows the culturist to grow his stock for a longer time, thus producing larger shrimp which can compete in the market with those taken by trawlers.

At present, the kuruma shrimp is the only species so intensively cultured, although in recent years Japanese scientists have been able to adapt Fujinaga's methods to the green tiger prawn and *Metapenaeus ensis*.

Yields attained by Japanese shrimp growers are far in excess of those achieved elsewhere, varying from 2000 to 6000 kg/ha, depending chiefly on whether running water can be supplied.

In nature, kuruma shrimp, like most Penaeid shrimps, mate and spawn at sea. Copulation between males and females normally takes place following each moult of the female. The sperm are encapsulated in spermatophores and inserted by the male into a special seminal receptacle of the female.

This may occur at any time of year, the unused spermatophores being rejected with the shell at each moult. A supply of sperm is thereby available to the female when spawning occurs. The spawning of the female lasts from mid-May to the end of September. During the spawning act, sperms deposited in the seminal receptacles are released and fertilization occurs as the eggs are discharged.

The fertilized eggs are freely dispersed throughout the water and hatch to nauplius larvae 13 to 14 hours after spawning. The nauplii moult six times within the following 36 hours, passing into the protozoea stage with the sixth moult.

The protozoeae, in turn, pass through three moults into the mysis stage during the following 5 days, and the mysis moult an additional three times during the next 5 days, then metamorphose into the first postlarval shrimp. At that stage, the animal ceases its planktonic existence and begins to crawl on the bottom, passing through an additional 20 to 22 moults, attaining adult characters and a body length of about 6 cm over a period of about 40 days.

The natural salinity at which larval development occurs ranges between 27 and 32%,. In culture this may exceed 35%$_{0}$ without adverse effects. The larvae and postlarvae also withstand a wide temperature range of 15 to 33°C, though development is most rapid at 28 to 30°C.

Beginning with the first protozoea stage, the larvae begin to feed, taking unicellular algae, small crustaceans, and a variety of other planktonic microorganisms. The postlarvae begin immediately to feed upon small benthic organisms and plant and animal debris. Some Japanese culturists engage in both spawning and rearing shrimp, but the majority of seedlings, as the juvenile, are called, are produced by specialists.

Some seedling producers grow their own brood stock, but most rely on fishermen to supply breeders. Only females are needed, due to their habit of storing sperm between moults. Spawners of 50 to 120 g are preferred to larger shrimp. Females may be easily distinguished from males by the dark grey ovaries visible between the carapace and the abdomen, but it is very difficult to determine the maturity of the ova.

Females suspected of being ready to spawn are placed, singly or in groups of two to five, in tanks 2 to 15 m^2 in surface area and 1 m deep, containing aged sea water, and left overnight. A mild water circulation is maintained to separate and aerate the eggs. If a female is ready to spawn, she will usually do so on the first night.

The act of spawning is quite vigorous and may be detected by the presence of foam on the surface of the water. Sometimes the water takes on a pinkish hue from a jellylike material which coats the newly spawned ova. Kuruma shrimp produce an average of 300,000 eggs and sometimes as many as 1.2 million.

The female is removed immediately after spawning to prevent her from eating the eggs. Spawning can be carried out at temperatures of 22 to 33°C and salinities of 28 to 36%, but 25 to 29°C and 32 to 35% are considered optimal. In nature, kuruma shrimp encounter a wide range of temperatures and salinities, but Japanese culturists prefer to keep these factors constant throughout the life cycle.

This is considered particularly important during hatching, for which most culturists employ a temperature-controlled room. Hatching takes place in 13 to 14 hours at 25°C. The newly hatched larvae may be transferred to larger tanks. The Shrimp Farming Co., Ltd., of Takamatsu uses 112- or 450-liter ceramic, tile-lined tanks stocked with 15,000 or 100,000 larvae, respectively.

These tanks are maintained under greenhouse conditions at 26 to 30°C and vigorously aerated. In the early part of the season (April to June) supplemental heating by means of water-jackets in the tanks is required.

A newer and less expensive technique involves 10-m X 10-m X 2-in deep concrete tanks placed outdoors in full sunlight and used for both spawning and larvae rearing. Thirty to one hundred females per tank are stocked for spawning. Slow water circulation is maintained at all times, and the water supply is recycled after passing through 80- to 100mesh/cm vinylon cloth filters.

Whatever type of tank is used for rearing the young shrimp, they remain in it throughout the 10- to 12-day larval period and for the first 20 days of postlarval life. The season for rearing larvae and postlarvae lasts from early April to mid-September.

The nauplii do not feed, but thereafter it is essential that each life stage receive a special diet. The protozoeae are fed mostly on diatoms, occasionally supplemented by the flagellates *Isochrysis galbana* and *Monochrysis lutheri*. The latter are considered particularly valuable for very young fry.

The original technique of diatom feeding, as developed by Fujinaga and still practiced by many culturists, involved pure cultures of *Skeletonema costatum* grown in separate tanks and pumped into the fry tanks. In 1964 Fujinaga developed a technique of culturing diatoms in the fry tank by merely adding 200 g of potassium nitrate and 20 g of potassium phosphate to each tank daily.

This not only greatly reduces labor and expense but produces a mixture of species, which has been found to be preferable to a single species. In 1966 30 species of diatoms were identified from a single culture tank.

Diatoms are included in the diet of mysis larvae, but 90% of their food consists of newly hatched nauplii of brine shrimp (*Artemia*), cultured at a density of 10 g of eggs per liter. Five liters of such a culture per 15,000 larvae per day are fed.

Clams and shrimp ground into 1-mm pieces may be used as a supplementary food, but brine shrimp nauplii have been found essential. When kuruma shrimp reach the postlarval stage and assume a benthic life it is advisable to begin to circulate, as well as aerate, the water in the rearing tank.

Brine shrimp may still be fed, but small pieces of annelids, nematodes, copepods, bivalves, and fish are the principal food. Cannibalism may begin to occur at this stage, so considerable amounts of food should be supplied, taking care not to overfeed and foul the water.

The starting rate for postlarvae is 20 g of food/(day) (10,000 individuals). This is increased to 80 to 120 g/day over the 20-day growing period, during which the postlarvae undergo three or four moults. When they reach 15 to 20 mm in length and 10 mg in weight they are ready for stocking in production ponds or sale as seedlings.

Total survival from egg to seedling stage averaged around 10% in the mid-1960s but rates as high as 50% have been reported in recent years. Transportation of seedlings to production ponds is complicated by their cannibalistic tendencies.

On short trips the seedlings are placed in 1-m × 0.7-m × 0.3-m deep boxes with fine mesh tops and bottoms. The boxes are placed in a tank with a water circulating system. At water temperatures above 25°C, losses to cannibalism of up to 30% are tolerated.

On longer trips (up to 10 hours) the seedlings are transported in trucks equipped with hermetically sealed refrigerated chambers to lower the metabolic rate of the shrimp and reduce cannibalism. The seedlings are placed in lots of 5000 to 10,000 in 20-liter polyethylene bags containing 6 to 8 liters of sea water and a supply of oxygen.

The temperature inside the chamber is initially set at 1 to 15°C and gradually raised during transport to the temperature of the receiving water so as to prevent thermal shock. Thus 600,000 to 700,000 seedlings can be transported in a 2-ton truck at a cost of about 3 to 5% of the price of the seedlings.

There are two basic methods used in growing kuruma shrimp for market; pond culture and "river" culture. Up to three times as many kilograms of shrimp per area of water surface are obtained by the river method, but due to the difficulty of supplying large amounts of running water it is not suitable for large-scale operations.

Attempts are being made to grow kuruma shrimp in net cages, a method which has to a large degree combined the virtues of running water culture and pond culture for many species of fish, but this is not being done on a commercial scale yet.

Kuruma shrimp production ponds vary greatly in size, from 0.01 to 1 t9 ha or more. Small ponds, which are usually constructed of concrete, arc more expensive to build but easier and more economical to maintain than the large earthen-banked ponds, which have a tendency to become choked with filamentous algae, which may suddenly die off and pollute the pond.

Some shrimp-growing concerns use a combination of small and large ponds with a total area of perhaps 10 ha. Whatever the surface area. growing ponds are 1 to 2 m deep and have sand bottoms. Interchange of sea water in pond culture is accomplished by means of one or two large (up to 1-m diameter) pipes which allow tidal filling and drainage.

The pipes are fitted with fine mesh screens to keep the shrimp in and extraneous organisms out. About one-fourth of the volume of water in a pond is normally exchanged at each tidal cycle, but the precise amount is highly variable.

If the amount of fresh tidal water entering the pond is not adequate to maintain a suitable concentration of dissolved oxygen, electric paddle wheels or some other means of aeration may be employed. If the tide level is such that interchange of water ceases altogether, pumping is recommended until natural circulation is restored.

Pumps may also be used when some other factor, such as an

overabundance of zooplankton, produces unusually low concentrations of dissolved oxygen.

The river-type culture facility consists of a series of oblong ponds, 0.5 to 0.7 m deep, supplied with water by an inlet pipe similar to that used in pond culture. Rapid exchange of water is achieved by pumping water out of the end pond rather than relying on tidal flow.

Usually two pumps, with a total exchange capacity of 80,000 liters/hour, are used; both are operated at night when the shrimp are active, but only one is run during the day when they are buried in the sand, hence consuming little oxygen.

The size of such culture systems is limited by the capabilities of available pumps. The Shrimp Farming Co., Ltd., operates a series of 28 ponds, each 100 m × 10 m (0.1 ha). Other operators use ponds as small as 0.02 ha.

The Shrimp Farming Co., Ltd., also grows shrimp in concrete or wooden tanks 50 m × 10 m × 1.3 m deep, with false bottoms made of fine screen. The false bottom is covered with about 2 cm of sand. Air is passed through a system of standpipes from beneath, forcing water up into the tank proper and creating a downward circulation through the sand, which acts as a filter.

This sort of aeration and filtration greatly reduces the need for constant interchange of water, although some circulation is maintained. The single most critical factor in stocking production ponds is the availability of dissolved oxygen; the minimum acceptable level is 3.5 ppm. Effective oxygen concentration can be increased by circulating the water more rapidly, thus more rapidly replacing the oxygen consumed by the shrimp.

There seems to be no simple stocking formula based on dissolved oxygen concentration and rate of circulation, but perhaps an example will demonstrate the sort of relationship which obtains. If the water temperature is 28°C and the dissolved oxygen level is at 80% of saturation (6.3 ppm) and 10% of the volume of water in the pond can be replaced hourly, the number of seedlings stocked should be as many as can be expected to produce 0.11 kg/m^2 of shrimp in September, the last hot month, allowing for 30% mortality.

If 33% of the water can be replaced per hour, the stocking density may be increased to whatever number will produce 0.50 kg/m^2 by September. Even under optimum conditions, high population densities retard the growth of kuruma shrimp, so that culturists aiming for large shrimp may stock considerably fewer than the maximum permissible numbers. The decision to be made here is an economic one. Based on current prices, which will bring the culturist a better return, a large crop of small-tomedium shrimp or a smaller crop of jumbo shrimp?

Another major factor in the growth rate of shrimp in Japan and other temperate zone countries is the date of stocking. Although kuruma shrimp can withstand temperatures as low as 4°C for short periods of time, they cease feeding below 10°C. Thus, if seedlings are stocked in the spring, they may be harvested after 6 months, but if stocking is carried out in the summer or fall, it may be necessary to hold the shrimp in ponds for as long as 9 months.

This of course results in increased mortality. One of the reasons shrimp and other crustaceans remain a luxury food is the poor efficiency of food conversion, necessitated largely by the great losses of energy involved in moulting.

The kuruma shrimp culturist should expect to produce 1 kg of shrimp for every 10 to 15 kg of feed at the optimum temperature, 25°C. Table elsewhere in this chapter is a feeding schedule which has been found adequate to prevent cannibalism and maximize growth of kuruma shrimp seedlings. Daytime feedings are discontinued after the seedlings reach about 1 g in weight, by which time they are almost exclusively nocturnal.

Diseases and parasites present little or no problem in growing kuruma shrimp from seedlings to marketable size and cannibalism is not a problem once the shrimp are past the postlarva stage. Survival between stocking and harvest varies from 60 to 100%.

In Japan, as elsewhere, one of the principal problems faced by the shrimp culturist is the low efficiency of harvesting. Conventional methods of netting and trapping are only partially effective and inevitably necessitate draining the pond and picking up by hand as many of the buried shrimp as can be found.

Better results have been obtained by use of a trawl with a high-pressure hose mounted in front to blast the shrimp from the sand, but the most effective piece of gear developed to date is an electric trawl. Some culturists simplify the harvesting problem by leaving the shrimp in ponds over the winter and harvesting a few at a time to take advantage of premium prices.

After harvest growing ponds are drained and dried for a few weeks and the algae are scraped off the concrete sides of small ponds. Sea water is introduced and allowed to sit in the ponds for a few days before restocking.

Table 12.2: Feeding schedule for kuruma shrimp (*Penaeus japonicus*). Cultured in Japan.

Weight of Individual Shrimp (G)	*Types of Food*	*Amount feed (% of total weight of Shrimp)*	*Frequency of feeding*
0.1- 0.5 (first few days after stocking)	Ground clams and shrimp	200-300	2-3 times daily
0.1- 0.5	Ground clams and shrimp	50	2-3 times daily
0.5- 1.0	Small whole shrimp or ground clams	25	2-3 times daily
1 - 2	Small whole shrimp or ground clams	25	1 feeding daily, just before sunset
2 -10	Minced fish or, preferably, low-fat meat or ground clams	15	1 feeding daily, just before sunset
10 -20	Minced fish or, preferably, low-fat meat or ground clams	5	1 feeding daily, just before sunset

Most shrimp sold in Japan are destined for use in the famous Japanese dish tempura, for which only very fresh shrimp are satisfactory. Thus it is necessary to ship shrimp live. This is made possible by chilling them to 12°C. At this temperature they can endure long periods out of water, maintaining their greatly reduced metabolic rate solely on the basis of oxygen in the water trapped in their gill cavities.

The chilled shrimp are packed in cedar sawdust, which is naturally repellant to insects. (Japanese cedar, *Cryptomeria japonica, is* not related to American cedars but is closely akin to the California redwood.) Due to the excellent insulating properties of sawdust, further refrigeration is not necessary for up to 2 days in the summer and 4 days in the winter. On arrival the shrimp may be revived by dropping them into warm water and sold live.

With the introduction in recent years of numerous technological improvements, Japanese shrimp culture has become so successful that cultured shrimp are being released in the Inland Sea to augment the shrimp fisheries. Local governmental units (prefectures) are responsible for stocking programs.

Most of the shrimp for stocking are produced by federal Propagation Centers, but some prefectures maintain their own hatcheries. Stocking is carried out in sandy-bottomed bays and inlets, geographically and oceanographically situated so that the shrimp are not likely to migrate out and are relatively free of predators.

Most of these areas once supported large populations of kuruma shrimp which for one reason or another, usually overfishing, have been depleted. Final selection of sites to be stocked is determined by the prefectural governments in consultation with Fishermen's Cooperatives.

Postlarvae, such as might be sold for use in commercial shrimp culture, were originally used in this program, but it was found that stocking larger shrimp resulted in better survival. Thus propagation centers now rear postlarvae in running water tanks to the length of 10 to 15 mm before distributing them for stocking.

Stocked waters are opened for fishing when it is judged that the shrimp have reached harvestable size. There has been no biological proof of the success of the stocking program, but studies are being carried out by the Nansei Regional Fisheries Research Laboratory. Shrimp fishermen, however, report that in their opinion the stocking program has been effective in increasing local populations of kuruma shrimp.

EXPERIMENTAL SHRIMP CULTURE

United States

The largest shrimp fishery in the world is that exploited by Cuban, Mexican, and American trawlers in the Gulf of Mexico. The brown shrimp (*Penaeus aztecus*), the white shrimp (*Penaeus seti ferns*), the pink shrimp (*Penaeus duorarum*), and, to a lesser extent, the Caribbean brown shrimp (*Penaeus brasiliensis*) and seabob (*Xiphopenaeus kroyeri*) form the basis for that fishery as well as a similar one along the Atlantic coast of the United States as far north as the Carolina banks.

Though yields of these fisheries have remained high, they have been barely able to supply half the demand for shrimp in the United States. For this reason, and because the pollution and filling of tidal swamps and estuaries may eventually significantly reduce the available nursery areas, in recent years there has been considerable interest in shrimp culture in the United States.

American biologists have of course long been aware of Asian shrimp culture practices, but for some reason it was generally assumed that American shrimps, despite their close resemblance to Asian species of *Penaeus*, were not susceptible to culture.

Recent years, however, have seen more or less successful experiments with both the Japanese and southeast Asian methods of shrimp culture, although there are as yet no commercially successful American shrimp farms.

It may be that there are estuaries in the United States which could be farmed using the Malayan method of stocking by natural recruitment, but thus far it has been found necessary to resort to artificial stocking to obtain satisfactory yields.

The practicability of pond stocking is presently limited by the availability of postlarval and juvenile shrimp. Stock for culture may be obtained from trawlers, but shrimp taken in trawls suffer 85 to 100% mortality no matter how they are handled. Even if the healthiest appearing survivors are selected from trawl catches, a further mortality of 25% or so may be expected when they are stocked.

The only capture device that does not produce high mortality is the cast net, but cast nets are practical only during the first few weeks of the year when shrimp are abundant in tidal streams. The problem of recruitment ceases to be of importance if reproduction can be controlled.

Attempts have been made to induce spawning of American Penaeids in ponds without success, and most authorities are in agreement that the future, if any, of American shrimp culture lies in adapting Japanese methods to American circumstances and species or, failing that, in introducing kuruma shrimp.

One dissenter is John H. Knox, a business management consultant who has immersed himself in shrimp culture biology and technology and believes that, with suitable modification, the Malayan system of continual stocking and harvest would produce commercially feasible yields of brown shrimp, white shrimp, and possibly pink shrimp in the United States.

Among the improved recruiting methods suggested by Knox are the construction of weirs to funnel postlarvae into a pond, driving shrimp by means of an electrical field, luring them by use of lights, and drawing them in with the type of bladeless impeller pump which is now routinely used in commercial handling of such fragile food items as eggs, tomatoes, and peaches. All of these methods have the common advantage of drawing in shrimp from a larger area than would be harvested by merely opening a sluice gate.

As in all forms of shrimp culture that depend on natural spawning and recruitment, the scheme envisioned by Knox depends largely on judicious site selection. The following factors appear to be crucial in growing American Penaeid shrimps:

Soil quality

The soil must be conducive to both the growth of shrimp and the construction of dikes. The latter factor of course implies little more than low porosity. Determining whether soil is chemically and physically compatible with shrimp is somewhat more complex.

Complicating this decision are the preferences of individual shrimp species. Brown shrimp and white shrimp generally prefer softer, muddier substrates than pink shrimp, which are commonly found on sandy bottom, A more general requirement is the absence of metallic oxides, which arc repellant, if not toxic, to shrimp.

Pollution

Domestic and industrial pollutants are of course detri mental to the welfare of shrimp, but a less obvious source of "pollution' is the mangrove tree. Although in Malaya shrimp ponds are built in mangrove swamps, the American species of mangrove at times impart to water a substance which is toxic to American shrimps.

Salinity

Postlarvae and juveniles of American Penaeid shrimps are tolerant of a wide range of salinities, but as they approach maturity it is important that excessive amounts of freshwater not enter the pond. The safe salinity range seems to be 22 to 37%.

Depth

Since high production of benthic organisms is desirable, 0.5 to 0.7 m is considered to be optimal, although depths up to 1.3 m may be satisfactory if the water is unusually clear.

In general, deeper holes are detrimental in that shrimp will congregate there rather than near the sluice gate when the pond is drained for harvest.

One or two deep holes of known location may, however, be advantageous in the Carolinas, where sudden chilling may occur. Large-scale mortality of shrimp, particularly white shrimp, has been known to occur in shallow ponds when air temperatures drop to around 4 to 5°C.

Land configuration

This is primarily an economic consideration. Construction costs may be minimized by taking advantage of natural impoundments formed by tidal creeks, swamps, or lagoons which can be adapted for shrimp culture by merely placing a sluice gate across the mouth.

Such sites, in addition to being rare, are often too deep or, if located on a creek, are subject to desalinization in the wake of heavy rainfall. In the majority of instances, a dike will have to be constructed.

The prospective culturist should thus seek to reduce construction costs by using existing land features such as river banks and railway embankments as part of the dike system and by constructing dikes using soil excavated at or near the pond site.

All ponds should be separated from the open sea by at least 15 m of marsh grass or other vegetation to break storm waves. Further details of pond culture of American shrimps have not been worked out, but Knox felt confident enough of the commercial feasibility of the process to undertake surveys of some 5000 miles of coastline to locate suitable sites for a shrimp farm.

Since the best type of marshland for this purpose is the least attractive for other forms of commercial development, he felt sure he could obtain the necessary property cheaply. Although he was successful in locating suitable sites, lie found that conservation laws and restrictions on tidelands leasing made it virtually impossible to lease acreage suitable for shrimp culture in any of the eight states where it would be feasible.

These laws, plus an entrenched emotional resistance on the part of the local citizenry to anything that would restrict access by sportsmen to marshy estuaries, have until recently thwarted all would-be shrimp farmers in the United States. This situation has begun to change as state and local governments realize the economic potential of estuarine aquaculture, but leases are still difficult to obtain.

The first tangible evidence of changing attitudes was the harvest, in 1970, of the first crop of shrimp (*Penaeus setiferus*) by Marifarms, Inc., a 1200-ha Japanese-American-owned farm near Panama City, Florida. The 1970 and 1971 harvests were experimental in nature, but in 1972 Marifarms moved into the commercial market.

The 1000 ha of estuary which comprise most of the farm are leased from the state of Florida with the stipulation that the company release 20 million shrimp annually into the natural environment.

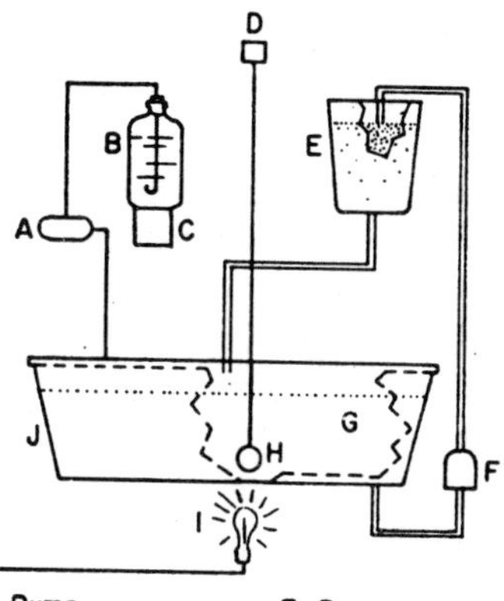

A Metering Pump
B Diatom Culture
C Magnetic Stirrer
D Air Pump
E Crushed Oyster Shell Filter
F Pump
G Plankton Screen
H Air Stone
I Light
J 100 Liter Fiberglass Aquarium

Figure 12.4: Setup in which shrimp are reared from egg to juvenile at National Marine Fisheries Service Laboratory, Galveston, Texas.

Marifarms has also moved to minimize land use conflict by permitting permanent full public access to the area. To most would-be American shrimp culturists, Knox's experiences still seem to constitute another good argument for controlled spawning of American Penaeids.

White, brown, and pink shrimp and seabobs have all been successfully spawned and reared in captivity, primarily at the United States Bureau of Commercial Fisheries Biological Laboratory, Galveston, Texas, and the University of Miami's Institute of Marine Science, using various adaptations of Fujinaga's original scheme.

Figure elsewhere in this chapter is a diagram of the type of setup in which shrimp are reared from egg to juvenile at Galveston. None of the three species can yet be produced in commercial quantities, but the greatest degree of success has been achieved using the white shrimp.

Thus far it has proven possible to rear up to 200 juvenile white shrimp per square meter in tanks 1.3 m deep, using sea water with salinities of 31.5 to 37.0%. White shrimp have also proven the most productive species for pond stocking.

Table elsewhere in this chapter lists the results of four experiments in which white shrimp were stocked in 0.05-ha ponds. In the Florida experiments, the shrimp were fed whatever amount of ground whole fish they would consume daily. At Galveston, fertilization, rather than direct feeding, was employed, I yard of chicken manure being deposited in a single location prior to stocking. Brown shrimp have not been investigated as fully as white shrimp, but it appears that they do not grow quite as well in ponds.

On the other hand, they are more hardy with respect to cold water. Pink shrimp, due to their preference for sandy bottoms, are less suitable for culture than white shrimp or brown shrimp in many areas. It seems almost certain that American researchers will eventually devise techniques as biologically efficient as those currently used by Japanese shrimp farmers.

Whether shrimp farming in the United States will ever become as economically rewarding as it is in Japan seems doubtful, although the interest shown by a number of large corporations argues in its favor. In addition to being confronted by high labor, site preparation, and equipment costs, American producers will be forced into more direct competition with shrimp fishermen than their Japanese counterparts.

In Japan the demand for live shrimp for use in tempura can only be satisfied by cultured shrimp. Since they have a monopoly on this portion of the market, Japanese shrimp culturists are thus able to charge very high prices. In the United States there would be no such discrimination between cultured shrimp and the fishery product.

The prospective American shrimp culturist must therefore ask himself how his anticipated production costs compare with the expense of outfitting, maintaining, and operating a trawler.

It may be that intensive culture will never be able to compete with trawling in the United States and that the primary function of American shrimp culture will be to compensate for the destruction of estuarine nurseries by stocking shrimp for eventual harvest by fishermen.

Latin America

Shrimp culture has yet to be accorded much consideration in Latin America, partly for economic reasons and partly because most Latin American shrimp fisheries have not been severely depleted. An exception occurs in the northern Gulf of California. Profligate use of Colorado River water for irrigation in California and Arizona has reduced that stream to a fraction of its natural volume by the time it enters Mexico and reaches the Gulf.

The resultant drying up and salinization of tidal swamps and estuaries have virtually eliminated the important fishery for cafe brown shrimp (*Penaeus cali forniensis*), blue shrimp (*Penaeus stylirostris*), and white shrimp (*Penaeus r annamei*) (not to be confused with the white shrimp of the Atlantic) in that region.

Mexican scientists are currently exploring the possibility of shrimp culture in ponds distant from the sea but connected with it by canals, as an alternative to this fishery.

Other experiments in culture of marine Penaeid shrimp in Latin America are those financed by U.S. capital in Mexico and Ecuador. In 1969 the first shrimp culture experiments were initiated in Honduras, using postlarvae supplied by the University of Miami.

Africa

Although significant shrimp fisheries are found in a number of African countries, commercial shrimp culture has not been attempted on that continent. Beginning in the mid-1960s pink shrimp were experimentally cultured in Nigeria, but the outbreak of civil war forced suspension the FAO-sponsored project.

To date most practical and experimental shrimp culture has take- ; place in tropical and subtropical regions, where catastrophic die-oils O stock in shallow ponds during cold weather are less likely to occtn However, extensive shrimp fisheries occur in temperate and even sub arctic regions and the highly successful kuruma shrimp industry of Japan demonstrates that shrimp can be successfully cultured well outside the tropics.

Korea

In 1968, South Korea became the second temperate zone country where shrimp are grown commercially. The successful experimental culture there of *Penaeus orienlalis* led to the establishment of about 50 ha of private shrimp ponds. Rapid expansion is foreseen.

Europe

Experimental culture of cold water species is currently under way in France, West Germany, and the United Kingdom. The French work is in the initial stages, kuruma shrimp having been imported from Japan in 1969.

West German biologists are further along, having succeeded in rearing the sand shrimp (*Crangon crangon*), which sustains an important fishery in the North Sea and the Baltic Sea, from the zoea stage to sexual maturity.

At present no attempt is being made to apply this experimental success on a practical basis. This might prove to be quite difficult since the sand shrimp is much more pronouncedly metamorphic than the commonly cultured Penaeid shrimps. One might therefore expect that the environmental and nutritional requirements of the various life stages would be more diverse and difficult to satisfy than those of Penaeids. Culture in the United Kingdom of the deepwater prawn (*Pandalus borealis*) and *Palaemon serratus* is also still in the laboratory stages but seems closer to commercial application.

Substantial numbers have been reared through all stages and the optimum conditions of temperature, salinity, light, and population density determined. Researchers are presently seeking means to control diseases and a cheaper substitute for brine shrimp as an early food. A number of authorities, however, consider these species too slow-growing for practical culture.

Freshwater Shrimp Culture

When shrimp are mentioned, one customarily thinks of a marine environment. But many of the largest and most desirable shrimps occur in freshwater. By far the best known of these is the giant freshwater prawn (*Macrobrachium, rosenbergi*) of the Indo-Pacific region.

Maximum length of *M. rosenbergi* is about 25 cm for males and 15 cm for females. Both sexes bring extremely high prices relative to other seafoods. Attempts have been made, with some success, to induce *M. rosenbergi* to enter impoundments for growing to marketable size, but the rather low natural population densities characteristic of this species render commercial culture by the methods used in southeast Asia for marine shrimps less than practical.

Accordingly, fishery workers in the Indo-Pacific countries have made efforts to spawn and rear *M. rosenbergi* in captivity. The first experimental success in this enterprise was achieved by an FAOsupported fisheries development project under the direction of S. W. Ling at the Fisheries Research Laboratory of the Fisheries Department of the Federation of Malaya at Glugor, Penang.

Commercial culture there is not yet a reality but might well prove feasible with some improvement in the efficiency of the methods practiced at the Penang hatchery. In nature, adult *M. rosenbergi* are found in virtually all types of fresh and brackish waters. Larval development, however, requires water of 8 to 22%$_c$ salinity.

Mating takes place a few hours after the female performs a premating moult in estuaries or in freshwater streams not far above tidewater. The male deposits sperm on the ventral thoracic legs of the female, but the sperm are not retained for long periods of time as in the marine Penaeids.

Rather the entire complement of eggs is deposited and fertilized in brood chambers at the base of the thoracic legs within 6 to 20 hours after mating. Unmated females also deposit eggs after moulting, but these fall off after 2 or 3 days.

It is believed that, in nature, females may spawn 3 to 4 times a year, producing up to 120,000 eggs each time. The eggs remain attached to the female, who aerates them by beating her pleopods and carefully removes dead eggs and foreign matter, using the first pair of thoracic legs, up to the time of hatching. The process of incubation usually requires about 19 days at 26 to 28°C.

From about the twelfth day the color of the eggs, originally bright orange, begins to fade to a pale grey. When this darkens to slate grey, hatching is imminent. From the first minutes of life, *M. rosenbergi* larvae are active swimmers, but they are not initially strong enough to hold their own against a current.

Thus river-hatched larvae are quickly swept downstream to a suitably saline environment. At first the larvae swim together in large groups, but after the tenth day of life they tend to separate. They feed primarily on zooplankton, but in the absence of an adequate supply of live animal food they will take minute bits of dead organic material or plants. Within 35 to 55 days the larvae have passed through 12 stages and metamorphose into juveniles.

Juveniles immediately adopt a benthic mode of life and commence to feed on benthic animals and organic detritus. Moulting occurs every 4 to 6 days. Juvenile *M. rosenbergi* are believed to crawl slowly upstream until, 2 to 3 months later, in the recognizable form of a young prawn, many of them have reached pure freshwater.

At this time young *M. rosenbergi* are 5 to 6 cm long (measured from eye socket to tip of telson) and weigh about 6 g each. The young prawns continue the migration begun as juveniles but swim and crawl at a much more rapid rate. Some may travel over 60 km upstream from the sea.

From this time on, *M. rosenbergi* will eat almost any piece of living or dead organic matter of suitable size. When sufficiently hungry they may resort to cannibalism. Under favorable conditions, sexual maturity is attained in 9 months, after which time there may be a downstream migration.

Sometimes egg-bearing or "berried" female *M. rosenbergi* can be captured from the wild for use in culture. Three methods of capture are employed: trap, hook and line, and hand net.

Prawn traps are funnel-shaped structures of split bamboo or galvanized wire mesh. In use they are baited with pieces of fish, shrimp, or baked coconut and set overnight near the banks of rivers. Hook and line fishing for prawns, using one or more barbless hooks baited with earthworms, small shrimp, or pieces of baked coconut, is practiced in both Malaysia and Thailand.

A small sinker, just heavy enough to hold the baited hooks on the bottom, is attached about 25 cm above the uppermost hook. When a bite is detected a few seconds are allowed for the prawn to hook itself, then the line is drawn up steadily, without jerking.

Berried female prawns caught on hook and line are kept for a day or so in submerged wire cages to ensure that they are not seriously injured. Hand netting is done at night, when prawns move into shallow water to feed.

A strong light temporarily stupefies the prawns and enables the fishermen to see the bright bluish reflection of their eyes. Specimens thus detected can be captured by careful netting from the rear. Transportation of live prawns from the field to the culture site presents few problems.

As long as they are kept moist, prawns will survive for several hours when packed in baskets between layers of soft plants. Longer journeys may require aerated tanks or plastic bags filled halfand-half with water and oxygen. If bags are used, the sharp tip of the rostrum must be cut off to prevent its puncturing the bags.

If berried females are not available in sufficient quantities, young prawns may easily be reared to maturity in captivity. Mature females are usually kept in groups in aerated 100- to 200-liter tanks. Such groups must be constantly watched for moulting.

Newly moulted females must be screened off from the rest, else they will he attacked while the shell soft. Males may fight at any time, so they are usually kept individually i·. 60-liter tanks.

When a female has moulted, 2 to 3 hours are allowed fw the shell to harden, then she is placed in the tank of a male. elating wila occur within a few hours, followed by egg laying within 24 hours. la sufficient freshly moulted females are available, group spawning may be practiced.

For this purpose 2 to 4 males are placed together with 8 to 20 females in a tank 2 to 3 m long, 1 to 1½ m wide, and 40 cm deep and mating and egg laying proceed as described. As in all stages of *M. rosenbergi* culture, vigorous aeration is essential. Both sexes are kept in freshwater through spawning.

Berried females, whether collected from the wild or mated in captivity, are transferred to individual 50- to 200-liter tanks. When the eggs begin to turn grey, sea water is added daily in small amounts so that by hatching time the salinity is 8 to 15%.

This is not only better for the larvae than freshwater, it seems to produce better rates of hatching. An average female produces about 50,000 larvae, which are almost immediately transferred to a rearing tank 2 to 3 m long and 50 to 70 cm wide containing 16 to 20 cm of water.

The bottom of the rearing tank slopes slightly to a collecting pit at one end. Larvae are captured for transfer by shading all but one corner of the hatching tank. The larvae are attracted to the lighted corner, where many of them may be captured by dipping with a cup. The remainder are siphoned into the rearing tank.

They are quite hardy with respect to water quality, but every effort is made to maximize growth and survival by providing near-optimal conditions: 12 to 14$\%_0$ salinity, a temperature of 26 to 28°C, and a pH of 7.0 to 8.0. Sudden changes in these environmental parameters are scrupulously avoided.

If the salinity of the water in the hatching tank is less than 12%, the rearing tank is initially filled to less than its capacity with water of the same salinity as that in the hatching tank. Gradual upward adjustment of salinity is made by slowly siphoning a predetermined amount of sea water into the tank.

An aerator and stirrer are used to keep the dissolved oxygen concentration near saturation. The basic larva food used at Penang is brine shrimp nauplii, which are hatched in the rearing tank, using eggs imported from the United States. Brine shrimp eggs are placed within a floating ring at one end of the tank, which is shaded.

The newly hatched nauplii are attracted to the lighted end of the tank and eaten. For the first few days of rearing the daily complement of brine shrimp eggs is about 31 teaspoonsful per batch of 50,000 larvae. This is gradually increased to 3 teaspoonsful per day when the larvae are 30 days old, then held at this level until they metamorphose to juveniles.

Some brine shrimp should he present in the rearing tank at all times to prevent cannibalism. Since brine shrimp eggs are quite expensive, supplementary feeds are used as much as possible. A suitable natural food is flesh ripe fish eggs, thoroughly washed to eliminate ovarian tissue and other foreign matter.

In 1968 workers at the Songkhla Marine Fisheries Station in Thailand succeeded in rearing *M. rosenbegi* larvae using mullet (*Mugil spp.*) eggs as the primary food with brine shrimp nauplii as an occasional supplement.

Prepared foods are also used, although brine shrimp nauplii appear to be essential during the first day of life. The current favorite at Penang is a vitamin-fortified mixture of fish flesh and egg custard steamed together, drained and passed through a screen to provide particles of an appropriate size.

Fish flesh or egg custard may also be fed separately. Powdered dried chicken blood is successfully used in Thailand. *M. rosenbergi* larvae will also eat phytoplankton, and the Hawaii Division of Fish and Game has found it convenient to grow larvae in "green water" for the first 12 days.

Prepared foods are provided at the rate of approximately 30% of the total body weight of larvae per day. For convenience in feeding, most of the rearing tank may be shaded at feeding time to concentrate the larvae in one place. Feed is gently spread on the surface of the water with a medicine dropper.

This should be done slowly enough that each larva has a chance to feed. If most of the larvae appear to be carrying food particles, they are being correctly fed.

Use of prepared feeds requires that great attention be paid to cleanliness. Uneaten food particles and fecal matter are siphoned off twice daily. Every 10 days or so a partial change of water is advisable. This is done by shading part of the tank and siphoning from that portion.

One of the disastrous consequences of overfeeding or lack of cleanliness may be an incurable fungus infection which manifests itself

Table 12.3: Practicle sizes of an artrificial feed fed to larvae of the giant freshwater prawn *(MaC)-obrachium rosenbergi)* in experiments at the fisheries research station, Glugor, Penang, Malaysia.

Age of Larvae (Days)	*Food Particle Size (mm)*
2—4	0.4
5—10	0.5
11—20	0.9
20+	1.4

as small white patches on the tails and at the bases of the appendages of if larvae. Infected larvae should be removed and destroyed. If a large percentage of any batch of larvae are infected, it is best to sacrifice them all.

Larval *M. rosenbergi* are also subject to a serious protozoal infection, which, if caught in the early stages, may be treated with 0.2 ppm c, malachite green for ½ hour daily, or for 6 hours with a single dose of 0.4 ppm copper sulfate.

Prawn larvae are sensitive to nicotine, so tobacco smoking should be prohibited in the vicinity of larvae rearing tanks. Yet another source of mortality among late larvae is jumping out of the water. Stranding may be averted by shading the sides of the tank to keep the larvae in the center.

When the larvae are ready to metamorphose, small branches, stones, shells, and so on, are placed on the bottom of the rearing tank to provide shelter for the freshly moulted juveniles, thus deterring cannibalism. When 90% of the larvae have metamorphosed, the remaining slow growers are transferred to another tank for further rearing.

The metamorphosed juveniles must next be acclimated to freshwater. This is accomplished within 3 to 8 hours by gradual replacement of the brackish water in the larvae rearing tank.

Juveniles may be reared in the same tanks used for the larvae, but it is better to provide more spacious quarters in the form of larger concrete tanks or earthen ponds with cemented brick walls.

These facilities vary in surface area from 5 to 50 m^2 and in depth from 15 cm to 1 m and are abundantly supplied with shelters for the young prawns. In addition to the usual aeration, it is desirable to maintain a slight flow of water through the tank or pond.

Stocking rates for juveniles vary from 2 to $10/m^2$. The juvenile prawns are very catholic in their food habits, but growth is maximized and cannibalism minimized by feeding fresh animal material as often as is economically feasible.

Fresh fish, mollusks, and earthworms cut into pieces according to the size of the juveniles are the principal food, although whole live aquatic worms and chironomid larvae are used when available.

Supplementary foods include dried animal material softened in freshwater for ½ hour before use and pieces of grains, peas, beans, and soft aquatic plants. Feeding is carried out four times daily; three daylight feedings and one at night. To avert cannibalism the amounts fed must be in excess of what the shrimp can consume.

Insofar as possible all uneaten food is siphoned out after each feeding. Juvenile *M. rosenbergi* are subject to the same diseases as larvae. As a preventive measure juvenile rearing ponds are completely dried, drained, and disinfected before and after each use.

Disease treatment is the same as described for larvae. With good management juveniles should grow to 2- to 3-cni prawns within about 30 days, with a survival rate of about 501y, When they reach about 4 cm in length the young prawns are suitable for stocking in production ponds.

Almost any sort of pond over 200 m^2 in surface area and 50 cm in depth, with a water temperature of 22 to 32°C, can be used for growing *M. rosenbergi,* but larger ponds, 1000 m^2 or more in area and 1 to 1 ½ m deep, are more economical.

Ponds for prawn culture are prepared in the same general manner as fish ponds in southeast Asia: predators are eradicated, inlets and outlets screened, and aquatic plants removed. It is desirable to have a gentle flow of water through the pond at least a few hours each day.

Prawns may be stocked alone or in combination with fish. One finds in the literature references to growing *M. rosenbergi* in combination with "carp." It should be emphasized that this refers to various of the Chinese carps, not to the common carp (*Cyprinus carpio*), which competes for food with prawns and brings a far lower price.

Fishes successfully used in culture with *M. rosenbergi* include such herbivores and/or plankton feeders as the big head (*Aristichthys nobilis*), grass carp (*Ctenopharyngodon idellus*), silver carp (*Hypophthalmichthys molitrix*), catla (*Catla eatla*), rohu (*Labeo rohita*), milkfish (*Chanos chanos*), *Osteochilus hasselti, Barbus gonionotus,* grey mullet (*Mugil cephalus*), kissing gourami (*Helostoma temmincki*), sepat siam (*Trichogaster pectoralis*), and threespot gourami (*Trichogaster trichopterus*).

Suitable stocking rates depend not only on the numbers and kinds of fish stocked, but on the quality of soil and water. Table 5 is a general guide to stocking practices. Natural production within the pond supplies most of the food for prawns at this stage. Productivity is enhanced by monthly application of 200 kg of cow dung and 10 kg of lime per hectare.

Supplementary feeding is also practiced, using 75% animal material, including small pieces of fish, mollusks, earthworms, offal, live insects, and silkworm pupae, and 25% plant material, such as various grains and rotten fruit.

Table 12.4: Stocking rates for giant freshwater prawns (*Macrobrachium rósenbergi*) cultured alone and with fish in southeast Asia.

Pond Conditions	*Stocking Rate (Prawns/ha)*	*Stocking Rate of Fish*
	Prawns Cultured Alone	
Rich	15,000	
Medium	10,000	
Poor	6,000	
	Prawns Cultured with Fish	
Rich	6,000	Full
	12,000	Half
Medium	4,000	Full
	8,000	Half
Poor	2,000	Full
	4,000	Half

Five percent of the total body weight of prawns is fed daily, half in the morning and half in the afternoon. Waste may be prevented by placing food in trays along the side of the pond. Both food and shelter for the prawns may be provided by growing small patches of *Ipomoea* in the pond.

The area covered by *Ipornoea* should not, however, exceed 10% of the area of the pond. Further shelter for moulting prawns may be supplied by placing branches on the bottom of the pond. The most serious management problem encountered in this phase of prawn culture is oxygen depletion, to which *M. rosenbergi is* more sensitive than most fishes.

When prawns migrate toward the edges of the pond and appear sluggish in their movements it is time to apply remedial measures to increase the supply of oxygen.

Under favorable conditions prawns in ponds should reach marketable size (15 cm and 100 g) in 5 months, at which time they may be harvested by draining the pond or seining.

Less intensive culture of *M. rosenbergi* in paddy fields is also practiced, but the future of this form of prawn farming is threatened by the increased use of insecticides on rice.

The bunds of paddy fields used for this purpose should be slightly raised so as to retain at least 12 cm of water throughout the 4-month growing period of the rice. Inlets and outlets should be equipped with screens to prevent the escape of prawns and entry of predators.

These screens should extend about 0.3 m above the water surface or prawns will climb over them and escape. One or two small sump pits 1 m × 2 m × 50 cm deep should be constructed near the outlet to trap the prawns when the field is drained.

Paddy fields should be stocked only after the rice seedlings are fairly well rooted. Due to the shorter growing season, older prawns 2 to 3 cm longer than those used in pond stocking are preferred. These are stocked at about 1 prawn/15 m^2 under average conditions. Supplementary feeding is not practiced.

Since culture of *M. rosenbergi is* still largely in the experimental stages, there are few data on the yields which may be achieved. However, a commercial, albeit pilot, operation on Oahu, Hawaii, under the supervision of the State's Department of Fish and Game can produce 3,000 kg/ha of giant prawns.

Larval survival rates in a highly automated hatchery are satisfactory even though they could still be improved. At moderate flowrates of water through the adult rearing ponds, limits on stocking are mostly conditioned by dangers of disease.

But even lacking experimentation with a more vigorous flow, *T. Fujimura*, who has pioneered this success, is confident that 4,000 kg/ha are attainable with continuous stocking and harvesting schedules. Large freshwater shrimps similar to *M. rosenbergi* are found in practically all tropical and subtropical regions, and *Macrobrachium rude is* coincidentally cultured along with *M. rosenbergi* in India, but the only other freshwater species thus far studied to any extent are *Macrobrachium malcolmsoni* and *Macrobrachium carcinus.*

In Pakistan, the Directorate of Fisheries has succeeded in experimentally breeding and rearing *M. malcolmsoni* in a freshwater pond (size not given). Stocking with about 15,000 young yielded 560 kg of adult shrimp. Breeding was accomplished by confining pairs in very fine-meshed cages, 68.5 cm × 35.5 cm × 18 cm deep at the side of the pond and feeding with rice bran each morning.

Macrobrachium carcinus has been experimentally reared through all larval stages at McGill University's field station in Barbados, but mortality has been too high for effective culture. As far as is known, neither spawning nor hatching of eggs in captivity has been accomplished.

It is reported that in Peru larvae of the freshwater shrimp *Macrobrachium caementarius* are harvested from the lower end of rivers, raised in tanks for a few months, and used to stock both private and public waters.

PROSPECTUS

Further growth of the shrimp culture industry will result from expansion into new parts of the world, improvements and innovations in culture techniques, and introduction to culture of new species.

Most of the countries which presently support commercial or experimental shrimp culture have been mentioned here. New additions to the list may be expected regularly, as virtually every country with a seacoast has some potential for shrimp culture.

NEW TECHNIQUES

A number of new and/or experimental techniques have also been 0 entioned here. At present the chief stumbling block in shrimp culture is poor survival of the larvae. The key to better survival is apparently a better diet.

Japanese culturists have achieved the greatest success in supplying the nutritional needs of young shrimp, but their reliance on imported brine shrimp is costly and, if imitated by many other countries, might result in the depletion of brine shrimp stocks in the United States.

Mention has already been made of the successful substitution in Thailand of fish eggs for brine shrimp in the diet of *Macrobrachium rosenbergi*. It has been suggested that amphipods or other locally available small crustaceans might be cultured as food for young shrimp in countries where brine shrimp are not available.

Improvement might also be effected in the feeding procedures for older shrimp. It would be particularly advantageous to culturists if a prepared food comparable to the pelleted feeds used in culture of carp, trout, and other fishes could be developed for shrimp.

A suitable food pellet would have to incorporate a superior binding agent, since shrimp, rather than ingesting pellets whole as do most fish, hold them and pick them apart. In a British study *Palaemon serratus* were fed with pellets containing one of eight different protein foods.

In each case the prepared feed produced much poorer growth than fresh food containing the same protein source. When, instead of a protein source, powdered polyethylene was added to the basic formula as a "nutritionally inert" filler, growth was better than that achieved using five of the other eight experimental feeds.

Experimental work on pelletized diets for shrimp was also carried out at Florida State University, where a food conversion ratio of 3:1 in pink shrimp under experimental conditions was reported.

Other promising experimental techniques include growing shrimp in thermal effluent and monosex culture. The former method is being studied chiefly in the United States where numerous large power plants release large quantities of heated water used for cooling purposes.

Conclusive results are not yet available, but indications are that growth and survival of Penaeid shrimps may be enhanced in "thermally enriched" environments.

Monosex culture has not yet been attempted, but its feasibility is suggested by the fact that female Penaeid shrimps of most, if not all species are larger than males of the same age; female sugpo prawns cultured in the Philippines average two to three times as large as the males at harvest.

Research in West Germany has disclosed that female sand shrimp convert food more efficiently than males. On the other hand, male *Macrobrachium rosenbergi* grow much larger than females. It seems likely that similar sexual dimorphisms exist in other groups of shrimp as well.

NEW SPECIES FOR CULTURE

Nearly all attempts at shrimp culture to date have involved Penaeid shrimps or members of the palaemonid genus *Macrobrachium*. Only a minority of these species have been cultured commercially and few of the remainder have been adequately studied, so additional members of these groups may be expected to enter the picture.

Of particular interest among the Penaeids are those exceptional species which are highly euryhaline. Notable among them are the Australian greentail prawn (*Metapenaeus benettae*) and *Metapenaeus ensis*, both of which spawn naturally in estuaries, a trait that could greatly simplify estuarine culture.

Postlarval greentail prawns apparently prefer water of less than $20\%_0$ salinity. Australian biologists are currently experimenting with the culture of these and/or similar species, locally called "greasy backs."

Edible non-Penaeid shrimps which possess the ability to reproduce in brackish water include *Caridina gracilirostris*, most species of *Macrobrachium*, *Palaemon*, and *Leander*, and some species of *Palaemonetes*. *Macrobrachium lanchesteri* of Malaysia will even reproduce in stagnant freshwater. In addition to possessing the considerable advantage of being very hardy with respect to high temperatures, low dissolved oxygen concentrations, and waters with low mineral content, *M. lanchesteri is* believed to be herbivorous.

In concentrating on members of the genera *Penaeus, Metapenaeus,* and *Macrobrachium,* shrimp culturists have overlooked species with less complex life cycles. Such species, if they could be cultured, would eliminate many of the difficulties now encountered in rearing young shrimp. These species may be roughly divided into four categories:

1. Species with no free-swimming larvae. In *Sclerocrangon boreas* of the North Atlantic and Pacific and *Sclerocrangon ferox* of the arctic Atlantic the young remain attached to the female's pleopods and do not feed up to the zoea stage.

   These two benthic species reach lengths of over 12 cm and appear potentially suitable for culture. Certain other members of their genus, however, produce pelagic larvae.

   There are species of shrimp which bypass the larval stages entirely and emerge from the egg as juveniles, but most of them are too small for human consumption. An exception is *Bythocaris leucopia,* which exceeds 9 cm in length. *B. leucopia is* a deep water species, however, and thus might not be amenable to culture.

   A better possibility might be the Japanese *Pandalopsis coccinata.* The 15-mm shrimp which emerges from the egg of this species is classified as a zoea, but is benthic and probably has feeding habits similar to the adult.

2. Species with larvae which do not feed. There are species of shrimp which have no functional mouth parts as zoea and subsist on yolk until they become juveniles.

   Most of these are deep water pelagic species and would probably be difficult to maintain in captivity. A possible exception is the benthic *Glyphocrangon spinicauda.*

3. Species with large larvae. Much of the difficulty in rearing shrimp larvae stems from their small size. Larger larvae could be fed such readily available animals as copepods or amphipods or might even take prepared foods.

   Large larvae, however, mean large eggs, hence these species produce less eggs than the commonly cultured shrimps. Extreme cases such as *Richardina spinicincta,* which may produce as few as six eggs, are obviously unsuitable for culture, but species which produce several hundred eggs might prove satisfactory if extremely high survival of larvae were achieved.

4. Species with few larval stages. *Pandalus kessleri,* which is fished, although not cultured, in northern Japan, hatches as a very advanced 8-mm zoea and moults to become a postlarva within a few days. *P. kessleri* has the disadvantage of being very stenohaline, thus unsuitable for tidewater culture.

   The same advantages and disadvantages apply to *Pandalus platyceros,* which is currently being cultured experimentally in the United Kingdom. Other species that appear to have similar rapid development include *Argis lar* and perhaps other members of that genus; the holarctic *Lebbeus polaris,* and *Lebbeus groenlandicus,* found from northeast Asia to Greenland.

The species just mentioned represent only a tiny fraction of the known species of Natantia. Many of the rest are obviously unsuited for culture by virtue of size, habits, or habitat. Nevertheless, there are undoubtedly others of potential value to the culturist.

It should be noted that almost all of the species discussed are boreal or tropical in distribution. It is thus particularly likely that additional cultivable species will be discovered in the South Temperate and Antarctic regions.

Whatever species or techniques are used in shrimp culture, it is unlikely that dramatic improvements will drive the price of shrimp down. The generally carnivorous habits of shrimp, along with the great amounts of energy lost in moulting, virtually guarantee that food conversion will be inefficient.

Thus as long as there are ample markets for luxury foods the profit potential of shrimp culture will remain high. But if worldwide or, in some instances, local food shortages develop, shrimp culture may be overshadowed by biologically and economically more efficient forms of brackish water aquaculture.

13

Culture of the Lobster

One of the most highly prized of all seafoods is lobster, and efforts have been made to culture this delicacy at least since the 1860s. From the biologist's or culturist's point of view "lobster" may indicate either of two very different types of animal.

Seafood gourmets find considerable difference between the two as well, but many consumers are less discriminating. The animals most of us visualize when lobster is mentioned are the American lobster (*Homarus americanus*) and its European counterpart, *Homarus vulgaris,* both of which are restricted to the North Atlantic.

However, much of the lobster tail of commerce (including that marketed as rock lobster, Australian lobster, or South African lobster) comes from one or another of the spiny lobsters, which are found virtually throughout the oceans.

There are many species of spiny lobsters belonging to several families, but all may be distinguished from *Homarus* by the lack of the formidable claws or chelipeds. A more important difference to the culturist is the much more complex larval development of spiny lobsters, which has kept spiny lobster culture lagging behind that of *Homarus,* although neither animal has yet been reared commercially.

CULTURE OF *HOMARUS SPP.*

Early Stocking Programs

Early attempts at culturing *Homarus* concentrated on hatching larvae for stocking in the sea. In 1885 the U.S. Fisheries Commission began releasing newly hatched lobster larvae along the northeastern coast of that country and by 1907 numerous federal or state-supported hatcheries were established in five states.

Canada and Newfoundland soon followed suit but found that hatcheries were neither biologically nor economically justifiable and discontinued stocking by 1917, although Canada still maintains a small experimental program.

The early boom in the United States fell off for the same reasons, but the practice of lobster culture never completely died and the state of Massachusetts still carries out a stocking program. A different sort of stocking program is contemplated in British Columbia and Oregon, where some biologists hope to establish naturally reproducing populations of *Homarus americanus.*

Though artificial propagation of *Homarus vulgaris* was achieved 20 years before the first success with *Homarus americanus,* lobster hatcheries were not established in Europe before 1921. Since then, experimental culture and stocking have been undertaken in Norway, Sweden, Denmark, Germany, France, the Netherlands, and the United Kingdom, with results no better than those achieved on the other side of the Atlantic.

Large-scale experiments are presently being conducted only in Norway and the United Kingdom. At one time British researchers were also experimenting with the culture of another homarid species, the "Dublin prawn" (*Nephrops*), but this work has apparently been discontinued.

Commercial rearing of edible size lobsters has been the subject of much speculation and occasional experimentation but has never been achieved in Europe or North America.

Natural History

As far as is known, the natural history of the two species of *Homarus is* virtually identical. Mating, which occurs in the summer months, follows the pattern for decapod crustaceans in that it is dependent on the moulting of the female.

According to some authorities copulation can occur up to 12 days after the female moults, but chances of success are much higher within 48 hours. The success of mating depends partly on the relative size of the male and female; if there is great disparity in size, it proceeds only with difficulty or not at all.

Courtship is apparently initiated by a pheromone secreted by the freshly moulted female. When a male is drawn to within a meter or so he responds by advancing on the very tips of his walking legs, with continuous rapid movement of the maxillipeds and side to side movement of the antennae.

Upon making contact, the two lobsters stroke each other with their antennae for up to 30 min. At the conclusion of this courtship, the male mounts the female, gently rolls her over, and they copulate in a head-to-head position.

Males appear limited to mating with one or two females in a period of a few days. Females may on occasion mate with more than one male. Sperm is stored in the female's seminal receptacle for 9 to 13 months, at which time the 5000 to 125,000 eggs are extruded, fertilized, and cemented to the nonplumose hairs of the swimmerets.

The eggs are carried by the female for 10 to 12 months before hatching. Thus the total time between mating and hatching may be as much as 2 years, though culturists have succeeded in reducing this period, by means of temperature control, to as little as 11 months.

During the period of incubation the eggs change color from nearly black to green to brown. Hatching has been recorded at temperatures as low as 9.4°C but usually takes place in spring or early summer at 15 to 20°C.

The newly hatched mysis larvae, which make their first moult almost immediately, assume a planktonic existence near the surface. After a few more moults they acquire well-developed claws and other external appearances of tiny lobsters.

At this time they are capable of swimming yet may still be found among the plankton, but soon they take up a benthic, nocturnal existence. Development to this stage takes 9 to 33 days, depending on temperature, but survival from hatching to the benthic form (fourth stage) is probably less than 0.1%.

Postlarval lobsters ordinarily undergo four more moults in the first season of life, from the date of hatching to the end of that calendar year, for a total of 10 moults, counting larval moults, in that season.

Thereafter moulting becomes less frequent, until by the attainment of sexual maturity at about 6 years moulting occurs no more than once annually.

Sexual maturity usually coincides with the attainment of commercial size (about 20 cm in length and 0.5 kg in weight), though the precise rate of growth is dependent on temperature. Data on lobster growth rates are scarce since all external indications of the individual identity of a lobster are lost with the shedding of the exoskeleton.

Captive lobsters kept individually have been observed to grow 9.5 to 17.4% in length and up to 50% in weight at a moult. There appear to be no significant differences in rate of growth due to sex.

Lobsters in Massachusetts have been observed to moult as early as April 25 and as late as December 29 at temperatures as low as 3.3°C, but most moulting occurs from May to October at temperatures of 15 to 20°C.

There are two seasonal moulting peaks, one in early summer when the water temperature first reaches 15 to 20°C and one in early fall. Fall moulting is probably a response to increase in volume of body tissue due to heavy feeding during the summer.

Homarus americanus has a life span of 50 to 100 years and attains weights as great as 19 kg.

HATCHING AND REARING THE YOUNG IN CAPTIVITY

Early lobster hatcheries relied on eggs taken from "berried" females and hatched separately with the aid of a device to agitate the water. It is currently believed that the female lobster is a more effective incubator than any man-made device.

Either way, hatching lobster larvae has always been easier than rearing them and, although first-stage larvae were stocked along the Atlantic coast of the United States and Canada from 1891 to 1917, it has been the opinion of most lobster culturists that for a stocking program to be effective the young lobsters must be capable of assuming a benthic life upon release.

Thus rearing of larvae has long been a preoccupation of lobster culturists. The largest lobster hatching and rearing operation today is that carried on by the state of Massachusetts on the island of Martha's Vineyard, under the direction of John T. Hughes. Hughes and his associates have succeeded in mating lobsters in captivity, but the chief source of eggs for hatching continues to be the lobster fishery.

Spring-caught females bearing brown eggs ("Brown eggers") are selected, since their eggs will hatch in a few months, whereas "green eggers" would have to be held over winter.

The prospective mothers are placed in running water (salinity 30 to 31%,) in hatching tanks 274 cm × 91.5 cm × 30 cm deep, divided into compartments for individually holding up to 70 lobsters. (Berried *Homarus r ulgaris* reportedly cannot be kept together because they will claw the eggs off each other, but this is not so with *Homarus americanus*.) They are fed on shellfish viscera and/or fish.

Hatching usually commences in mid-May, when the water temperature reaches 15°C, and becomes intensive during a 2-week period in June and July.

The newly hatched larvae are swept away by the current and collected in a wire screen box then transferred to circular fiberglass tanks with a diameter of 400 mm and concave bottoms. Experienced workers estimate the number of larvae by eye and place about 3000 in each tank.

Water is circulated through the rearing tanks to keep the larvae drifting in midwater. If they were to accumulate on the bottom, cannibalism would severely decimate their numbers. Water enters the tank from the bottom through an inverted, perforated plastic cup, which breaks up the flow and keeps water circulating evenly in all parts of the tank.

The outlet is an overflow pipe equipped with a similar device. The first fry feed used at Martha's Vineyard, and still used in Norwegian hatcheries, was finely ground beef liver, but ground clams and frozen adult brine shrimp (Artemia) have been found to produce much better survival.

Crab viscera are another acceptable food. Ground clams or brine shrimp are mixed with sea water in a proportion determined by the demands of the larvae, and one tablespoon of the mixture fed every three hours throughout the larvae's stay in the hatchery.

Heavy feeding helps avert cannibalism, but overfeeding may clog the inlet and outlet pipes, thus reducing circulation and increasing cannibalism as well as raising the threat of pollution.

Using these methods an average of 22% survival to the third moult has been attained, with a record season's survival of 42.6%. Next to cannibalism the major cause of mortality is a gas disease caused by supersaturation of the water with nitrogen, a condition brought on by air leaks in the circulating system.

Lobster larvae are sensitive to certain metal ions, but this has become less of a problem at the Martha's Vineyard hatchery since lead piping was replaced by plastic.

In Norway, lobster fry in hatcheries are attacked by a parasitic suctorian (*Euphelota sp.*). Heavy infestations cause mass mortality by offsetting the larvae's buoyancy and forcing them to the bottom.

Chemical treatment has proved futile, but *Euphelota* can apparently be excluded from hatcheries by filtering sea water through sand before it is used.

Current Stocking Programs

When the lobster fry reach the fourth or fifth stage (between third and fifth moults) they are planted at selected points along the Massachusetts coast. The assumption is that they soon settle to the bottom where natural mortality is much less than that for planktonic larvae.

The repeated presence of fourth-stage larvae in plankton catches, however, indicates that they do not all settle immediately, or perhaps none of them do. The logical way to eliminate this cause of concern is to grow all of the larvae to fifth stage.

A more gratuitous assumption is that stocking lobster larvae contributes substantially to the fishery. There is circumstantial evidence suggesting that the first large-scale propagation program, put into operation by the state of Rhode Island in 1901, improved the fishery off that state.

In 1904 the Rhode Island catch had declined to 169,747 kg or 20 kg/pot. In 1919, after 17 years of stocking, the catch was up to 736,422 kg or 35 kg/pot. These data were used as a rationale for further efforts on both sides of the Atlantic, but there is no evidence that any of the subsequent stocking programs paid dividends.

Rhode Island eventually gave up on lobster culture as being "uneconomical." The precise fate of lobster larvae released into the sea cannot be determined for the same reason that growth rates of wild lobsters cannot be studied, the impossibility of tagging (a satisfactory internal tag has reportedly been developed in Maine, but details are not yet available), but statistical inferences can be made as to the practical value of lobster culture as currently carried out.

In 1950 Clyde C. Taylor of the U.S. Fish and Wildlife Service made the first critical evaluation of a hatchery program. He demonstrated that if 10% (a rather optimistic figure) of the lobster larvae reared and stocked in Maine in 1943 had survived to commercial size and were captured in 1949, they would have constituted only $0.015\%_{o}$ of the fishery for that year. There is no indication that the situation is or ever was substantially different anywhere else.

Recent Applied Research

Biologists at the Martha's Vineyard hatchery have succeeded in selectively breeding various odd-colored lobsters, which could serve as natural tags for growth studies and assessment of stocking programs. Although odd colors have persisted through ten moults in the laboratory, it is known that food affects the color of lobsters and it is conceivable that odd-colored lobsters released in the sea might change diets and therefore color.

According to Hughes, however, certain genetically determined colors are permanent and so distinctive as to rule out confusion with any environmentally induced colors. The rate of development of both eggs and larvae can be accelerated by raising the water temperature.

Eggs held at or above 20°C will hatch about 3 months sooner than eggs started in sea water at normal winter temperatures, with no apparent harm to the resulting larvae. Similarly, the rate of moulting of larval lobsters may be increased by a factor of 2 to 5 by heating the water.

The upper limit of temperature for first stage larvae appears to be 27°C, but third- and fourth-stage larvae can endure constant temperatures as high as 31°C. A factor that might affect the feasibility of rearing larvae to fifth stage is population density. Density has been shown to affect survival to fourth stage, but little is known as to what constitutes the optimum density at any stage.

Adult lobsters in hatcheries are usually kept in very shallow water, for reasons of convenience. There has never been any problem in getting lobsters to mate under these conditions, but until recently females would ettison their eggs before fertilization.

This problem was alleviated at Martha's Vineyard by the simple expedient of raising the water depth from 15 to 45 cm. No one knows just why this works, but it has enabled Massachusetts biologists to contain the entire life cycle of *Honiarus americanus* within the laboratory and opened up the possibility of selective breeding.

Among the goals of selection, in addition to the "natural tags" described, are higher growth rate, larger claws, more meat in relation to body size, and resistance to disease.

POSSIBILITY OF COMMERCIAL CULTURE

As intriguing as the possibilities of lobster breeding appear, the economic prospects for self-contained lobster culture in the near future do not look bright, at least not in the United States or the United Kingdom.

It appears that at present commercial lobster culturists would be more likely to succeed by growing juvenile lobsters to marketable size. The principal source of stock for such an operation would likely be the lobster fishery.

In some places there would need to be legislative changes to allow fishermen to retain small lobsters for this purpose. Before such legislation could be rationally considered it would be necessary to weigh the economic and gustatory benefits of lobster culture against the possible effects of reduction of wild breeding stocks.

If any method of growing marketable size lobsters in captivity achieves economic success, the state of Massachusetts can take much of the credit for laying the groundwork. Biologists at the Martha's Vineyard hatchery have succeeded in raising lobsters up to the age of 10 years and as large as 154 min in carapace length.

Fifth-stage lobsters to be retained for growth to maturity are stocked in individual 15 cm × 15 cm compartments in a trough containing 15 cm of water. After about 2 years it becomes necessary to provide larger compartments, but individuals must always be isolated or given abundant hiding places to prevent cannibalism on freshly moulted lobsters.

The only alternative to isolation is to stock lobsters at very low densities. All of these methods present obvious drawbacks to commercial culture. Captive lobsters are ordinarily fed fresh fish or shellfish. If either food is not fresh, it will be rejected. Each lobster at Martha's Vineyard is fed as much as it will consume daily, except during the winter when they are fed but once a week.

It is estimated that it takes about 8 kg of food to produce 1 kg of lobster. Lobster culture could be made more efficient if a pelleted feed, such as those used in culture of catfish and trout, were available.

In addition to sinking, a satisfactory lobster pellet would have to be of a texture to accommodate the lobster's feeding habits without dissolving or crumbling.

Unlike fin fish, which engulf pellets whole, lobsters grasp and chew their food. By using the seaweed gel carrageenin, pellets with the consistency of used chewing gum can be manufactured. Such pellets, incorporating commercial trout chow, dog food, or cat food as foods, are now being tested at Martha's Vineyard.

These pellets are stable in water and accepted by lobsters, but whether they will produce growth comparable to that achieved with fresh foods is as yet unknown. In nature it takes 5 to 7 years from hatching to produce a marketable size lobster.

During much of this time little or no growth is going on, due to water temperatures below 10°C. By maintaining year-round high temperatures it is possible to greatly accelerate growth rates.

Lobsters kept at a constant 15.6°C moult twice as often, hence grow twice as fast as those exposed to the full range of natural temperatures in the North Atlantic. Further, lobsters will adapt to temperatures as high as 30°C-16 to 21' above normal summer water temperatures in their natural habitat.

This knowledge is the basis for current work on *Homarus* culture on the Pacific coast of the United States, where they are not native. Lobsters are being experimentally grown at San Diego, California, in heated discharge from a San Diego Gas and Electric Co. power plant.

Growth rate is probably capable of further improvement, independent of thermal manipulation; great individual differences in growth rates have been observed in stock of both sexes kept under identical conditions, suggesting that selective breeding for rapid growth would be practicable.

By using heated water and other intensive care techniques biologists at Martha's Vineyard have in at least one instance produced a marketable size lobster in a little over 2 years after hatching, and marketable 3-yearolds are a commonplace.

It would also be propitious for the future of lobster culture if the public could be educated to accept smaller lobsters or lobster meat processed so that the original size of the lobster could not be determined.

Hughes believes that commercial lobster culture, using heated water, is now feasible. Perhaps even more optimistic are some members of the staff of a West German marine biological station on the island of Helgoland, in the North Sea.

They have launched an ambitious project to investigate the possibility of culturing *H. vulgaris* from larvae to commercial size in cages on the sea floor, under virtually natural conditions.

The optimism of Hughes and the German researchers notwithstanding, we feel that for the present any sort of commercial culture of either species of *Homarus* seems at best an intriguing gamble.

CULTURE OF PALINURID LOSBSTERS

Natural History

There are 7 genera and about 30 species of spiny lobsters (superfamily Scyllaridea), of which at least 15, all members of the family Palinuridae, are commercially important. So far as is known, all the commercially important species have similar but very complex life histories.

Mating occurs in inshore waters at various times of year, depending on species and age of females. Old females mate earlier than young and some of them are thought to mate twice a year.

In mating, males extrude sperm in the form of a viscous fluid which attaches to the underside of the female. There the surface rapidly hardens to form a sperm sac.

Table 13.1: The commercially important species of spiny lobsters and thedir ranges.

Species	*Range*
Jasus lalandii	Australia, Juan Fernandez Islands (*off* coast of Chile), New Zealand, South Africa, Tasmania, Tristan da Cunha
Jasus verreauxi	Southern Australia, New Zealand, Tasmania
Palinurus elephas	Great Britain to the Mediterranean
Panulirus argus	Florida, the Caribbean area, the Atlantic coast of South America, Bermuda
Panulirus gracilis	Southern Mexico to Ecuador
Panulirus inflatus	Gulf of California to Southern Mexico
Panulirus interruptus	Southern California, Lower California (Mexico)
Panulirus japonicus	Japan
Panulirus laevicauda	Bermuda to northeastern South America
Panulirus longipes	Western Australia, Ryukyu Islands, Taiwan, Philippines, New Caledonia
Panulirus marginatus	Hawaiian Islands
Panulirus ornatus	Indian Ocean, Ryukyu Islands, Taiwan, Philippines
Panulirus penicillatus	Indo-Pacific, Korea, Lower California (Mexico), Galapagos, Costa Rica
Panulirus regius	Western Mediterranean, West Africa
Panulirus versicolor	Indo-Pacific

Some time later, the eggs are extruded and pass over the sperm sac. At that time the female breaks the sperm sac by scratching it with her legs, thus fertilizing the eggs. They are then passed on to the swimmerets where they are attached, to remain until hatching.

The number of eggs produced by a female varies with size and species. Estimates as low as 50,000 and as high as 4,000,000 have been recorded. The time between mating and fertilization is probably dependent on water temperature. In general it appears to be less than that for *Homarus.*

Certainly hatching occurs much sooner than in *Homarus;* only 3 weeks are required in some species. During this time the eggs change color from bright red-orange to a dark brown which fades until they are almost colorless just before hatching.

If, from the culturist's point of view, the reproductive process of spiny lobsters is more efficient than that of *Homarus,* the spiny lobsters more than make up for it with protracted and complex larval development.

The newly hatched larva is a flat, leaflike, and unusually delicate animal 2 to 3 mm long, known as a phyllosoma. Phyllosomas are planktonic and float horizontally with the legs extended.

At least some species are negatively phototropic and make fairly extensive diurnal vertical migrations. The larvae remain planktonic while passing through a large number of moults, most of which do not result in metamorphosis, although progressive changes in form may be detected.

Usually 3 to 6 months and 6 or more metamorphoses are required to reach the puerulus stage, but in one laboratory experiment on

Figure 13.1: Young spiny lobster (Phyllosoma).

Panulirus aponicus, 16 moults were passed through in 178 days without metamorphosis. It is possible that the number of larval moults is not fixed for a species and that frequency of metamorphosis is partially dependent on nutrition or some such factor.

The puerulus is superficially similar to the adult but is transparent, lacks lime in the skeleton, and may still be planktonic. Finally, the puerulus moults to become a juvenile about 2.1 cm long and settles to the bottom.

After two or three more moults it acquires the reddish-brown color of adult spiny lobsters. Survival to this point is extremely low since predation is extensive at all stages. Juvenile and adult spiny lobsters are also subject to predation but avoid it to some extent by hiding under rocks and other cover during the day and foraging at night.

Muddy bottoms and strong currents are avoided. In nature adult spiny lobsters consume a wide variety of foods, including fish, worms, mollusks, and smaller crustaceans. Cannibalism may occur if foods containing calcium carbonate are not available.

Spiny lobsters may act as scavengers but exhibit a marked preference for fresh food. Frequency of moulting, and therefore rate of growth, varies with food supply, water temperature, and sex. Mature females moult but once or twice a year, before mating and sometimes after hatching or otherwise disposing of their eggs.

Males grow larger than females and may moult at any time of year, thus are thought to moult more often. Growth between moults is about 5 to 10% of body length for *Panulirus argus.* ;Maximum size and age varies with species.

Panulirus interruptus is said to reach a weight of over 13 kg, but such specimens are rare, and 3 kg would be considered large. In California this species is believed to take at least 7 to 9 years to reach the legal minimum size of 10½ in. (27 cm), although *P. argus* may attain this length in 3 years.

Attempts at Culture

Obvious difficulties notwithstanding, many attempts have been made to rear spiny lobsters from the egg in captivity. Perhaps the first efforts were those of the California Department of Fish and Game, starting in 1911, with *Panulirus interruptus.*

Sporadic efforts with that species have continued, but little progress has been made, though Margaret Knight at Scripps Institute of Oceanography in La Jolla, California, has been able to hold larvae in finger bowls for up to 4 months. Soviet scientists also report some success in holding and rearing *Palinurus elephas* in aquaria and nursery ponds.

Other members of the family Palinuridae which have been hatched and held in the laboratory for 5 to 10 moults include *Panulirus japonicus* in Japan, *Panulirus argus* in Florida, and *Jasus lalandii* in South Africa. Mention should be made of the confusion between the terms "stage" and "moult."

There are descriptions in the literature of rearing *Panulirus japonicus* and other species as far as the "tenth stage," but when compared to natural larvae of *Panulirus interruptus,* for which the larval stages have been thoroughly described, the supposed tenth-stage larvae appear to be third or fourth stage.

This confusion is occasioned by the lack of any direct correspondence between developmental stage and number of moults. Under unfavorable conditions of temperature or food supply, spiny lobster larvae may moult without appreciable growth or morphological change.

The term "stage" should be used only to refer to morphologically distinct forms. Other Palinurid species which have been hatched in captivity but not reared beyond the very early stages include *Panulirus in flatus* in California, *Panulirus longipes* in Japan, and *Panulirus polyphagus* in Malaysia.

The necessity of unpolluted water free from silt or small bits of detritus on which the larvae may entangle their long legs and the need for nearly constant temperature would certainly constitute serious restraints to commercial culture, but the main problem at present is feeding.

Early larvae of most species accept brine shrimp nauplii quite readily, but attempts to feed older larvae on adult brine shrimp, sea urchin eggs, and larval gobiid fishes have met with slight success. Complicating the situation is the fact that almost nothing is known of the natural food of spiny lobster larvae.

CULTURE OF SCYHLLARID LOBSTERS

All of the commercially important spiny lobsters belong to the family Palinuridae. The related Scyllaridae are scarcely exploited. However, it should be pointed out that those species whose habits are most conducive to fishery exploitation are not necessarily those best suited for culture.

Some Scyllarid lobsters possess the advantage for culture of having shorter and less complex larval development. In general they also appear to be hardier animals.

The Scyllarids *Ibacus ciliatus, Ibacus novemdentatus, Parribacus antarcticus,* and *Scyllarus bicuspidatus* have been hatched in Japan but have not been reared for more than a few days. Similar lack of success has been experienced in India with *Scyllarus sordidus.*

However, Phillip B. Robertson of the University of Miami's Institute of Marine and Atmospheric Sciences has become the first to rear any spiny lobster to the juvenile stage.

He reared the sand lobster (*Scyllarus americanus*) from the egg through 6 to 8 phyllosoma stages to metamorphosis in 32 to 40 days at 25°C and salinities of 23.2 to 38.6%.

Most important from the culturist's point of view, Robertson was able to achieve this on an exclusive diet of brine shrimp nauplii. Robertson's success notwithstanding, it will almost certainly be a long time before larval culture of the sand lobster or any other scyllarid lobster can be recommended for other than experimental purposes.

REARING OF SPINY LOSTER PUERULI OR JUVENILES TO MARKETABLE SIZE

Clearly, if there is to be commercial culture of Palinurid or Scyllarid lobsters in the near future it will involve capturing pueruli or juveniles and growing them in confinement. This possibility has been considered in Australia where young *Panulirus longipes* can be captured in abundance on the west coast.

To retain these young for culture would presently be illegal, but if it could be shown that culture was economically feasible and would not deplete natural stocks, the legal restraints might be removed. Most undersize *P. longipes* taken off Australia are 2 to 3 years old and would need to be held for only 1 to 2 years to reach marketable size.

Experiments have shown that the food conversion ratio of such animals fed on fish or abalone is about 6:1, which is quite efficient for a crustacean. However, taking into consideration the costs of food, capture of stock, pond construction, maintenance, and so forth, it seems unlikely that such culture would be profitable in Australia at this time.

The type of culture suggested for Australia has reportedly been attempted with *Panulirus japonicus* by Japanese researchers. Young *P. japonicus* caught in traps have been held in ponds or shallow bays and fed trash fish.

The results indicate that it may be feasible to produce salable lobsters at a profit. There may be other countries where the practice of capturing and growing young spiny lobsters will prove profitable.

The feasibility of such culture would be enhanced if growth rates could be increased as has been done with *Homarus americanus*. This might be done by improving the quality of food fed to spiny lobsters. Most Palinurids in captivity are fed fish, probably for reasons of availability, but crustaceans have been shown to produce better results.

A better possibility for increasing growth rates is the use of heated water. Steven A. Serfling of San Diego State College in California has been able to increase the growth rate of young *Panulirus interruptus* in the laboratory by as much as 260% over average natural rates by maintaining them at 28°C. It is not known whether this would be feasible within the framework of commercial culture.

14

Culture of Freshwater Crayfish

Among the best known and meost highly esteemed crustaceans are the lobsters (*Homarus* spp.), but they are rivaled as a delicacy by their smaller freshwater counterparts, the crayfishes or crawfishes (family Astacidae). (Not to be confused with the marine spiny lobsters, family Palinuridae, sometimes marketed as crayfish or crawfish.) True crayfish comprise more than 300 species and are found on all the continents except Africa.

Although crayfish are esteemed as a gourmet food in several European countries and are the primary source of protein for certain tribes in New Guinea, they are generally underutilized by man.

Crayfish have attained importance as a commercial food product in parts of Europe and the United States. The most enthusiastic consumers of crayfish are the French, and crayfish farms have been in operation in France since 1880.

But the most important crayfish producing area is Louisiana, the only American state with a history of French culture. In a good year more than 800,000 kg of "wild" crayfish may be caught arrd marketed in Louisiana; during bad years the yield may be less than half that figure.

Fishery production is supplemented annually by 1.2 million kg produced on the 6000 to 7000 ha of crayfish farms in the state. Details are not available on techniques of crayfish culture in Europe, hence this report concentrates on practices in Louisiana.

NATURAL HISTORY OF THE PRINICIPAL CULTURED SPECIES

There are twenty-nine species of crayfish known to inhabit the waters of Louisiana, but only two are cultured. On most farms the dominant species is the red crayfish (*Procambarus clarkii*), but a few areas produce chiefly white crayfish (*Procambarus blandingi*).

The natural history of the two species is similar. Mating occurs in open water in the late spring, when the water level in the Louisiana swamps is high. At that time the male crayfish deposits sperm in an external receptacle on the female.

Shortly after the peak of the breeding season, female crayfish come out on shore and dig burrows near the water's edge. Since they are exposed to terrestrial predators at this time, areas well protected by emergent plants are preferred.

Burrows are essentially vertical and usually 0.7 to 1.0 m deep, unless the water table is unusually high, in which case burrows half that depth may be found. By the end of July, all adult females have constructed burrows, which are then usually occupied by a single male, along with the female. Each burrow is capped with a plug of dirt.

Young crayfish and unpaired males also seek shelter in the mud or in naturally occurring holes during the summer, but they do not burrow. Some additional mating may occur in the burrows, but the crayfish are thought to be essentially inactive until September, when egg laying occurs.

Eggs and sperm are simultaneously released by the female and the fertilized eggs attached to the underside of her tail until hatching, which occurs in 14 to 21 days with red crayfish and 17 to 29 days with white crayfish.

The adults die soon after hatching. An average hatch is about 400 red crayfish (maximum 700) and somewhat less for white crayfish. Fertilization and egg laying often occur in the burrow, but growth and survival of the 25-mm, free-swimming young is greatly enhanced if open water is available.

In years when the water is low in the fall, hatching may occur in the burrow, in which case the young suffer from overcrowding and lack of food. Or the female may crawl off overland in search of water and die of dehydration or be captured by a predator.

Young crayfish usually seek shelter in dense plant growth near shore, then move out to deeper water as they mature. Both red and white crayfish are annual animals, and maturity may be reached in less than 6 months after hatching. Crayfish of all ages are omnivorous but prefer animal matter. Nevertheless, most crayfish, both in nature and in culture, must subsist on a predominantly vegetable diet.

POND CULTURE IN LOUISIANA

Crayfish culture is practiced in two types of water in Louisiana: rice fields and artificial impoundments. The latter, though its large-scale use dates back little more than 20 years, now accounts for more than 80% of the area devoted to crayfish farming.

Site Selection and Construction

As in most other forms of aquaculture, site selection is crucial in pond culture of crayfish. Due to the shallowness of crayfish ponds, it is essential that the land chosen be relatively flat.

When the highest point in the pond bottom is covered by 0.3 m of water, depths of over 1 m should not occur in more than 25% of the remaining area. It is not, however, of any particular value if the pond bottom is level. In fact, small elevations in the bottom have the favorable effect of increasing the area available for burrowing of early breeders.

Densely wooded areas are not favored, since dense shrubbery and trees along pond banks hinder harvesting, shade out desirable aquatic plants, add leaves and debris which decay and reduce oxygen levels, and may keep temperatures in the shallows below optimum.

It was in such environments, however, that pond culture of crayfish had its start in Louisiana and 2400 ha of densely wooded swampland are still in use in an area just west of the Atchafalaya Basin, where conventional pond construction would be extremely difficult.

These leveed swamplands are also heavily used by waterfowl, which are extensively hunted in Louisiana. Soil quality surely has some effect on crayfish production but, in Louisiana at least, the primary consideration is that the soil hold water.

Water supply is of course important, but crayfish are very tolerant of naturally occurring physical and chemical conditions. Aspects of water quality which are of particular importance to the crayfish farmer are temperature and hardness.

Optimum temperatures for red crayfish are thought to be 21 to 29°C, but growth is not drastically reduced until the temperature falls below 13°C. Above 32°C, red crayfish burrow into the mud and become inactive. White crayfish do better at slightly lower temperatures and begin to burrow at temperatures as low as 27°C.

Growth is the primary reason for the culturist to be concerned with water temperature, since neither species is likely to suffer significant thermally induced mortality at temperatures common in Louisiana. For the same reason, dissolved oxygen concentration, though unlikely to be a cause of mortality, should be kept as high as possible.

Cultured crayfish have been observed to do well at pH levels as low as 5.8 and as high as 8.2. Crayfish in acid waters tend to have thinner shells. Soft water also results in thin, soft shells as well as poor growth and survival. It appears that the water in crayfish ponds should have a total hardness of at least 50 ppm, and that up to 200 ppm is desirable.

In recent years interest in crayfish farming in the coastal swamps of southern Louisiana has increased, and some attention has been paid to the effect of salinity on crayfish. Preliminary experiments indicate that crayfish will reproduce and grow fairly well at salinities of 6 to 10%.

"Tolerant as crayfish are to natural conditions, they are extremely sensitive to synthetic chemicals and other substances which may find their way into agricultural water supplies. Such commonly used compounds as Pyrethrum, creosote, orthodichlorobenzene, sodium cyanide, turpentine, orthocresole, cresylic acid, pine oil, nicotine, carbon bisulfide, phenothiazine, calcium cyanamid, and chlorinated hydrocarbon pesticides have all been shown to be toxic to crayfish.

The last-named group presents particular problems because of the possible danger to human health from dosages sublethal for crayfish and because the crayfish farmer may find it difficult to prevent contamination of his water supply by pesticides used on nearby agricultural land. It is recommended that crayfish culturists located in the vicinity of intensive terrestrial farming operations alert neighboring farmers and crop-dusting pilots of the location of their crayfish ponds and attempt to secure their cooperation in averting contamination.

When spraying is going on nearby, pumping of water from streams and ditches into crayfish ponds should be suspended. The danger of contamination by pesticides and otheipoll tall is greatly reduced if the water source is a deep well, but maa farmers, for reasons of necessity or economy, use surface water. When ever type of water is used, it is best if each unit of the farm is providefrith its own pump.

Units need not be discrete but may be portions (iarger ponds separated by inside levees. The smaller the units, the greacr the ease of water quality control and general management. On the oi°.er hand, the more small units are built, the greater the construction cost ger hectare of water surface. A large farm might consist of one or two .0- to 300-ha ponds broken up into 10 or so units. One-family farms ac mall as 8 ha exist but do not provide a full family income.

Detailed advice on levee construction may be obtainedfrom the Soil Conservation Service, county agricultural agents, or commercial contractors. In general, levees should be high enough to keep out flood waters and wide enough to permit access to vehicles.

Water circulation has been found to be a deciding factoiin the success or failure of many crayfish farms. To facilitate circulationil is necessary to provide not only an adequate inflow of water but good drainage as well.

Drain pipes, which must be screened with 12-mm crsinaller wire mesh, should be located as far away from inlet pipes ss possible to permit thorough mixing of water. Drains should be lai;t enough to permit complete draining in 30 days.

Stocking

Although some ponds contain natural populations of crzfish, stocking is nevertheless necessary the first year, after which the popcation should be self-sustaining. The usual procedure is to stock ponds rill' adults in May to July, at which time crayfish are "tough" and Picts low. The pond should be flooded for at least 2 weeks before stockin;and arrangements made to purchase freshly caught crayfish.

Stock hey in captivity for even so short a period as overnight should not be accepted. Large specimens, about 30 to 45/kg, are preferable. Suggested pocking rates for red crayfish vary according to the amount of cover!n the pond.

At least 80% of most lots of crayfish purchased for stacking in most parts of Louisiana will be red crayfish. If, as occasionally happens,

Table 14.1: Suggested stocking rates for crayfish in different types of ponds in Louisiana.

Wild Grayfish Present	*Types of Pond*	*Stocking Rate (Kg/Ha)*
Yes	—	20-25
No	Densely vegetated	40-45
No	Wooded	45-60
No	Open, sparse cover	45-60
No	Open, very little cover	60-100

a stock of predominantly white crayfish is obtained, the figures in Table elsewhere in this chapter should be increased by 25%.

Crayfish of either species should be placed in the pond as soon as possible and kept cool and damp until that time. Predaion on newly stocked crayfish will be reduced if they are released in densely vegetated areas or, if the pond is sparsely vegetated, in deep water fir from shore.

J. G. Broom at Auburn University obtained experimental evidence that stocking young red crayfish in March at 42,500 to 85,000/ha would produce better yields than the conventional stocking system, but as far as is known this method has not been put into practice, perhaps due to the difficulty of capturing young crayfish for stocking. Broom suggests the following stocking formula:

$$\frac{\text{desired yield (kg/ha)}}{\text{weight at harvest}} \times \frac{100}{\text{expected survival}} \times \text{number of ha to be stocked} = \text{number of crayfish to stock}$$

Manipulation of the Water Level

The most important management techniques in crayfish culture involve manipulation of water level and quality. Each year ponds are drained in late June or early July, when the females have started burrowing.

Slow draining is preferable, for fast draining will strand some crayfish which are not ready to burrow and expose them to predators. Similarly, slow draining allows young crayfish to seek hiding places for the summer.

Ponds are reflooded in September to ensure that the newly hatched young will have ample water. If growth rates are normal, they should be ready for harvest starting in late November or early December.

The culturist should keep an eye on rainfall, which is the principal controlling factor on wild crayfish harvests, and time reflooding so that he can begin harvesting before the wild crop comes in. Early crayfish bring the best prices and may spell the difference between economic success and failure.

Ordinarily, harvesting lasts until the pond is drained the following summer. Between reflooding and the onset of the harvest season in ponds having heavy cover, water levels 50 cm or so lower than those recommended above can be maintained to furnish more shallow water for young crayfish.

During the harvesting season the water level should be kept fairly stable. This requires frequent pumping to replace water lost by evaporation. Pumping must also be resorted to to replace deoxygenated water. Any abrupt reduction in harvest is usually a sign of deoxygenation or some such condition and calls for partial replacement of water.

Food Supply

Any animal food that cultured crayfish get is the result of natural production and their own foraging, but successful culturists encourage suitable food plants and discourage large, tough plants which interfere with harvesting, shade out smaller, more desirable plants, and are inedible by crayfish.

Crayfish from ponds that do not contain adequate amounts of edible plants often have brown or black "fat" or livers, and tails which are not filled out, and are considered to be of inferior quality to well nourished crayfish with full tails and yellow livers.

Plants used as food and/or cover in crayfish ponds must be capable of survival both while the pond is flooded and when it is dry. The most desired food and cover plant in crayfish ponds is alligator grass (*Alternanthera phylloxeroides*).

It can be seeded into a pond by raking it out of ditches and scattering it in the pond during drawdown in June and uly. Alligator grass may, on occasion, grow too thick and hinder harvesting. If harvesting is done by boat, boat trails may be disked or raked on the bottom during the summer.

Although cattle should generally be kept out of crayfish culture areas, grazing them on the dry pond bottom may help retard alligator grass. Water primrose (*Jussiaea spp.*) *is* now considered as good as or better than alligator grass and may be planted together with it.

Water primrose has the advantages of not growing as thick as alligator grass and being more tolerant of cold weather. A number of other plants which occur naturally in crayfish ponds, including pondweeds (*Potamogeton spp.*), *Elodea,* and duckweed (*Lemna*), are fair food and/or cover plants and should not ordinarily be discouraged.

It is certain that fertilization of dry ponds would benefit all of these and other plants, but techniques to encourage desired species have yet to be worked out. Crayfish will also eat almost any soft terrestrial plant. Some farmers have planted sorghum or millet as feed for crayfish and claim increased yields, but there is as yet no experimental evidence for this conclusion.

It is likely that supplemental feeding with animal matter would increase production, but it is doubtful whether it would be economically feasible. Experiments with feeding young red crayfish at Auburn University showed that growth was better on a diet of *Elodea* and ground *Tilapia* than on either component alone.

Research is currently being carried out at Louisiana State University with the aim of developing an economical, high-protein artificial feed for crayfish.

Problems

The most common pest plants in crayfish ponds are cattails (*Typha spp.*). They can usually be controlled only if caught early, at which time individual plants can be pulled out manually. If dense growths occur, disking and raking the pond immediately on drying may be helpful.

Otherwise, it is necessary to call on state or federal agencies for assistance. Outside help is also usually necessary to control water hyacinth (*Eichornia crassipes*) which, unchecked, may completely cover the surface of a pond.

A number of emergent plants other than cattails are usually present but seldom reach problematical densities in ponds which are drained and dried annually. Filamentous green algae, which occur principally during the winter, also may hinder harvesting operations.

Further, they are prone to die off suddenly in warm weather, creating a pollution problem. Partial removal of floating algal mats may be effected by vigorous circulation of the water. Man is by no means the only animal which is fond of crayfish, and predation by fish, birds, raccoons, bullfrogs, snakes, turtles, salamanders, large water beetles, and others, is a problem confronting every crayfish culturist.

The best protection against most of these predators is abundant cover in the pond, but fish, the most serious predators, may require additional measures. Annual draining and drying of course substantially reduce fish populations, but some of the worst predators, notably green sunfish (*Lepomis cyanellus*), bowfin (*Amia calva*), and bullheads (*Ictalurus* spp.), may survive in potholes until reflooding time.

Rotenone at 2 to 3 ppm will destroy such fish. Great care should be exercised in its use, however, and a biologist consulted if possible, since 5 ppm of rotenone will kill some young crayfish. It is standard practice to screen pond outlets to prevent fish from entering, but opinions differ as to the feasibility of screening inflow pipes.

Many successful operators reason that most, large fish are killed by the pump impellers and do not screen inflow pipes. In any event, the large 0.3- to 0.7-m pumps employed on most ponds move great volumes of water and make screening difficult.

It is recommended that, on new ponds supplied by surface waters, a temporary screen be installed on the inflow pipe and checked frequently during the first few days.

If considerable numbers of large predatory fish are captured, a permanent screen should be employed. A suitable design consists of a cylinder of 25-cm weldwire about 1 m in diameter and 4 m long. Such a screen will allow young of predatory fish to enter the pond, but finer screens clog up very rapidly and require constant cleaning.

Harvesting

One of the most difficult aspects of pond culture of crayfish is harvesting. The most frequently used harvesting device is an 0.8 to 1.0 m long funnelshaped trap made of 21-cm mesh chicken wire and so constructed that it folds flat for hauling.

Shorter traps are fully as effective for capturing crayfish, but dissolved oxygen concentrations may become very low in crowded, submerged traps, causing mortality. Long traps, however, may be propped up at an angle so that a small portion is above the surface of the water, and trapped crayfish can obtain air.

Traps are commonly baited with fish heads or chunks of gizzard shad (*Dorosoma cepedianum*), which is considered more effective than any other fish. Fresh fish may be scarce during the winter, and soybean cake, perforated cans of dog food, or almost any high-protein substance may be substituted. About 25 traps/ha are set out.

Most of the harvesting is done by professional fishermen hired by the culturist. This compounds the culturist's harvesting problems, since lie is seldom able to maintain a crew of fishermen throughout a harvest season. But to realize maximum yields and fulfill contracts to buyers it is essential that harvesting be intensive throughout the season.

The problem is particularly acute during cold weather, when fishermen may be reluctant to run their traps frequently, and during the height of the wild crayfish season, when they may be able to make more money harvesting wild stocks on their own.

The demand for labor is particularly great at the start of the season, in late November and early December, when many culturists prefer to harvest as heavily as possible to beat the peak of the wild crop, to utilize adults which have spawned and will die shortly and reduce the danger of crowding of the young crayfish.

Table 14.2: Schedule of procedures for pond culturee of crayfish in Louisiana.

Activity	*Dates*
Construction of new ponds and flooding	By May 15
Stocking June 1-30	
Draining after stocking)	June 15-July 15 (begin 2 weeks
Fish control July 15-August 1	
Repairs, improvement, planting, and weed control	July 15-August 15 (as soon as possible after most of the pond is dry)
Reflooding	By September 15
Harvest	November 25-June 30 (begin 1 month later for new ponds)

Some farmers circumvent harvesting problems by opening their ponds to the public, either for a set fee or by charging substantially less than the retail price for the crayfish which are caught.

A summary and schedule of procedures for pond culture of crayfish in Louisiana is given in Table elsewhere in this chapter.

RICE FIELD CULTURE IN LOUISIANA

Crayfish have long been harvested as an incidental crop from rice fields in Louisiana, but it is only in the last 15 years that intensive cultivation has become common. Today, nearly 1000 ha of rice fields are operated in 2-year rotation as crayfish ponds and pastures.

The approximate schedule for this sort of rotation is given in Table elsewhere in this chapter. There are usually enough crayfish present in a Louisiana rice field to serve as broodstock. If not, adults may be stocked at 6 to 12 kg/ha during May.

Some crayfish leave the drained fields in July and August, but most of them burrow into the moist soil. Rice stubble resprouts about a week after harvest, at which time the fields are reflooded to a depth of 15 to 45 cm.

Crayfish in rice fields feed mainly on rice stubble and various aquatic plants which find their way into the fields. Rice-crayfish farmers should not use rice seed treated with aldrin, which may be toxic to crayfish.

Table 14.3: Schedule of procedures for rice field culture of crayfish in Louisaiana.

Activity	*Dates*
Plowing	March 1-April 30
Replowing and planting rice	April 15-May 15
Flooding and stocking, if necessary	May 1-May 31
Draining	July 15-August 15
Harvesting rice, followed by reflooding	August 1-September 1
Harvesting crayfish	December 1-June 15
Drain and use as pasture	June 15-March 1

Harvesting crayfish from rice fields, although tedious, is easier and cheaper than in ponds. Due to the more regular bottom, nets may be employed. The usual type, called a drop net or umbrella net, consists of a rectangular piece of netting, each corner of which is connected by a wire or rod to a ring located over the center of the net.

A pole or other lifting device is inserted in this ring and the net laid flat on the bottom. Crayfish are baited into it with beef pancreas or other offal and captured by lifting the pole. Ordinary farm laborers rather than professional fishermen may be hired to do this chore.

Growth to the minimum marketable size of 10 to 15 g is rapid in either type of culture, requiring little more than 6 months. Larger 40- to 45-g crayfish, which bring the best prices, are harvested principally in the early part of the season and may be 8 to 14 months old.

Well-managed ponds and rice fields commonly produce 400 to 700 kg/ha of crayfish, and yields of better than 1100 kg/ha have been achieved.

Marketing in Louiciana

Marketing is by no means organized. Crayfish may be sold live, boiled, or as peeled tails to wholesale dealers, restaurants, or individuals. Production of peeled tails may be increased if a mechanical crayfish peeler, currently being developed at Louisiana State University, is perfected.

Diseases and Parasites

Disease is not a major problem to crayfish culturists in Louisiana. A bacterial rot causing decay of the rostrum was observed in red crayfish in Alabama but was readily cured by treatment with potassium permanganate at 3 ppm. An extremely heavy infestation of both red and white crayfish with larvae of the water boatman *Ramphocorixa acuminata* occurred at the U.S. Fish Farming Experimental Station, Stuttgart, Arkansas, but this insect has never presented serious problems in commercial culture.

CULTURE OUTSIDE OF LOUISIANA

Some gourmets find three large crayfish native to the Pacific Northwest of the United States superior to the Louisiana varieties. *Pacifastacus klamathensis, Pacifastacus leniusculus,* and *Pacifastacus trowbridgii,* sometimes marketed as "short lobster" (a term also used to refer to undersized lobsters taken illegally) are principally fishery products, but, in Whatcom County, Washington, they are beginning to be cultured.

Most existing crayfish farms in Washington utilize ponds originally constructed for other purposes, such as irrigation, but ponds built specifically for crayfish are likely to become more prevalent.

Crayfish of several species are also raised for use as bait by sport fishermen in various parts of the United States. In the Finger Lakes region of New York, *Orconectes immunis* has been successfully raised in ponds with various species of bait fish.

With supplementary feeding on soybean meal, fish meal, cracked corn, potatoes, and cut hay, 40 to 350 kg/ha were produced and higher yields are believed possible. Yields of up to 1000 kg/ha of *Orconectes rusticus* have been reported from fish ponds in Ohio.

Methods of raising crayfish for bait are by no means standardized. The essential difference from culture for human consumption is that young, rather than adults, are harvested. One successful grower in Missouri uses 12- × 6-m spawning ponds, 1 m deep.

When spawning and hatching are complete, the adults are removed using a heavily weighted minnow seine. Some of the larger ones (20 to 28 cm long) are marketed as food, but this is of secondary importance. The young are fed on cornmeal mush supplemented with cut fish and commercial fish food pellets and harvested in small lots on demand.

As mentioned earlier, there is a considerable demand for crayfish in a number of European countries, and crayfish culture in Europe might have developed to a greater importance were it not for a recurring "plague" specific to *Astacus astacus,* the principal European commercial species.

Crayfish plague is caused by the fungus *Aphomyces astact* and is presently considered incurable. Nor does there appear to be any tendency on the part of *Astacus astacus* to develop a natural immunity. The history of the crayfish fishery in Finland illustrates the severity of tile crayfish plague. In 1900 that country exported 15.5 million crayfish, but in ill(' 1960s only 0.3 to 0.4 million were exported annually.

The reduction is attributed solely to the plague. The plague-resistant American crayfish *Pacifastacus leniusculu.s* has already been introduced to Finland and is being artificially propagated there so that more extensive introduction. may be made.

Recently, Soviet biologists developed a hatchery technique which is claimed to have saved *A. astacus* from extinction in Lithuania. It is not known if the crayfish plague had anything to do with the impending doom of the Lithuanian crayfish.

In 1969, hatcheries in east Lithuania were expected to release about 500,000 young crayfish into lakes and rivers. The hatchery technique involves stripping the eggs from the females; up to 90 young have been produced from one female.

POSSIBILITIES FOR EXPANSION

There are a number of edible European crayfish other than *A. astacus,* and it is surprising that their culture has not been attempted. In fact, the nearly worldwide neglect of crayfish by aquaculturists is amazing.

Opportunities for expansion of the crayfish industry would appear to be particularly plentiful in the United States. In addition to the species already discussed, a small commercial fishery for *Orconectes virilis* exists in Wisconsin, but otherwise crayfish are virtually neglected as a food resource in North America.

A number of the species cultured as fish bait are large enough to be edible and surely it would be a relatively simple matter to adapt existing culture techniques for production of large, edible specimens.

Where expansion of crayfish culture outside of Europe has been attempted, it has usually involved introduction of red crayfish from Louisiana. It is likely, however, that in most countries there are indigenous species suitable for culture, and certainly these should be tried first.

The giant crayfish (*Astacopsis gouldi*) of Tasmania, which reportedly reaches lengths of over 40 cm and weights of 3 to 4 kg is particularly intriguing in this regard. In Japan, where red crayfish were introduced in 1918 as food for bullfrogs, they have become a serious agricultural pest. Populations of up to 1200 kg/ha exist in some rice fields in western Honshu, where they nibble off rice shoots and weaken dikes by their burrowing activities.

A similar situation exists in taro (*Colocasia esculenta*) fields in Hawaii. It is surprising that the Japanese, normally so quick to utilize aquatic and marine resources, have for more than 50 years failed to adopt rice-crayfish culture methods similar to those used in Louisiana or otherwise turn the presence of the red crayfish to their advantage.

Perhaps the progress of crayfish culture has been impeded by rather unfortunate publicity implying that fortunes can be made by simply stocking any rice field or leveed tract of swampland with crayfish and harvesting it a year later.

Nevertheless, there is money to be made, with hard work, from crayfish farming, and it would seem that crayfish are overdue to assume an important role in aquaculture. At present, they seem best suited for marketing as a luxury food, but if more intensive culture methods, particularly more efficient harvesting techniques, are developed, the tribesmen of New Guinea may not be alone in regarding crayfish as an important nutritional resource.

INDEX

B

C

F

G

J

K

L

M

N

Q

R

S

T

U